Reinhabiting Reality

SUNY series in Environmental Philosophy and Ethics
J. Baird Callicott and John van Buren, editors

Reinhabiting Reality

Towards a Recovery of Culture

FREYA MATHEWS

STATE UNIVERSITY OF NEW YORK PRESS

Published by
State University of New York Press, Albany

© 2005 State University of New York

All rights reserved

Printed in the United States of America

No part of this book may be used or reproduced in any manner whatsoever
without written permission. No part of this book may be stored in a retrieval system
or transmitted in any form or by any means including electronic,
electrostatic, magnetic tape, mechanical, photocopying, recording, or otherwise without the prior permission in writing of the publisher.

For information, address State University of New York Press,
90 State Street, Suite 700, Albany, NY 12207

Production by Judith Block
Marketing by Susan Petrie

Library of Congress Cataloging in Publication Data

Mathews, Freya
   Reinhabiting reality : towards a recovery of culture / Freya Mathews.
      p. cm. — (SUNY series in environmental philosophy and ethics)
   Includes bibliographical references and index.
   ISBN 0–7914–6307–9 (alk. paper) — ISBN 0–7914–6308–7 (pbk. : alk. paper)
   1. Human ecology—Australia—Merri Creek Region (Vic.) 3. Environmental
   ethics—Australia—Merri Creek Region (Vic.) 4. Environmental degradation—
   Australia—Merri Creek Region (Vic.) 5. Merri Creek Region (Vic.)—
   Environmental conditions. I. Title. II. Series.

GF802.M47M37 2004
304.2′8′09945—dc22

                                                                    2004042985

10 9 8 7 6 5 4 3 2 1

For Jenny Kemp
Companion on the Way

Contents

Acknowledgments

ix

Part 1
Culture: The Love of Ground

Chapter 1

The Last Crane: Modernity and the End of Grace

3

Chapter 2

Letting the World Grow Old

25

Chapter 3

Becoming Native

49

Part 2
Ground Studies

Chapter 4

Julia's Farm: Fertility

87

Chapter 5
Hamilton Downs:
Philosophy in the Field . . . of Being
101

Chapter 6
The White Heron: Grace and the Native Self
115

Part 3
Views from the Ground

Chapter 7
The Merri Creek: To the Source of the Given
133

Chapter 8
Barramunga: Return to the Doorstep of Night
165

Afterword
Singing the Ground
199

Notes
205

Index
225

Acknowledgments

It is with real pleasure that I take the opportunity here to thank and acknowledge the people who were important to this book, whether in providing inspiration, support, or company on the various adventures and journeys. These people include Julia Bell, for the sustenance she has given my imagination through many long city-locked years; Norm and May Gardner, for their example of eldership and for opening up their home and hearts to me; Maya Ward and Cinnamon Evans, intrepid pilgrims; the many individuals who offered us assistance and hospitality on the Journey to the Source; the Finders, for our attempt to discover together an emotional base for reinhabitation; the folk at CERES, the Center for Education and Research in Environmental Strategies, especially Noel Blencowe for his wisdom in holding the centre; John Cameron, for first sparking my thinking about place with the series of Sense of Place colloquia that began in 1996; Craig San Roque, for the spellbinding event at Hamilton Downs; my colleagues in the Philosophy Program at Latrobe University, for their patience with my philosophical experiments and their support during my absences; Deborah Rose, for her profound understanding of indigenous cultures and her generosity in sharing her insights; Helen Turner, for many fairy godmother, or godsister, interventions at moments of crisis; Peter Lloyd, for sanctuary in the animistic domains of Bindara Farm; Jeff and Margaret Malpas, for warm hospitality during the very last revising phase; Rainer Mathews, for faithfully holding the fort.

I am also grateful for helpful comments on the manuscript by two State University of New York readers, Glen Mazis and Michael P. Nelson. (Mazis's recent book, *Earthbodies: Rediscovering our Planetary Senses*, also published by State University of New York Press, in 2002, intersects intriguingly with mine at many points.)

I would also like to thank the people of One Arm Point, for all they taught me, and also the Wurundjeri people, for their endurance and grace in the face of the ongoing obtuseness of those who have appropriated their lands. My love and thanks go out too to the country of my childhood, Braeside, and to the country that has nourished me and my thought during the seven years gestation of this book: Merri Creek country, where I now live; Barramunga country; and Ninghan country.

My sincere thanks too to the ever-courteous and friendly team at State University of New York Press, especially Jane Bunker, Judith Block, and Susan Petrie.

Chapter 2 and chapter 3 are adapted from papers entitled "Letting the World Grow Old: An Ethos of Countermodernity I" and "Becoming Native: An Ethos of Countermodernity II," which appeared in *Worldviews: Environment Culture Religion* no. 2, vol. 3, 1999, and no. 3, vol. 3, 1999, respectively, and "Letting The World Do The Doing," *Australian Humanities Review* 33, 2004; chapter 7 was published as *Journey to the Source of the Merri*, Ginninderra Press, Canberra, 2003. Thanks to Sister Felicitas Corrigan and Miss Mollie Martin for their kind permission to quote Helen Waddell's translation of "The Old Man of Verona."

Part 1
Culture: The Love of Ground

Chapter 1

The Last Crane: Modernity and the End of Grace

It is dawn. I jump out of bed and pull my dusky pink jeans on over my pajama pants. It's too cold to bother with dressing properly. I run down to the back of the garage and take the saddle and bridle from their pegs. They are dank to the touch. I cross the big vegetable patch that is also a poultry run. The hens and geese are still fast asleep in their fibro shed, safely locked up against foxes. They make a few sleepy little comments as I pass. Big be-dewed spiders' webs adorn the young almond trees in the orchard that is just becoming established in the chook run. I climb the wooden stile over the fence. There is ice on the steps and my fingers, already swollen with chilblains, are very red. But I don't care. I can see my pony at the far end of the paddock. She is a little grey Welsh Mountain mare, and she is just a shadow in the mist that is thick along the creek. I walk into the mist, calling to her. A spectral crane poised on a blanched stag beside the creek flaps soundlessly away. There are always cranes here by the creek, always. (Technically, they are herons, but we call them cranes.) My pony pricks her ears and ambles up to me, rug askew. She whickers a contented greeting as I put my arms around her damp but warm neck. Her lower legs and fetlocks are caked with mud. I tie her to the fence and saddle up. I am seven or eight years old.

The sun is rising and the mist is lifting a little as I ride along the gravel road. To the north of our house there are paddocks dotted with huge old manna gums, their bark scarred with shield cuttings from a time unimaginable. The slab house and poultry farm that our neighbors-to-be, the Hunts, will soon erect on the block next to ours has not yet been built and I can still walk through paddocks to the one-room primary school my brother and I attend. At least, we attend it until our parents realize that the curriculum consists mainly of profane language instruction and treehouse construction. But on this morning I am not riding towards the school. I am riding south. I pass our already installed neighbors, the Cannons. Mick has built roomy stables down by the creek for his trotters, the horses he trains each day, but Mrs. Cannon still lives in a fibro hut in the middle of their paddock, a hut not much bigger than our chookshed. One day handsome Mick will build for her the large double-fronted creambrick veneer of her dreams. But that day has not yet come. Beyond the Cannons it is just vacant paddocks down to the aptly named golf course, Woodlands. The track beside Woodlands exerts an attraction, because there I can sometimes find flax lilies, chocolate lilies, and egg-and-bacon flowers—and golf balls, for which my mother pays me threepence apiece. But I am not going to Woodlands today.

I look across the paddocks to the old forgotten mansion, Mayfield, its tall chimneys and half-glimpsed grandeur framed among palms and pines on the far side of the creek. Mayfield! Mayfield! My enchanted domain. There is no bridge over our creek and I am not allowed into the wide paddock with the sign Trespassers Prosecuted that separates our place from this numinous zone. One night I do try to sneak across, with a plucky friend, but we don't get far. A year or two later, with another friend, I brave the crossing in broad daylight. It is unnaturally shady in the grounds of the old chateau. All the blinds in its windows are drawn. The empty house hugs its secrets, its memories, to itself. No one hereabouts seems to know its story. No one even asks for it. Mysteries are let lie. A once-lovely garden has grown rank in the shadows of the great pines. The garden, the outhouses, the dark grounds are all deserted. But a father and son do occupy the caretaker's quarters. The young son is riding a palomino pony in a stockyard. Around and around. Shafts of sunlight manage to penetrate the gloom to illumine this beautiful boy and horse. I never see either of them again, nor do I ever forget.

I turn left from Boundary Road into Mills Road. Mills Road is dirt, not gravel, hardly more than a tire track. Mills Road is mine. There is not much to see. A market garden at the Boundary Road corner, otherwise just paddocks, part of a small dairy farm. The farmhouse is situated halfway down the road. Rundown, ugly. My family buys unpasteurized milk in a bucket from the farmer's wife. The road ends in a fence, the boundary of a great expanse of original swamp and bushland reserved by the Board of Works for sewerage purposes. There is an even more rundown house on a tiny allotment at the very end of the road. For a short while it is rented out to a poor family before it is allowed to fall into ruins. I am told by someone that the father of the family earns the Basic Wage. I don't understand the significance of this in the slightest, but it is clearly a solemn matter.

There is a gap in the wire fence at this far end of the road and I ride my pony into a lush paddock. I am on forbidden ground. The grey skeletons of a few fallen giants are scattered around. Logs have a special attraction for me: they can be jumped. But I don't attempt to jump these particular specimens until I am given a larger horse, some years later. The new horse turns out to be not much of a jumper anyway, and gets beached on these monsters. But I am not thinking about jumping today. I am looking for something in the wet grass. Here they are! The snowdrops! A whole circle of them, growing out in the middle of this paddock unbeknownst to anyone. I dismount and sit, shivering, in the center of the circle. It feels very special.

The year is 1999. It is a Sunday and I am driving home from an outing on the far side of town with my twenty-four-year-old son. Our route takes us along Boundary Road. It is now an eight-lane drag lined with huge factories and warehouses. Not long after my family shifted, when I was fifteen years old, Braeside was zoned heavy industrial. ("Braeside" of course means "creekside" or "brookside"; it seems strange, when I think about it, that the suburb was named after the creek, though the creek itself never had a name.) A few factories had already been built before we left, but they, as it turned out, were the merest beginning. I did not return to Braeside for almost twenty years, and by the time I did, it was much as it is today. There was no trace of our old home. The creek had been concreted into an open drain. (It seems stranger still that a suburb named "Braeside" should see fit so to obliterate its eponymous "brook" or "brae.") A network of industrial streets was now overlaid on the paddocks across which I had moseyed and meandered. Mills Road was part of this network. It provided entry into a series of luxuriously sealed and kerbed crescents accommodating large-scale warehouses. Braeside had suffered the full catastrophe. But Woodlands remained, and, by some miracle, so did Mayfield. Now a paved street ran past the house, but the house still nestled within its old grove of pines and palms and retained a few acres of grounds. As vacant and neglected as ever, it still emanated discouraging signals to would-be trespassers and was surrounded by a high cyclone wire fence. The property lay within the extensive grounds of a concrete works. One day I had made polite inquiries at the concrete works' office as to whether I could visit the house, but to my astonishment my request was met with almost threatening hostility. Over the years however I continued, very occasionally, to drive past what was left of the old estate. To take the route through Braeside always made me cry, and there always seemed to be some fresh inroad into any remnant of the former landscape. Despite this, Mayfield drew me back, even though the bulldozers were obviously closing in.

So now, on this Sunday in 1999, I am puttering along Boundary Road in my ancient Datsun 120Y, describing the country as I once knew it to my son. I take the turnoff to Mayfield. But a surprise awaits me. About a quarter of Mayfield's ever-shrinking grounds have been taken over by a huge new factory. "Factory" is not quite the word for the structure in question. I'm not sure if there is a word. The mentality behind the language of "blocks"— blocks of land, blocks of flats—seems to have found its ultimate expression here. This is, quite simply, an immense concrete block, hundreds of meters long, with a single steel door in each wall. No windows. No feature of any kind. It is almost comical, like a cartoonist's caricature of the instrumentalism of late industrialism. Or Uncle Scrooge's money bin. The negation of architecture, a final reductio ad absurdum of modern civilization. The ground around the block is also concreted, so, this being Sunday and the whole of Braeside being deserted, we drive in. Walking to the rear of the block, we find another strip of cyclone mesh separating the property both from Mayfield and from adjoining Woodlands, but there is a hole in the fence! I feel brave with my big son beside me, so we step through.

The hole gives us access to the back of the golf course, though not to Mayfield. What a dreamlike transition! It is like slipping "behind the appearances", from the nightmare of the present to the lost world of the past. On the other side of that strip of mesh are the trees and shrubs of my childhood. There is enough of a little wood here that we feel enclosed. A fairway is just visible through the trees and we wander through the scrub—which has the scruffy feel of neglected remnants—past Mayfield, until we come out to a tee. Not wishing to be seen, we turn back. My heart is singing and hurting simultaneously. Here I am in a tiny capsule of my own country. I look avidly at all the plants. The dark little eucalypts are familiar, but I can't identify them. Nor can I identify the main understorey shrub. But there is a herb growing freely that looks like asparagus—and I wonder if it *is* asparagus, asparagus escaped from our garden of forty years ago, and still running wild? And then, there at my feet, a spray of tiny purple faces springs into view! Can this be true? Can these treasures still be clinging to the edges of existence? Yes, a flax lily!

Now we are walking away from Mayfield, with the fenced-off creek on our left. We wander down to where the creek passes under Boundary Road, and there, perched in a battered treetop, high above the coarse grass, is a familiar form. Next to eight lanes of transit traffic and a narrow drain in a concrete culvert, looking out over an expanse of steel, concrete, and signage—space inhabited by nobody, though used by many—stands Crane, the graceful guardian of my childhood. Still here! It alone has not abandoned its country. I feel like dropping to my knees and kissing the ground out of which the tree that holds this beloved sentinel grows! It doesn't fly away as we walk by, but watches quietly.

Now my son and I find a hole in the cyclone mesh that fences off the creek. The hole is cut conspicuously beside a sign forbidding entry and warning of sudden water rises and noxious airs! Again we step through and follow the deep channel right around to the rear of the site of my old home. The floor of the channel is like a spacious concrete footpath. At intervals the drain at its center opens out into a square holding pool and one of these pools is located where the creek runs through the back of the site of my home. Unbelievably, here, in a pile-up of silt, some waterplants are growing—reeds, a clump of large, ornamental-looking leaves, and a film of pondweed. The only sign of life along the entire length of the culvert!

We follow the culvert back until we can climb up into one of the streets that crosses it. Then we walk around to the front of the homesite. There is nothing to identify it except, on one side, the brick veneer that our neighbor, Mick, had finally built for his houseproud Dot. Now stripped of all the domestic respectability for which Dot Cannon had pined, the house has been converted into a crude office with an advertisement for tires blazoned across the front bedroom windows. It looks very small. On the other side the Hunts' slab house has been incorporated into a showroom and office complex, behind which shelters a little pocket of their English garden, and an original shed. But between the remnants of our neighbors' houses, not a single blade of grass from my home remains. The entire three-acre site is occupied by a warehouse and, at the rear, a car graveyard, with crushed cars neatly stacked in rows, each stack six or seven cars high.

It is a familiar story, but no less desolating for that. In a sense I was losing Braeside from the very start, because it was visibly slipping away from the time my family first settled there. Perhaps that is why I loved it, even as a child, with such an aching love—a love for which our modern languages lack words. For this love of place is not like other loves, of people or animals, artefacts, activities, causes. A loved being or thing or idea is held by us, held in our arms, in our imagination; our love casts a glow around it. But a loved place holds *us*, even if it exists only in memory; it causes everything within it, including ourselves, to glow. A loved place is not encompassed by our love; we are encompassed, loved, breathed into life, by it. There is little recognition or articulation of this kind of relation between self and world in modern Western thought—little attention to categories that express the way the world *makes room* for us as opposed to the way we act on it, impose ourselves upon it. But many of us sense this accommodation, sense that we are indeed received, and feel a huge but nameless emotion in response. When we witness a place in which the world has made room for us overlaid with cement and tarmac, banded in steel, so that every last breath—the breath it imparted to us—is pressed from it, we feel a nameless pain. Being nameless, we have no option but to treat it as of little consequence, never suspecting how we ourselves are diminished by the violent termination of these holdings, these impartings, that are, in fact, foundational to our being.

What kind of society is capable of effecting such wholesale terminations as those that occurred at Braeside? This is a question that far exceeds that of the destruction of ecosystems. Certainly the original open woodland ecosystem of Braeside has been dramatically erased in the process of industrialization. But this is not all that has been erased. The concrete "blocks" that now encroach on Mayfield from every side signal a crisis more encompassing than the ecological crisis. The ecological crisis is a symptom of a deeper, metaphysical crisis in human consciousness and an accompanying crisis of culture. A reorientation to the living world will be possible only in the context of a reorientation to materiality per se and a new appreciation of the possibilities inherent in our relation to world, and its local modality, place.

What *are* the possibilities inherent in our relation to world, to place, and what would it take to realize them? These are the questions explored in the present book. They are possibilities of allegiance, faithfulness to world, to place, as sovereign, solace, beloved, its ends our own, its will our command. Such a reorientation can emanate only from a metaphysical outlook dramatically counter to the definitive temper of modernity. The modern period, ushered in by the scientific revolution of the seventeenth century, has rested on, and reinforced, a thoroughly secular view of empirical reality. From the viewpoint of this secularism, empirical reality is empty of any conative or communicative capacity, any capacity to "mystify" rational observers by overriding their observations and calculations via revelatory initiatives of its own. The object of our observations is expected to unfold in a lawlike way, undisrupted by dialogue with its observers or eruptions of poetic self-disclosure or promptings of inner will. In this sense that world is conceived as without an informing principle of its own: in itself it lacks any attribute analogous to mentality, subjectivity, soul, or spirit and is devoid of the meanings, purposes, or values to which such attributes give rise. We, and other beings like us in respect of rationality or perhaps sentience, are the sole locus of mentality. All the rest of the colorful, variegated, teeming world that we see and hear, taste and touch around us is ultimately nothing but empty matter or physicality, conceptually drained of any presence or interiority, and hence of any meaning-giving principle. This is the great—dualistic—premise of modern civilization: there is nothing akin to mind in basic matter.[1]

Let us describe this dualistic view of matter as *materialist*. A materialist view of matter, according to this usage, is simply one that characterizes matter or physicality generally in terms of categories that exclude reference to mentality or any analog thereof. Regardless of whether a materialist view of matter is conjoined with some kind of immaterial mentalism, as in Cartesian dualism or theism, or whether it dispenses with mentality, metaphysically, as a phenomenon that emerges at a certain level of physical organization and can be reductively analyzed in terms of physical categories, it is this view of matter which, I want to suggest here, forms the cornerstone of modern civilization.

In order to appreciate this cornerstone significance of a materialist view of matter for modernity, let us consider, in briefest outline, some of the ways in which the various projects and values that have been constitutive of modernity have in fact rested on such materialist presuppositions. These projects and values include science, an extractive profit-driven economics such as capitalism, an ideology of progress, a liberal polity, an ethos of consumerism, and an international regime of colonialism. Let us summarily examine each of these projects or values in turn.

That matter is unendowed with meaning, purpose, or agency, either in its own right or as a result of "occult" interventions (by deity, for instance), is the very premise of the *scientific* project. Unless it is assumed in this way that the world is pure object, incapable of any kind of moral ownership of itself, the scientific interrogation of the world is morally indefensible.[2] It is this assumption, moreover, that grounds the confidence of scientific investigators that the world will prove transparent to scientific reason. The nature of a world informed with, or under the influence of, "spiritual" presences capable of engaging communicatively and responsively with inquirers could not be exhausted by scientific methods of investigation.

The objectification of the natural world implicit in a materialist view of matter also dissolves cultural prohibitions or taboos with regard to its exploitation, thereby paving the way for a maximally *extractive profit-driven economics* as opposed to a custodial one: economics is in this case no longer a medium of dialogical exchange between a community and its world, as in subsistence economies, but a unilateral extraction.[3] The paradigmatic form of such an economics is of course capitalism.[4]

When matter is defined dualistically, in purely materialist terms, then a tendency towards "strict materialism," which is to say materialism in its narrower, traditional sense, involving the analytical reduction of any kind of ideality or mentality to pure physicality, is set in motion. If the workings of the natural world can be analyzed in purely materialist terms, then appeal to ideal or transcendent agencies, such as Cartesian minds or theological entities, is no longer required for explanatory purposes. Moreover, since the possibility of ideal or transcendent intervention in natural affairs also seems foreclosed by a materialist account of matter, the potential for occult agencies to influence human lives is diminished. To the degree that our view of matter is materialized then, the status of any purportedly transcendent forms of mentality is on both these counts rendered increasingly epiphenomenal to the worldview that informs our actual praxis.

When strict materialism is established as the tacit consequence of a materialist view of matter, and theism or other forms of transcendent mentality are quietly set aside, then it is understood that human beings must negotiate their meanings and values among themselves. There are no longer any external or objective points of reference for meaning or for notions of the good or the proper ends of human life. The good is not the good per se, but simply the good for us. This entails that political regimes can no longer adopt authoritarian stances in the name of metaphysical imperatives. Rulers may continue to define the good in terms of ideologies that serve ruling-class interests, and they may insist, coercively, on obedience to these ideologies. But as long as they adhere to a materialist frame of reference they cannot claim any metaphysical authority for their ideological prescriptions: they can no longer characterize their version of the "good" as tributary to the unfolding of a cosmic order.[5] Ultimately then society premised on materialism has little alternative but to set aside a polity based on objective conceptions of the good. No one has the moral authority definitively to overturn or override another's conception of their own good. It is accordingly arguable that any legitimizable polity for a materialist society must enshrine the political entitlement of every individual to work out their own good in their own way, subject only to the condition that their doing so does not compromise the like entitlement of others to do the same.

In this way strict materialism in the metaphysical sphere lays the foundation for *liberalism* in the political sphere. Under a liberal regime individuals are free to recuperate occult beliefs if they choose, but this is now a strictly private affair, a consequence of a public commitment to materialism. In this sense the (hidden) materialist premise of liberalism covertly nullifies the metaphysical pluralism to which liberalism pays lip service.

Members of liberal societies sense the illusoriness of this pluralism, and in time tend to discard values inconsistent with strict materialism: without guiding goals emanating from a larger scheme of things acknowledged by society, they pursue their own immediate welfare interests. A welfare interest in this context is an interest in social and material satisfactions that do not depend for their realization on larger meanings or purposes. The pursuit of such interests generally translates, in contemporary idiom, into a form of competitive *consumerism,* and since success as a consumer depends, in modern contexts, on financial status, dedication to competitive consumerism entails dedication to financial goals, where this in turn reinforces the profit imperative of *capitalism*.

In tacit compliance with their materialist base, modern societies define their "standard of living" in basically economic terms and, in the absence, again, of constraints emanating from a larger scheme of things, they seek to increase this "standard of living" indefinitely. The prospect of such increase is the chief legitimation for capitalist overproduction, which is in reality a function of the profit motive. Every obstacle to increase is met with capitalist organizational and technological determination and ingenuity: the drive ever to raise the standard of living is a spur to organizational and technological innovation. In the face of such innovation, and with the assistance of science, obstacles are surmounted and the technical capability of society is perpetually—and exponentially—expanded.[6] This process is known as *progress*.

As many commentators have noted, commitment to progress is at the core of modern civilization. Modernity rests on the assumption that scientific reason will lead to ever greater understanding of the world and hence, provided that society keeps in step with science, to an increasingly advanced or "enlightened" civilization.[7] This commitment to progress conjoins with an even deeper commitment of the modern mind, viz a commitment to change per se, entailing a shift of attention to the frontiers of the episteme and a quest for the newest and latest in every field of experience. The commitment to the new derives, as I explain in chapter 3, from a wholesale embrace of discursivity that is a corollary of materialism, of disenchantment with the concrete dimension of reality: when the concrete, rendered inert, no longer appoints the ends of life, humanity has to search for its sustaining meanings in the realm of ideas, of discourse. But the sustaining or energizing power of ideas depends upon their novelty—it is *new* insights, *new* conceptual or philosophical horizons, that mobilize the mind. Fed by ideas rather than by the nourishing presences within matter, the modern is in a continuous state of searching for the next conceptual or philosophical fix. This existential commitment to the new combines with the commitment to progress to produce the distinctive profile of modernity: a chronic dissatisfaction with the given resulting in a regime of perpetual change, a perpetual quest to improve the world, to make it over in accordance with our own latest designs. In this respect, modern civilization is *radical* as perhaps no previous culture has ever been. Its dedication to a continual unveiling of the new is reflected in the etymology of the word "modern," which is derived from "mode," meaning "of the present," as in "a la mode," keeping up with the latest. Modernity is a restless condition, a condition of discontinuity with the past and of dissociation from tradition. A modern society will turn its face implacably towards the future, reaching beyond the given for new and ideal forms of life.

It is, again, the materialist premise of modernity that enables modern societies to discard the traditions that had perennially served to safeguard cultural continuity by placing all kinds of conditions and constraints on change. For traditions generally derive their prescriptive authority from extramaterial sources—gods, scriptures, spiritual teachers, ancestors, revelations, the poetic pronouncements of the land itself. Without the authorization of such sources, there would be nothing to hold traditions in place. Within the materialist context of modernity, there is, of course, precisely nothing so to secure them. So the drive towards progress, the drive continually to replace one set of things, beliefs, systems, or practices with another, better set, takes the normative place of tradition.

Confidence in scientific rationality as a privileged mode of understanding reality, embrace of a liberal polity, faith in a profit-driven economics to produce material progress and reliance on human discourse itself to furnish meaning together constituted the secular Enlightenment of the eighteenth century, the definitive epoch in the history of modernity. In the name of the Enlightenment, and buoyed by the sense of superiority that accrued from it, Western societies engaged in an expansionist program of *colonialism*, subordinating countless other cultures to their own and subjecting new continents to their extractive economy.

However, when it is understood that no external or objective points of reference for meaning or for notions of the good exist, a further ideological tendency is set in train—a tendency towards *derealization*, the kind of constructivism that results in a collective human solipsism. When matter is thought to appoint no ends or purposes for us, then that same matter becomes increasingly irrelevant to the way we experience our lives: it is perceived merely as the inert backdrop to our meaning-making, a backdrop that can be epistemically constructed in countless ways. Salience is now vested in the play of different meanings projected by different cultures or individuals onto this inert backdrop. Matter drops increasingly out of the picture, and human discourse fills the stage. The putative emergence of mentality out of materiality is forgotten or backgrounded and the omnipotence of human mentality, at the level of meaning, is assumed. A full spectrum of different value systems and worldviews is affirmed and celebrated as evidence of this human omnipotence. Liberal insistence on metaphysical pluralism gains new force and urgency, but the derivation of this pluralism from a particular metaphysical premise—the materialist view of matter that denies the world ends or meanings that it can communicate to us—sinks even deeper into unconsciousness in this nominally "postmodern" phase of modernity, even as postmodern emphasis on the primacy of discursivity powerfully reinforces the modern investment in the ideal and consequently the new.[8]

As a cultural movement then, the kind of deconstructive postmodernism that substitutes the discursive for the real and hence rejects the claims of metaphysics in fact represents a further unfolding of the dualistic logic of modernity. The argument of such deconstructionism is epistemological in its overt thrust. It repudiates metaphysics (where this includes the metaphysical presuppositions of science) on the grounds that metaphysics is a totalizing form of discourse or knowledge, a form of discourse or knowledge that claims privileged status for itself on account of its rational methodologies. The real motivation behind this repudiation however is not so much episte-mological as political: there is no attempt to provide a logical refutation of metaphysical postulates or a rational demonstration of the relativity of reason. Instead deconstructionists discredit Western epistemological preten-sions by arguing from the political loadings of Enlightenment forms of knowledge and by pointing to the ways in which colonial and other systems of oppression have historically been legitimated and enforced by appeal to these forms of knowledge.

The position from which deconstructive critiques of modernity are launched is liberal in tenor. While the classical liberal holds that every indi-vidual in a given (tacitly Western) society is entitled to work out his own good in his own way—provided his doing so does not impinge on the free-dom of other individuals to do the same—the deconstuctionist applies this principle both within and across societies. Not only all individuals, but all peoples, are entitled to their own discursive articulations of the good, where such articulations are inevitably informed with different metaphysical assumptions, assumptions which are inevitably the bearers of their authors' interests and standpoints.

The epistemological pluralism thus espoused by deconstructive postmod-ernists is politically unimpeachable. But it is, again, made possible only by the hidden metaphysical premise that such postmodernism shares with moder-nity. For in insisting, in accordance with the antiessentialist, antimetaphysical agenda that defines such postmodernism, that the self is entitled to realize itself in whichever way it deems best, the discreteness of self vis a vis world has already been presupposed. What has, in other words, been presupposed is that self can be realized independently of whether or not or in what way world is realized. This assumption, that self is not implicated in world, rests on a subject-object form of dualism derived from mind-matter dualism. From a *non*dualist perspective, a self cannot realize itself independently of the world in which all selves are nested. Indeed, the notion of "self-realization" itself makes little sense in this connection, for self cannot realize itself but is real-ized through world. The "each to their own" perspective of deconstructive postmodernism has thus already foreclosed the metaphysical issue that it prides itself on keeping open. It has already decided that the subjectivity of human individuals is not implicated in a wider subjectivity—of some greater whole—which must be realized before individuals themselves can be realized. In short, from this kind of postmodern as from the modern point of view, world is ultimately backdrop, inert object to human subject—if indeed its independent existence is conceded at all. This is so despite the postmodern avowal of metaphysical pluralism.

In both its classical and nonclassical (postmodern in the sense of deconstructive) forms then, modernity may be seen as resting on a particular—dualist—metaphysical premise, viz materialism, and any challenge to modernity must involve the substitution of a nondualist premise for that dualist one. If mind is restored to matter, then modern assumptions about the scope and limits of knowledge, technology, politics, economics, even psychology, are turned on their heads. The new premise becomes the substratum of public and political life. The question How shall we live? is then no longer a question that can be negotiated by us among ourselves, but must be negotiated within a much wider field of mentality than was ever envisaged by the modern imagination. The world can no longer be discounted as brute matter or unknowable background, but must be included and accommodated as active presence in all our deliberations.

I describe nondualist outlooks as broadly *panpsychist*, inasmuch as they ascribe a "psychist" or mentalistic dimension to all of matter, or to the physical realm generally. While it is true that casual references to panpsychism are sometimes taken to denote the unlikely view that material objects, such as chairs and dinner plates and tennis balls, are also subjects, or centers of subjectivity, actual theorizations of panpsychism in the history of philosophy have rarely conformed to this interpretation of the term. Panpsychist accounts of reality have rather tended to ascribe mentality to objects as an aspect of their materiality per se rather than characterizing those objects as necessarily individual subjects in their own right. In the prequel to the present book I have elaborated a particular version of panpsychism, according to which the physical manifold may be understood both as a unity that possesses a subjectival dimension of its own and as a field of differentia, a subset of which constitute relatively distinct individual subjects. In other words, this universe is a One, a field of subjectivity, which also self-differentiates into a Many, a manifold of individual subjects. The subjectival dimension of this universe renders it an arena not merely for causality but for communication.[9] In the same book I have explored the psychology of the panpsychist self seeking communicative engagement with such a world. The aim of the present book is to discover the *praxis* of panpsychism, a praxis which, as we shall see, stands in deepest contrast to the praxes of modernity that have led to the forsaking, at a metaphysical level, of our now lonely world.

Societies that forsake their world, in deference to the materialist commitments of modernity, pay a high price for what is, from a panpsychist point of view, their faithlessness. This is the price that is currently being enacted in almost caricature fashion on the industrial fields of Braeside. The present book is more about the cultural costs—the costs to us—of our materialism than its costs to the environment. For when the entire world is treated as raw resource, inert and unspeaking, then the fundamental modus operandi of society must, from a panpsychist point of view, be one of callous insensitivity. To represent the world as brute and blind requires that we ourselves assume an attitude of bruteness and blindness. We must march through the world unseeing and unfeeling, turning away from the poetic order that unfurls about us, closing our ears to the inexhaustible eloquence of things, trampling underfoot the exuberant infinity of tendrils reaching out to us. How can we cultivate such a habit of insensitivity towards the world around us without this insensitivity creeping into all our dealings? It will make little difference then if we extract from the background of inconsiderable matter certain living elements we are prepared to treat as morally considerable. We might set up flora reserves and societies for the prevention of cruelty to animals, for instance. But the basic—crude and careless—tone of our relation to reality has been set. All our activities henceforth are tinged with the bruteness and blindness of this basic attitude.

This attitude finds its quintessential expression in the image and language of the "block." The block sees, hears, feels nothing. Lacking windows, it is blind. Made of concrete or other solid stuff, it is without inner fluidity or feeling. Stripped of any but the most basic geometrical configuration, it is unable to adapt to influences from without: it retains the same rectangular disposition, unchanged, in all circumstances. Lacking any means of expression, it cannot speak; lacking receptors of any kind, it cannot listen. It is the very image of inert existence, pure thinghood, locked up inside itself, oblivious to the existence of others. Bereft of any but primary qualities, the block stolidly refuses to acknowledge all that is fluid, living, expressive, responsive, subtle, multivalent, multilayered, interleaved, elusive *and* present, capable of self-veiling *and* self-revelation. Block-logic, the blind logic of the one, is antithetical to "dia-logic", the communicative logic of attunement to the subjectival dimension of self and others.[10]

The attitude of the block then is the attitude of one whose communicative function has been disabled. This attitude is exemplified in a tendency to describe both self and world in *quantitative* (or *metrical*) and *universal* (or *abstract*) terms. Resort to a *quantitative* perspective betrays a desensitization to subjectivity and a negation of the possibility of dialogue because the nature of subjectivity is, properly, unrepresentable in metrical terms: subjectivity, as experienced by the subject, is not locatable in space—it is neither large nor small, at rest or in motion; it is unbounded and diffuse, with different aspects and elements of experience permeating one another. Though experience does unfold through time, the temporality of subjectivity does not conform to a metric: time as immediately experienced dilates and contracts in accordance with emotional and other psychic states. When one subject seeks to communicate its selfhood to another then, it will not employ quantitative terms to do so. But when a subject has been rendered impervious to the subjectivity of the wider world, it will become desensitized to subjectivity in itself and others; it will begin to identify with externality and characterize that externality in metrical terms.

Resort to a *universal* perspective—which is to say, retreat from the particularity of things—likewise betrays desensitization to subjectivity and a refusal of dialogue. This is because the subjectivity of others is communicated to us via particulars. Communicative cues reside deep within the particularity of things: communicative intent is recognizable only at the level of the particular instance, at those junctures at which behavior departs from an anticipated norm. Recognition that a wild creature is responding to our signals, for instance, will not occur until its behavior ceases to conform to instinctual patterns—patterns that are universal for its kind—but assumes an unpredictable and singular character instead.[11] For us communicatively to engage such a creature then, we must be acquainted with it under both its universal and its particular aspects. Similarly in the case of the world at large. To initiate communication with it we must address it at the level of particulars. This requires awareness of intricate patterns of unfolding, attunement to the minutest details in the order and sequence of things; we must be prepared to pay attention to things in their infinite variability. The modern subject, perceiving reality through the universalizing lenses of science, is from the very start insensible to the communicative cues on which engagement with world depends.

This lack of attunement to particularity in our habits of perception will carry over, to some degree, into those—social and interpersonal—contexts in which we do admit the possibility of communicative engagement. Moderns will tend to perceive one another discursively, under this or that description, as falling into this class or that class, rather than encountering one another concretely, energically, in all the unanalyzable richness of one another's embodied particularity. I recall in this connection a story once told me by an acquaintance who had just returned from a stint of work as a nurse in a hospital in Alice Springs. She described how a group of Aboriginal people had come from a camp in the Todd riverbed to identify a body. They entered the morgue and before she had a chance to draw the cover sheet from the body in question, they all said, oh yes, that was old so-and-so alright! She was puzzled. How could they have known? They pointed to the dead man's feet, which were just protruding from under the sheet. The people had recognized their friend by the soles of his feet![12] How many of those whose lives are lived in the inattentive modality of modernity would recognize even their own nearest and dearest, let alone their drinking mates, by the soles of their feet? Or the palms of their hands?[13] And what is this inattentiveness in the end but indifference? A failure really to register others, except as discursive ciphers, of interest not for their own sake, as unique ends in themselves, but only for the discursive role they play in one's own story. Even within the confines of the "humanism" that is the intended correlate of materialism then, the habit of inattentiveness that is the legacy of materialism locks us into an effective, if inadvertent, solipsism. Thus while materialism paves the way for humanism—the view that humanity is necessarily the exclusive architect of the meanings and values by which it must live—it also simultaneously vitiates even that position: when the world doesn't matter to us, *nothing* other than our own selves can really matter to us, since our basic attitude to the world directs and frames our basic mode of perception.

The failure really to register others except as discursive ciphers in one's own story is inevitable in a culture in which all "speaking," all attunement to the poetics of existence, all aptitude for the nuanced synergies of eros, is discouraged at the level of the basic attitude, the attitude to reality per se. In such a culture the consciousness of individual human beings itself becomes increasingly blocklike; each individual is eventually capable only of sitting in himself or herself and saying, *This is me. Here I am. These are my goals. This is what they are worth. There lies the straightest path between my goals and me. That is the railway track of my life: I will follow that track. Anything that comes between me and my goals is an obstacle. I shall brook no obstacles. This is all there is.*

To entrench ourselves in this antidialogical attitude and at the same time to shield ourselves from the meaninglessness of existence in the monological mode, we members of modern societies piously deliver ourselves to "careers" (oh hectic word!), to the hustle and bustle of our chronic "busyness," our compulsive "industriousness." Career, business, and industry not only relieve us of leisure to reflect on our condition; they also conveniently afford a modus vivendi oriented to a quantitative and abstract outlook. Organizing life in accordance with professional protocols and schedules, gauging supply and demand, calculating costs and profits, converting diverse environments into uniform "resource bases," our daily attention is deflected from the qualitative and particular and hence from the danger of dialogical engagement: the world is perceived through a veil of managerial, economistic, and techno-scientific formulae which render it effectively uncommunicative in itself and beyond communicative reach.

Let me expand on the latter point a little. A subject that has already come to represent its own existence in the desubjectified—quantitative and universalistic—terms of the block will a fortiori represent the world at large in like terms and it will make that world over to match its representations. It will divide that world up, conceptually and physically, into self-contained units describable in quantitative and universalistic terms. Thus, in the grip of blockmindedness, agents of modernity partition land, for instance, into blocks and on those blocks they erect blocky buildings laid out in city blocks and industrial blocks. The land is farmed in blocks, with any variegation—of crops or herds or timber types—eliminated in favor of the blocklike simpification or uniformity represented by monoculture. Manufacture is likewise conducted in block fashion, via the standardizing techniques of mass production. Even knowledge is divided into discrete disciplinary blocks and education is organized via subject units worth this or that many points; to complete a block of subjects, comprising the required number of points, qualifies the student for the degree. Objects and human activities generally are quantified and increasingly, in recent times, commodified, conceptually rendered down into an economic substratum that is progressively displacing the phenomenal level of reality in our thinking: every object and activity is equated with an economic unit—its ontological indicator in a world discursively reprised as market.[14]

Wherever the logic of the block has been materially imposed, there the absence of dialogue will be assured. Land partitioned into blocks loses the conversation of its parts that emanated in the thematic unities and coherencies of organic place. Foods grown by industrial methods carry no message from grower to consumer and establish no communicative bond between either grower and world or consumer and world: in the monocultural mass production of food, the reciprocal intimacies between ourselves and other species that commensality and cultivation traditionally entrained are rudely terminated: who now is privy to the wider-than-human horizons of the pig or the duck, for instance? Certainly not the factory farmer or the consumer of factory-farmed produce! Who can join in the multivocal conversation of plants with other plant species and with the vastly variegated communities of insects, birds, and elements? Certainly neither the modern farmer, inescapably indentured to Monsanto, nor the alienated consumer of the corporate end product. Similarly with other forms of mass production. The product conveys no message from the maker to the user, and the making of it establishes no communicative bond between either maker and world or user and world.

Services too—from those involved in education and medicine to those pertaining to the domestic sphere—have lost their dialogical function. Where once a service was given and received as part of the elaboration and maintenance of an intricate mythopolitical order—lawmen imparting knowledge to initiates, for instance, or sons-in-law herding goats for mothers-in-law—and where the services thus rendered were themselves colored with narrative intent and ritual elements of gift or sacrifice, services are now strictly functional and contractual in form, rendered by anyone for anyone in exchange for cash. Since it was dialogical intent that stylized services and embroidered the products of human handiwork with poetry of form, and since it was this same intent that added to both services and goods the signature of care, the termination of dialogue with world results in the disappearance of both poetry and care from our day-to-day transactions with one another and with world.

It is worth noting in this connection the parallel between life, viewed in these monological terms, and a certain sphere of endeavor that is assuming a hegemonic cultural significance in contemporary modern societies—namely the sphere of competitive sports. Members of modern societies are increasingly using the discourses of sport as a major currency of sociality, while sporting celebrities are widely adopted in such societies as models of identity. The kinds of sports I have in mind here are the heroic sports in which an athlete aspires to achieve a record-breaking performance of some particular physical feat, such as running, jumping, or throwing. Such competitive sports offer a particularly faithful reflection of life in the materialist mode, of human activity stripped of intrinsic significance. The activities selected for the athletic arena are basically arbitrary sets of movements with conventionally constituted rules of execution: the right way and wrong way of executing them is decided by fiat. In a world that is itself empty of significance and that appoints no goals for us, such sporting activity becomes a paradigm of human endeavor per se. Human activity is accepted as an end in itself. The activity of flexing and stretching muscles may serve no meaningful further end, but we shall glory in it for its own sake. We shall confer a relative meaning on such intrinsically meaningless activity by subjecting it to competition: we shall each strive to excel at some such activity, to become the best at it. Through competition we collude with one another to hide from ourselves the intrinsic futility of our striving.

But activities such as running, jumping, throwing, swimming, and paddling that are now the province of athletic sports were once the ways in which we entered the flow of a wider field of life. Running enabled us to escape danger, track animals. Catching, throwing, and hitting stones or other missiles were likewise techniques of the hunt, enabling us not only to survive, but to participate in the life rhythms of other species. Paddling allowed us to ride the river, to become inducted into its watery spirit. Such activities were cultivated and prowess in them was encouraged because they drew us into deeper engagement with reality. They constituted dialogical modalities.[15] But what are these activities without the world that provided their context and significance? What is the point of indoor "rock climbing," for instance? How does paddling around obstacles in an artificial "white water" course in record time and with a minimum of penalty points differ, at bottom, from sitting in a chair and executing a complicated and arbitrary set of finger and arm movements? While sport might once have served as a school for fitness and skill that would eventually facilitate fuller encounter with world, it has now become a model for life in the materialist mode.[16] "This is me," the sportsperson says. "I program myself to execute a particular arbitrary action in a prescribed way. My goal is to outperform other executors of this action. I will dedicate all my energy to this goal. Nothing else exists for me." This is the testimony of the block, the sole remaining telos of one whose eyes are no longer for seeing the world or exchanging glances with it, whose ears are no longer for hearing the voices of the world, and whose limbs are no longer for reaching out to it. Locked in monologue, the block seeks affirmation of its existence by measuring itself and comparing its dimensions with those of others. Such sport thus unconsciously affords a reflection of the intrinsic purposelessness of activity in a society that has lost its dialogical dimension, while at the same time offering a surrogate sense of purpose in keeping with the insensate mentality of the block.[17]

Now let us compare modern cultures—which are at their root, I have suggested, cultures of crude indifference, on account of their materialist premise—with cultures premised on sensitivity to the psychic dimension of world. The fundamental attitude to reality will, again, in the latter case set the tone for the culture in its entirety. When the culture rests on a broadly panpsychist premise and the fundamental attitude is accordingly dialogical and devotional, every activity will be tinged with devotionalism and the poetry of dialogue. This is partly because all activities involve some kind of exchange with world, and each exchange with world presents an opportunity for dialogue. But the main reason for the devotional tenor of everyday life will be that devotion is here simply the attitudinal field in which the elements of the culture constellate. Every aspect of the culture takes on the color of its basic attitude to reality. This means not only that every activity will be laced with love of world, but also that every activity will care about *itself* as an expression of the unfolding of world: in each activity there will accordingly be attentiveness to form, to the fidelity and communicativeness of form. No longer simply utilitarian in intent, daily activities will be transformed into a gift of celebration and thanks, intimately attuned in their form to the particularities of the situations in which they are performed. As a result the whole of life will assume an aspect that has in modern societies become the exclusive province of "art": the practical and the functional will incorporate a dimension of address expressed through poetic, decorative, musical, performative, and ritual elements. Although cultures premised on panpsychism may not be affluent in material terms, they will be affectively rich, votary in tenor, and abundant in graces.

In light of this contrast between materialist cultures of essential bruteness-and-blindness and panpsychist cultures of essential attentiveness, we might ask whether a "culture" of bruteness and blindness is in fact a culture at all. Under conditions of modernity, societies increasingly represent little more than highly sophisticated instruments of human assault on world. Every aspect of social organization—from the economic to the ideological— serves the purpose of optimizing extraction of "profit" or other unilateral advantage from matter. Can this be described as culture? The word "culture" derives from the same root as "cultivate," viz the Latin *cultura*, meaning a tending; *cultura* is in turn derived from *colere*, to till or cherish. Culture is essentially to do with cherishing, with developing expressive forms of life within a field of cherishing. But what can this cherishing be but the cherishing of existence itself, the orchestration of praise—via praxis—for the ground beneath our feet, the ground we must tend and husband, attentively, if we are to remain in psychic dialogue with the sources of our being.

From this point of view then, culture is the communicative exchange between a people and its world, an exchange that takes place daily, hourly, in every sphere of life. The everyday activities of a people constitute the medium of this exchange; the activities of walking, hunting, growing and preparing food, eating, drawing water, courting, building, healing, teaching, dying, and farewelling the dead are not only requisites for living but opportunities for communicative encounter with world.

The fundamental modality of panpsychist culture is, from this point of view, *grace*. If culture is a matter of cherishing the ground of our existence and expressing this cherishing in the collective forms of our life, thereby raising that life above a brutish level, grace expresses the sense of gratitude for existence that underlies this cherishing. "Grace" is, etymologically, derived from the Latin *gratia*, favor or thanks. Grace on the part of a giver is giving for giving's sake, without any view to a return. Grace on the part of a receiver is appreciation and gratitude rather than expectation and demand. If a happy event is said to occur "by God's grace," this means it is a contingency gratuitously bestowed by God. In saying "grace" before a meal one offers thanks for sustenance rather than accepting it as one's due. If one submits to adversity "with good grace" then one submits without the anger or indignation that might be understandable in the circumstances: one acquiesces in "the given." One remains mindful of existence as a gift rather than a right, and therefore maintains an appreciative attitude. If one lives with grace one exhibits this basic attitude of appreciation in all one's affairs. Such an attitude is revealed in a noninsistence on "rights," a lack of self-righteousness, of indignation, of envy; it involves an ultimate reconciliation to all that is, even if it is not that which one has sought or on which one has set one's heart.

Grace is associated with beauty, particularly beauty of movement. To be endowed with physical grace is to move freely and fluidly, without striving or strain, following the path of least resistance. A person or animal is said to possess grace when their bodily movements are characterized by this kind of effortless flow. As such, grace might be regarded as a manifestation of the Taoist state of "inaction," the state of existing and acting within the parameters of one's own and one's environment's capabilities—within the parameters of the given. One who exhibits grace is active, in motion, but free of all stress and strain and in harmony with the field of movement in which she finds herself. To accommodate oneself in this way to the parameters of the given one must be deeply imbued with a sense of the rightness of things, a sense that life, however dislocated in the present moment, is a gift that, in a larger frame, is unfolding towards a perfect end. Various spiritual traditions afford such a perspective, inasmuch as they affirm the goodness of existence. But panpsychism is perhaps even more conducive to this perspective than theistic traditions, since it appoints no gods as rule makers, dispensers of stone tablets for our improvement and edification. From a panpsychist perspective there is no need for straining after prescribed goals, whether these are handed down by society or by deity. (Grace, let it be noted, is not a *moral* virtue. There is no edict that thou shalt act with grace. If there were such an edict, it would be self-defeating, for grace is always supererogatory; it cannot be commanded or compelled. Grace is an emanation of gift-consciousness.) Instead of straining after—material or moral—goals, all that is required, from a panpsychist perspective, is that one attune to the intelligence already at work within the given, and align one's own ends with those towards which things are already unfolding.

What a contrast between cultures whose primary modality is that of grace and the "cultures" of modernity! Modernity is most deeply characterized by its materialist dissatisfaction with the given, its determination to remold the inert putty of the world, reshape it in accordance with our own sense of what is right and proper. Without any inkling of immanent meaning or purpose in the existing scheme of things, moderns set goals of their own and then strive to meet them. Striving to transcend the status quo itself becomes their source of meaning. Moderns pit themselves against every level of the given: the corporeal, in sport and fashion and medicine, for instance; the mental, in intellectual endeavor; the social, in competition and contention; the environmental, via the technological surmounting of limits and boundaries. No sense of gratitude animates this attitude to reality. As masters of the universe, moderns regard life as nothing less than their due. Misfortune is met not with the acquiescence of one who understands that life is lent not owned, but with the indignation of the wronged. There is thus little grace in the forms of modern life. The basic attitude expressed in those forms is one of instrumentalization tinged with self-righteousness and anger. Modern society does not engage with world but encroaches upon it. It does not tend and cherish the ground of being, bringing forth in new poetic forms that which is already potentiality within it, but blasts and quarries this ground, imposing its own alien designs upon it. The world is a field, not for dialogue, but for the purely self-referential striving of the brute-and-blind.

Even if the natural world proves capable of surviving the heavy hand of modernity, can society itself survive the demise of culture in its original sense? Isn't social breakdown preordained in the solipsistic mindset of modernity, the basic attitude of crude indifference to reality that contractual-izes care and relegates poetics and grace to the little token sideshow of "art"? In the demise of culture are we not witnessing the demise of a distinctively human consciousness, that *votary* mode of consciousness, born of cherishing, which exceeded the requirements of biological necessity and found a new layer of expressive potentiality by engaging the world in communicative exchange?

Chapter 2

Letting the World Grow Old

To adopt a panpsychist premise is, according to the argument of chapter 1, to remove the metaphysical cornerstone from the edifice of modernity. It is to assume a communicative relation with world, thereby transforming our sense of the ends of human life. But if science, an extractive economics, and technological progress have constituted the praxis of materialist modernity, and liberalism and colonialism its politics, what is the praxis and politics of a votary culture resting on a panpsychist premise?

To recognize that in a panpsychist universe everything is unfolding toward a greater end, an end of cosmological self-increase that is already immanent in the very sources of Creation, clearly calls for an attitude of respect on our part: we should acknowledge the basic rightness of things as they are, independently of our interventions, and allow them to unfold unimpeded. In this sense, panpsychism entails an attitude of affirming the given. But panpsychism also implies that the world is capable of responding to us. We are therefore called to seek communicative engagement with it—though not in any way that constitutes an imposition upon it. However, communicative engagement is possible only to the extent that the other party is present and available to us. Engagement with world then can proceed only via its local modality, place. So the affirmation of the given that flows from panpsychism can be understood in two, complementary senses: as an affirmation of the actual, as opposed to the abstractly imagined possible, and as an affirmation of the local, that which is accessible to us here and now in place. Affirming the given in the former sense will be explored in the present chapter; affirming the given in the latter sense will be explored in the next.

WHAT IS NATURE?

Where are we to turn, in contemporary Western culture, for intimations of a panpsychist metaphysics, a truly nondualist worldview, which would force us to renegotiate the entire multilayered relationship of humanity to its world and hence to itself? Only at the radical end of the environment movement, among the various ecological philosophies, do we find such a program apparently already underway.[1] Drawing for inspiration largely on non-Western and indigenous and pagan traditions, ecophilosophers have for a couple of decades now been urging their societies to set aside the crude materialism that engenders anthropocentrism and acknowledge that the natural world is informed with ends and meanings of its own. We are encouraged to honor these ends and meanings for their own sake and live *with* the grain of nature rather than *against* it.

Is the reanimated "nature" which is respected for its own sake and protected by radical environmentalists equivalent to panpsychist reality? Is radical environmentalism already in fact the praxis of panpsychism? Let us test the validity of such an equivalence. What is this "nature" which radical environmentalists revere and with which they enjoin us to live in harmony? Is the metaphysics to which they subscribe sufficiently nondualist to enable them truly to slip the net of modernity, or is ecophilosophy itself, like deconstructive postmodernism, simply latterday modernity in another, cannier guise?

There are of course innumerable answers to the question, what is nature?[2] One of the most common is that "nature" denotes the domain of physics—either the physical universe in its entirety or the laws that undergird it. In this widest sense, nature will not be of particular interest to environmentalists, since such a nature cannot be threatened, and does not, on the face of it at any rate, stand in need of human protection or conservation. In what sense then is nature understood by ecophilosophers and eco-activists as in need of defense? It is often assumed that, in speaking about nature, ecophilosophers and eco-activists are referring to the domain of biology, the realm of living things—forests and swamps, for instance, or plants and animals generally, or wildlife in particular—since it is this biological realm which is clearly under threat from the engines of industry and the appetites of global markets today. However, where the cosmological definition is too wide, this strictly biological definition of nature will usually turn out to be too narrow for environmental purposes, since many environmental battles are fought over inorganic, or only partly organic, features of the environment, such as rivers, dunefields, caves, mountains and rock formations, as well as over organic systems.

What ecophilosophers and eco-activists in fact usually seem to have in mind, in their references to nature, is elements or aspects of the world that have not been created or unduly modified by human agency.[3] Implied in this definition is a categorical contrast between the artefactual and the natural. Is a reanimated nature, in this sense of "nature," equivalent to the reanimation of the world envisioned in panpsychist metaphysics? And, it has to be asked, is such a definition of nature really tenable at all? The answers to both these questions would appear to be no. Since all matter is, from a panpsychist point of view, endowed with an interior or subjectival as well as an externalized aspect, no categorical distinction can be drawn between products of human agency on the one hand and products of nonhuman agency on the other. All material form is to some extent, from a panpsychist point of view, a manifestation of mentality; therefore to regard trees and rocks and animals, not to mention webs, hives, termite mounds, and coral reefs, as falling within nature, and cars and fax machines and cities as falling outside it, seems to be a case of oversimplifying the issue, to say the least.[4] Any form of environmentalism resting on such a dichotomization of the human and the nonhuman will undoubtedly end up reinstating dualistic fault lines in the terrain of modern thought and practice, despite its own best intentions.

The ecophilosophical contrast between the artefactual and the natural does not then lead to a fully nondualist or panpsychist metaphysic, and the praxis that arises from this contrast is not equivalent to the praxis of panpsychism. However, this is not to say that there is not a definition of nature buried within this distinction that *is* consistent with panpsychism, and that is, accordingly, fully nondualist. This definition lies in the distinction between what happens when things are allowed to unfold in their own way, or run their own course, and what happens when, *under the direction of abstract thought*, agents intentionally intervene in a course of events to superimpose on it a set of abstractly conceived ends of their own. The sense of abstractness involved in this reference to abstract thought relates not so much to a capacity to discover universals through abstraction from the particular as to a capacity mentally to reduce that which is actual to a blank slate for the abstractly imagined possible. In this latter sense, abstraction, or as I shall characterize it here, *abstractiveness,* is a matter of finding one's starting point for a course of action in the realm of the abstractly conceived or imagined rather than finding it within the reference frame of the actual. *Nature* then is understood as whatever happens when we, or other agents potentially under the direction of abstractive thought, let things be, while *artifice* is what happens as a result of the intervention of such agents.[5] The radical environmental injunction to live with rather than against the grain of nature then translates into a panpsychist injunction to *let things be*.

What is implied in this notion of letting things be? It is a truism to say that all things, whether animate or inanimate, have laws of their own unfolding. In the case of the inanimate, these laws may be embodied in the physical and chemical dispositions of the things in question. In the case of the animate, they may reside in biological or instinctual dispositions. Even the unfolding of conscious beings such as ourselves conforms to certain ground plans that are not invented by us but already to some degree organize our instincts, intuitions, reflexes, emotions, and other spontaneous responses.[6] However, a materialist perspective offers no assurance that allowing all things to unfold according to these laws will perpetuate the larger processes of life on earth. From a materialist perspective, life is not the outer expression of a meaning or purpose intrinsic to matter, but is an accidental outcome of particular material circumstances. There is thus no prima facie reason to suppose that materiality, left to its own devices, will cohere into an ongoing life process. The dispositions of animate and inanimate elements, and even of different animate elements, might ultimately be mutually contradictory, from a materialist point of view, so that it could never be asserted with confidence by a materialist that, left to itself, life will take care of itself.

From a panpsychist perspective, however, life, in the sense of an informing mentality or subjectivity that shapes matter, is already intrinsic to reality, so the unfolding of matter, left to itself, is already an unfolding of life. According to the version of panpsychism developed in the prequel to the present book, the universe is a unity imbued with its own conatus, its own will to maintain and increase itself.[7] Individual things, whether animate or inanimate, are modes of this greater unity, and are consequently enfolded in the processes of its self-realization. Organisms and other living systems are also imbued with conative directions of their own, but the conativity of individual modes is mutualistic, so that in conatively realizing themselves individual modes are also facilitating the realization of other modes. In this way the conatus of each individual is tributary to that of greater wholes. Left to themselves then, things unfold in ways that by and large assure their own actualization and the further unfolding of the greater systems in which they are enmeshed.

All processes however, whether in ourselves or the world, are capable of being co-opted by the interventions of abstractive agents. Inorganic physical processes can obviously be terminated or diverted by such intervention; the behavior of organisms can likewise be manipulated; and the conativity of human beings can become self-alienated via deliberate conditioning. At each level a contrast can be drawn between an undisturbed state of affairs, in which everything unfolds or behaves in accordance with its intrinsic dispositions or, in the case of living things, an innate conatus,[8] and a state of affairs in which the dispositions of things are diverted by agents to produce end states that match those agents' abstract ideals or imagined scenarios. The undisturbed unfolding of events may be described as *natural*, according to the present usage, and an end produced by deliberate manipulation of such a course of events as *artificial*.

When agents under the direction of abstractive thought do take control of events, the process of life on earth is anything but assured. In accordance with their decontextualized intentions, such agents may make arbitrary interventions: they may cut through hills to straighten a road, for instance, or pollute a lake with manufacturing dye for the sake of people who have decided they want purple hair. With our abstractive powers we can conjure up inexhaustible numbers of ways the world could be, ways ranging from the demonic or the absurd and whimsical through to the humanitarian or utopian; and with the same powers of abstractive thought we can, increasingly, devise means for making the actual world conform to our fantasies, at least in the short term.

Historically speaking, abstractive thought has developed hand in hand with civilizations, where civilizations are dedicated to the remaking of the world in accordance with variable human interests, values, dreams, and conceits. By "civilization" here I mean that form of social organization that was initially characterized by a settled way of life involving both the building of cities and the practice of agriculture and animal husbandry. The salient feature of civilization as a form of life is, in this context, its refusal to live within the terms of the given, as earlier hunter-gatherer societies had by and large done. Instead, civilized societies have sought to change those terms—they have striven to reshape the world to suit their own purposes. They imagine categories of possibility beyond the already manifest—new kinds and classes of things in addition to those already in existence: houses to provide shelter, for instance, and wheels for transport; animals subdued into pulling the wheeled vehicles; succulent leafy vegetables growing in neat rows right at the back door of the houses. In order to conceive of these new kinds and classes of things, it was necessary to abstract quite radically from the world as it was, to look beneath the appearances to the underlying structures, and then to imagine ways those structures could be reassembled. This kind of thinking involves a different level of abstraction from that of the hunter imagining a kangaroo roasting on the fire at the day's end. Hunters and gatherers seek to satisfy their material and spiritual needs and desires within the categories of the given. They carefully study all the subtle particularities of life's tides, and learn to swim intelligently with those tides in order to achieve their ends. Civilized societies, in contrast, seek to transcend those particularities—the various vicissitudes of fortune, the reversals of the seasons, the manifold burdens of the flesh—by remaking the world to their own design. Rather than swimming with the tides, they try to uncover the laws of hydrodynamics and gravitation, in the hope of reorchestrating—and maybe even abolishing—tides.

At the level of self, latterday civilizations have involved the redeployment of our conativity—our instinctual self-realizing energies—in the service of socially prescribed ideals of individual selfhood. Our intelligence has been harnessed to abstract self-images and self-stories rather than to the deeper imperatives emanating from our conatus. Instead of letting ourselves be, we compulsively make ourselves over to match discursive ideals, where this can result in all kinds of aberrations, from neurotic individualism to fanatical collectivism or nationalism.

At the level of both world and self then, civilization tends to induce a preference for the abstractly imagined over the given, and seeks to substitute the possible for the actual. This tendency of civilization has become progressively more pronounced in the modern period, with its repudiation of tradition and its exponentially increasing power to manipulate matter, until it has resulted, today, in the dizzying regime of international capitalism, involving almost incessant, runaway erasure of the actual in favor of the possible—a regime euphemistically going under the name of "development."

When human beings refrain from excessively abstractive thought however, and reclaim their conative nature, then the world is relatively safe from such "development." For the conative natures of all beings are relatively trustworthy, not only because they are, as panpsychists aver, tributary to the conativity of a greater whole, but also simply because all have evolved in concert with one another, with the consequence that their natures are mutually cross-referencing. The actualization of individual beings is achieved, at the conative level, within the parameters of the already existent rather than the merely possible, and thus, at that conative level, all beings have a broad interest in maintaining the world as it is.

To recapitulate then, when nature is defined, as it has been here, in contrast with artifice and relative to a panpsychist premise, it is arguable that generally, on the terrestrial scale, though not perhaps in every conceivable circumstance, nature knows best.[9] By this I mean that when things are left to themselves, the biosphere is likely to fare better than it is when things are subject to our arbitrary interventions. There will of course be casualties at the level of individuals and smaller-scale systems when things are left to unfold in their own way, and as beings with a constitutive interest in our own self-preservation and the preservation of our nearest and dearest, we shall have to evolve modalities of self-preservation consistent with a general attitude of letting-be.[10] In what would such modalities consist? This is a question that will be explored in the third section of the present chapter.

RETURNING TO NATURE

The trap for environmentalists, in thinking about nature, is to reify it, to conceive of it in terms of things rather than processes. When we think of it in this way, we understand it as consisting of all those things that are not the product of abstract human design: forests, swamps, mountains, oceans, and so on. We then contrast nature with the human-made environment, consisting of cities, artefacts, technologies, and such like. We make the same mistake in thinking about nature at the level of the self: the *natural* self is equated with the body, the instincts, intuitions, and senses, and this is contrasted with the civilized self, consisting of the controlled rational ego. The environmentalist's defense of nature is accordingly read as a project not only to save existing swamps and forests, but to restore lost ones. Introspectively it is taken to imply a countercultural ethos of spontaneity, intuitiveness, and sensuality.

From the present point of view, this is a mistaken reading. To "return to nature" is not to restore a set of lost things or attributes, but rather to allow a certain process to begin anew. This is the process that takes over when we step back, when we cease intervening and making things over in accordance with our own—decontextualized—designs. Such a process can recommence anywhere, any time. It is not logically tied to those aspects of the world that we mistakenly reify as nature—the forests, swamps, instincts, and bodily functions—but can start to unfold again in the midst of the most intensively urbanized and industrialized environments on earth and in the most controlled and civilized of persons.

In a world already urbanized, "returning to nature" means not tearing down the cities and factories and planting woods and gardens in their stead. Such action would merely perpetuate the cycle of making the world over in accordance with abstract designs—albeit in this case ecological designs—and would reinforce the mindset involved in living against nature. Rather, returning to nature in an urbanized world means allowing this world to go its own way. It means letting the apartment blocks and warehouses and roads grow old. Yes, we will have to service and maintain them, since we will need to continue to use and inhabit them. Inhabitation will also call for adaptation and aesthetic enhancement. But this is compatible with a fundamental attitude of letting-be, of acquiescence in the given, and of working within its terms of reference, rather than insisting upon further cycles of demolition and "redevelopment."

Gradually such a world, left to grow old rather than erased for the sake of something entirely new, will be absorbed into the larger process of life on earth. Concrete and bricks will become weathered and worn. Moss and ivy may take over the walls. Birds and insects may colonize overhangs and cavities within buildings. Green fingers will open up cracks in pavements. Bright surfaces will fade, acquiring natural patinas. Under the influence of gravity, the hard edges of modern architecture will soften, and imitate the molded contours of landforms. Given time, everything is touched by the processes of life, and eventually taken over by them, to be fed into the cycle of decay and rebirth. Left to itself, the living world reclaims its own. Things that initially seemed discordant and out of place gradually fall into step with the rest of Creation. Old cars take their place beside old dogs and old trees; antiquity naturalizes even the most jarring of trash.[11]

The unfolding of the biosphere—which is to say, the course of life on earth—involves a pattern of gradual but continuous change—a pattern of aging and decomposition followed by spontaneous reconstitution into new forms. This is what happens to things when we let them be. Artifice, as here understood, correspondingly consists in any regime of abrupt, wholesale change, change that involves the erasure of one environment, or order of things, and its replacement with an entirely new one. Such regimes generally come about only at the instigation of agents in the grip of abstract ideas or imaginings that they are intent on actualizing irrespective of context—irrespective of what existed before and what surrounds the new "development." In this sense an old factory site, overlaid with grime and saturated with heavy metals, but in its cracks and neglected crannies also burgeoning with hardy and creative biological and social forms of life, is more natural than a town planner's lush park stocked with store-bought indigenous plants and subject to wholesale redesign or "redevelopment" at any time.[12]

Our own relationship with the things that surround us is transformed when those things are allowed to endure. Beings and objects become dear to us, acquire an irreplaceable significance for us, as they become woven into the fabric of our lives. The bone-handled knives that my aunt passed on to me; the scrolled top-piece of an ornate mirror that stood in the ruins of a farmhouse in which I stayed as a child; the mohair skirt I bought when I was sixteen; the sturdy ice cream container that has been my tuckerbox on many a bushwalk through the years; the swallows that have returned summer after summer to the mudnest on the front verandah; the venerable camellia tree in the quadrangle; such things and beings become party to my life's journey and intimate witnesses of it. Allowing things to be then not only marks a "return to nature," thereby assuring the viability of life on earth; it also engenders in us an attitude of cherishing the given, transforming us from indifferent exploiters of the things that surround us into their custodians.[13]

Of course, by making the point that nature, in its deeper sense, denotes not trees and grass and wildlife but the processes that occur to any and all things when they are no longer subject to the manipulations of agents in the grip of abstractive thought, I am by no means wanting to say that the conservation of trees and grass and wildlife—which is to say, environmentalism in its traditional form—becomes superfluous. Existing ecosystems should, like cities and selves, be allowed to unfold in their own way, free from undue human disturbance. Where such ecosystems have already been modified by the introduction of exotic species however, the application of the principle of letting-be is more complex. One might on the one hand infer that the new and old species should in principle be left to sort the conflict out themselves. To respect nature in this situation may not imply that we should eradicate the exotics and restore the indigenous. It might mean that we should forego interventionist "management" and allow natural processes to reassert themselves, however distressing it might be to watch native plants and animals disappearing under the onslaught of aggressive invaders. Such stepping back is, according to one reading of the principle, the course that would allow for a true "return to nature": some of the original species would presumably decline, and new ones would steal their niches, but as soon as competition had stabilized, speciation would begin again in situ, because we would no longer be intervening to reverse this trend.

However, in situations in which custody has properly been assumed by one party for another, it might seem that a balance needs to be struck between the attitude of letting-be, on the one hand, and due responsibility, on the other. The attitude of letting-be must not be allowed to degenerate, when applied to living systems that have already been annexed into our care, and deprived of their own conativity, into mere neglect, an ethos of letting-die. In the next section I shall suggest modalities of proactivity that would to a degree enable us to protect and preserve not only ourselves but other species and lands in a manner consistent with the principle of letting-be.

The general thrust of what has been said so far is that a certain stepping back from our usual interventionism is what is involved in "returning to nature." This applies not only at the level of the external environment but also at the level of self: making the transition from the psychology of civilization to a more natural state is no more a matter of trying to reinstate an instinctual, free-and-easy, impulsive regime than returning the world to nature is a matter of restoring lost forests and swamps. To try to transform the tense and guarded self of civilized society in this way would only be to perpetuate the process of control—the process of making the self over to match a socially approved ideal. At deeper psychic and perhaps somatic levels, such an attempt, with the self-rejection it implies, would presumably only exacerbate the tension to which the self in question is subject. The way for a self-censuring self to "return to nature" is simply for it to stop altogether the business of attempting to make itself over in accordance with abstract ideals and surrender instead to what it already is. When we give up being dissatisfied with ourselves and reconcile ourselves to our "unnaturalness," our tedious uptightness, for instance, then, ironically, we start to relax anyway; as we stop forcing ourselves to follow the latest social prescriptions, our own instinctual conatus has a chance to recuperate, to make itself felt again. Gradually we become reanimated with our native will to self-realization.

I am not suggesting here, by the way, that continuing to be repressed and civilized does not itself require effort. Clearly it involves enormous effort. But since this is a form of effort to which we may already be habituated, it is not likely to be as great as the effort that would be required to convert our entire system of response to a more spontaneous, impulsive mode. Nor am I suggesting that the self animated by its own conatus is a passive, nothing-is-worth-the-effort kind of self. Conatus in humans, as in other animals, involves quantities of striving. People will go to great lengths to find food to satisfy their hunger, for instance. They will expend themselves utterly in sexual activity. But these are exertions that the organism *wants* to perform—the effort is made with rather than against the grain of its innate desire. In this sense it is no effort for the organism to make such an effort, whereas the effort required for an organism to act against its innate tendency, in favor of socially prescribed ideals, for instance, is immense.

At the level of both self and world then, it is never too late to return to nature. No matter how artificial our self or world has become, each can always, at any given moment, become subject again to natural processes, simply by our decision to call a halt to "development" and "progress" and "self-improvement," and to allow things to remain as they are, to be retained rather than replaced. In saying this I am not of course intending to ban change altogether, but to insist that change should not disrupt the general unfolding of things. It should not raze the old and superimpose on the space that is left something unrelated to what preceded it. Change should carry us gently and smoothly into the future, respecting the cycles of creation, decay, and regeneration. It should grow from within the shell of the given.

It might be objected at this point that an attitude of letting things be is too passive to be compatible with (let alone considered an extension of) radical environmentalism. Doesn't it in the end amount to little more than a laissez-faire acquiescence in the political status quo? In response to this, let me explain how such an attitude would, if adopted by a significant proportion of the populace, in its quiet way thoroughly disable the economic basis of modernity—particularly as this is exemplified in capitalism—by systematically negating the following values, which are definitive of that economic basis.[14]

Consumerism. To allow things to be is to embrace those things that are already at hand, rather than seeking to replace them with new ones. Such embracing of the given is thus an antidote to the culture of disposability and conspicuous consumption fostered by capitalism. From the viewpoint of letting things be, we would be most pleased, not with our brightest and newest things, but with those that had endured the longest and which were accordingly our oldest and most well worn. Such things, having long figured in our lives and mingled their identity and destiny with ours, would be our most precious. "Keeping up with the Joneses," if it applied at all in the letting-be scenario, would entail having fewer and older things than the Joneses. (Of course it would not apply, since in that scenario we would not be measuring ourselves against the kind of social expectations personified by the Joneses.) Acquisitiveness, and hence consumerism, melt away in the face of an attitude of letting things be.

Commodification. When we become sensitized, through the ethos of letting-be, to the preciousness of things that have become invested with meaning via our own life experience and relationship with them, we remove them from the market place. They cannot be replaced by other things, even things of the same type, since the substitutes will not share our history nor hence be imbued with the same meaning for us. From this point of view, I could no more buy or sell things that had become part of the landscape of my life, part of my very identity, than I could buy or sell members of my family. Thus the pool of commodities is continually diminished.

Productivity. When we embrace the world as it is and are no longer forever seeking to make it better, according to abstract conceptions of the good, then greed is effectively abolished. We no longer crave bigger and better houses, cars, roads, cities, whatever. We are instead attached to what is already given. There is thus no call for ever-increasing productivity.

Progress. When people no longer wish to see the world forever "improved," the slate wiped clean and a "better" world, a utopian alternative, inscribed on it, then the ideological rationalization for capitalism viz that it can continue to improve peoples' standard of living indefinitely, collapses.

Efficiency. In late capitalism, efficiency—patently a notion pertaining to means—has acquired an almost fetishistic status. Tools (where this includes all kinds of techniques and procedures as well as implements and technologies) are valued not so much for what they do as for their efficiency, and they are retained only so long as their efficiency is perceived as maximal. When the attitude of letting-be is assumed however, tools are valued not merely for their efficiency, but for their givenness. I may continue to use an old plough, or a leaky fountain pen, or a certain laborious method for making dough, simply because this is the plough, or pen, or method, that my teacher or my friend's mother used; it is for me embedded in the fabric of the given. Efficiency may still be a consideration, but it will be only one factor determining the means I choose to achieve my ends.

Industry/business. These are the two definitive modalities of capitalism—industriousness and busy-ness—both connoting a certain kind of externally driven, externally focused, hectic state of doing or acting. Those who are busy and industrious act on the world, they take initiatives and make things happen. When we assume the attitude of letting-be however, we let the world do the doing, and we fit in with it. We favor "inaction" in something like the Taoist sense of that term; such "inaction" is not equivalent to passivity, but is a form of action that is effortless because emanating from our own conatus and meshed with the conatus of other beings rather than driven by external social expectations or ideologies.

Development. When we are committed to the processes of transformation and regeneration that eventually transpire when things are left to grow old, to unfold in their own way, then we will not tolerate the erasure of the given that is the precondition and prelude to "development" in the capitalist sense—that is, the replacement of the given by the decontextualized, abstractly imagined new.

Profit. If we do elect to let things be, it is on the assumption, as I explained earlier, that nature knows best—that nature, left to itself, conserves itself, does not exhaust itself, but rather replenishes itself, in accordance with the law of birth, decay, and rebirth. To sustain itself in this way, nature returns *everything* to the life cycle, it recycles everything. There is no "surplus" in this system and hence no accumulation. The law of return makes nonsense of the notion of "profit." "Profit" in one part of the system merely signals loss and depletion in another part.[15]

Property. When we honor the world as it is, honor its capacity to unfold in its own way, we of course no longer seek to *own* the world. Instead we find that by remaining faithful to the things our world contains, keeping and tending them and letting the world manifest through them as they endure, we are drawn increasingly into them. The world expresses itself, reveals itself, through the changes it induces in these things, through the lichen on the walls, the cracks in the glaze, the slow, stooping, inevitable return to earth. By continually replacing things we never witness the way the world reclaims its own, so we miss out on knowing it, encountering it, belonging to it. We comport ourselves as invaders, conquerors, buying up the matter that means nothing to us, and trashing it when we are tired of it. We treat ourselves, our own bodies, in the same way, truculently professing to own them and reluctant to allow them to be reclaimed by the world, reluctant to see the world tenderly revealing itself to us through them, through the fading and crazy-work and mute surrender of flesh to gravity. But of course, at the final call, the world claims us anyway, and we go, back into the earth, but no wiser, and a lot lonelier, strangers to the end.

To assume a panpsychist worldview, and to express this worldview via an attitude of letting-be, is inevitably to shift towards a form of management of the material dimension of life—in other words, to an economics, or way of ensuring the satisfaction of our material wants and needs—that is entirely different from modern economics. Since economics involves a certain engagement on our part with the world of matter, an economics with a panpsychist premise will obviously differ from one with a materialist premise. For when the physical world is viewed as a subject, or as a manifold of subjects, then economics constitutes an opportunity for encounter: the ways in which we utilize matter must not conflict with but rather enhance our inter-subjective engagement with it. The basis of an economics structured in accordance with the principle of letting-be will be briefly sketched in the next section.

From a panpsychist perspective then, respect for nature is, as we have seen, a matter of protecting not only ecosystems but *all* things from undue human disturbance, including things that do not usually arouse the concern of environmentalists, even nonanthropocentric environmentalists, such as deep ecologists. This view of nature, and what it is to live with rather than against it, implies an ethos that is far more encompassing than that of the traditional environment movement. It is an ethos as encompassing in fact as the ethos of modernity that it seeks to discredit. For the hallmark of moder-nity is, as was observed in the previous chapter, radical change in the intended direction of progress; such change manifests as development, con-trol, management, design, improvement, even salvation. The ethos of let-ting-be challenges modernity head on, trusting as it does the innate wisdom of things and eschewing as it does the definitive ambition of modernity to remake the world. From the present point of view, environmentalism, even in its deep-ecological forms, is not only missing the larger metaphysical pic-ture in its approach to modernity; it is also itself deeply entangled or imbued with the modernist ethos in its understanding of its own mission. Environmentalism is thus in danger of constituting just another trojan horse for the rapacious attitudes of modernity. It needs to extricate its legitimate concern for nature from heroic modernist assumptions about its own world-changing, world-saving role.

I am suggesting that instead of perpetuating this profoundly modernist ethos of changing or saving the world, the environment movement could assume an attitude of letting-be. We could step right outside the presupposi-tions of modernity, and dare *not* to try to make things better, at any rate if "making things better" is a rationalization for continually replacing one regime with another. When we say, "let's fix the world up—let's pull down these slummy old tenement blocks and build a brand new permacultural-urban-eco-village in their stead"—we are just as much in the grip of the old ethos of dom-ination and control as the city fathers were. We are rejecting the given in favor of an abstract or imagined alternative of our own—we are refusing to let things be—and it is this hubristic mentality which is the motor of modern civilization and the source of the environmental crisis. In remaining in the grip of the old ethos, in nursing the desire to make things better, we are simply continuing to water the modernist roots of the present predatory system.

An ethos that tries to avoid the pitfalls of this mentality will, of course, be an ethos of conservatism rather than radicalism. This conservatism has always been implicit in the environment movement, as plainly betokened by the fact that the term "conservation" is often regarded as synonymous with "environmentalism." The aim of such a conservative ethos then is not a brave new world but an old world, a world unfolding naturally, redolent with meaning, beauty, and its own life and terms. The only way of achieving such a world, without engaging in further interventions, is, as I have already explained, to let the present world grow old—to let the cities weather and fade and the ivy creep up the walls.

It is worth noting that an attitude of letting-be steers a middle course politically between the historical left and the historical right. The historical right was conservative, that is, committed to the given; it was accordingly comparatively lacking in ideology. The historical left was opposed to the given, committed to the utopian, and hence deeply abstractive and ideological. The historical right however, though conservative, differed from the present position inasmuch as it was at heart a defense of social, political, and economic privilege. It insisted on the preservation of traditions and institutions because it was through these traditions and institutions that the upper classes retained their privileges. A degree of true, concrete conservatism—the conservation of architecture and landscapes, for instance—was indeed implicit in this position, but this conservatism was in reality a mere spinoff from a self-interested politics of oppression. The historical left rejected this politics of oppression and demanded the overthrow—and ongoing readjustment—of the existing order, with a view to ending the systematic privileging of the powerful few at the expense of the many. This revolutionary or radical politics however sustained an unremitting antagonism to traditions and institutions generally, and this legacy has served, in the long run, to legitimate the rapacious contempt for the given in all its forms that is the hallmark of late capitalist modernity.[16]

The attitude of letting things be, in contrast, is conservative out of genuine respect for the world, for the capacity of things to unfold in their own way. Its conservatism is not motivated by a desire to preserve the privileges of the few, as that of the historical right has been. Indeed it tends, almost incidentally, as we shall see in chapter 3, to iron out wrinkles in the social fabric, but without succumbing to the radicalism, the ethos of intervention and overthrow, of the historical left. So, without itself resorting to utopian morality or ideology, it reconciles the custodial role of the right with the moral intent of the left. In this respect it is in fact the mirror image of the market-driven politics that is achieving hegemony in the industrialized world today, and is also neither of the left nor the right. This new economism combines the old rightwing investment in the perpetuation of minority privilege and moral indifference to the suffering of the majority, with the old radicalism of the left, its dissociation from tradition per se, and its dedication to building ever new, ever more fanciful worlds. In other words, economism has managed to combine the downsides of both the right and the left. In this unholy new regime, nothing is sacred, everything—every being, every object, every place, every institution, every element of culture and society, every relationship—is subject to obliteration or co-optation by a commerce that sustains fewer and fewer. The attitude of letting things be effectively inverts this nightmare and, by stepping outside the game of left and right altogether, incidentally combines the essence of the upside of each of the old right and left.

AGENCY IN A SYNERGISTIC MODE

To many people concerned about the fate of the global environment, the principle of letting-be, as here outlined, may appear unduly quietistic. How are we to wrest a living from the world without subordinating its ends to ours? How are we to address environmental degradation and biodiversity loss caused by human intervention if we simply step back and let things take their course? How are we to defend our world and all its human and other-than-human inhabitants against those with the political will and muscle to oppress if we merely acquiesce in the given and decline to take up a posture of resistance? Yes, the attitude of letting-be may represent the deepest challenge that can be issued to the mindset of modernity, but if it does not also prescribe positive modes of agency it must ultimately be self-defeating.

However, the principle of letting-be is not, as it turns out, entirely inconsistent with certain modes of proactivity, including modes of resistance. The modes of proactivity in question are those that work with, rather than against, the grain of the given. By this I mean that there are forms of action that achieve their ends by engaging with pathways of energic flow and communicative influence already at play in the world. An agent in this mode is a kind of metaphysical hitchhiker, catching a ride in a vehicle that is already bound for her destination. Or, more usually, via the hitchhiker's communicative engagement with the driver of the vehicle, both the hitchhiker's own plans and those of the driver are changed. The vehicle heads for a destination that neither hitchhiker nor driver had previously entertained, but which now seems more in accordance with their true will than either of their previous destinations.

The hitchhiker lets things be in the sense that she does not seek to turn back processes and conative unfoldings already in train. Her mode of proactivity, in seeking her own conative fulfilment, is through engagement with these existing unfoldings. It necessarily follows that the matrix of these unfoldings sets limiting conditions on her agency: she does not entertain ends or means defined outside the reference frame of the already given. This is a mode of agency that I have elsewhere termed *synergy*.[17] In synergistic mode, the agent can pursue ends of her own and can even seek to transform the status quo, but not by abstracting from the given and trying to replace it, holus bolus, with an arbitrary design of her own. She does not seek to erase the given, or contradict it, but by joining her own conativity to its she elicits from it a new response, a spontaneous unfolding in a new direction.

Let's consider, in briefest outline, how a synergistic mode of agency would operate in the economic, environmental, and political contexts fore-shadowed in the questions posed at the beginning of this section. These examples of synergistic agency are intended merely to illustrate the manifold possibilities for activity consistent with the principle of letting-be. They are not put forward as themselves a design for an alternative society!

Economics in synergistic mode. Extractive economics, based on the inactivation, the rendering inert, of "natural resources," can readily be reformed along synergistic lines; mutualistic partnership with animate natural processes then replaces the inactivation of those processes, their subordination to our ends. Such synergistic possibilities have already been extensively explored in the literature of alternative economics under the rubric of environmental sustainability: sustainability is in this sense already an inherently synergistic mode. Prime examples of synergy in this context are the alternative energy industries, employing techniques for harnessing energy from renewable sources; wind and sun, for instance, are not diminished or denatured by being temporarily diverted to serve our purposes. Windflows and lightflows are tapped without basic meteorological and solar patterns being fractured. (Water, though a renewable source of energy, is more problematic in this context: diversions and dammings of water often do result in the death of rivers and valleys.)

The ecological disposal of "waste" is another example of synergistic praxis. Much of our productive activity could be conceptualized ecologically as accessing elements and energies ("resources") not otherwise available to ecosystems, then, incidentally to our productive intentions, converting them into forms available for reuse by other species. Like nitrogen-fixing plants, whose metabolism benefits the entire ecological system, the side effects of our productive activities could vastly enhance rather than diminish the biosphere.[18]

Similarly, primary industries such as agriculture and pastoralism could be organized with a view to their potential for enhancing rather than degrading the environment. Pastoralism has brought water, in the shape of wells, to the arid rangelands of Australia, for instance, and has in this respect enhanced conditions for wildlife there, though the introduction of exotic grazers and browsers has at the same time reduced biodiversity. But there is no reason why a pastoral agenda could not bring net benefits to these lands, if pastoralism were conducted on synergistic lines. Provision of water together with the judicious harvesting of certain wild species rather than the husbanding of domestic ones, for instance, could possibly lead both to an increase in biodiversity and an increase in profitability for pastoralists.[19] Similar possibilities are well recognized, though little practiced, in agriculture: hedgerows and wildlife corridors restore lost habitat while providing refuge for insectivorous birds and mammals that control crop pests. Even more directly, authorities are now suggesting that farmers be encouraged to produce environmental goods, such as pollen, in addition to traditional crops, as the economic value of environmental goods is finally being recognized and factored into production.[20]

Environmentalism in synergistic mode. Where ecosystems are disrupted or degraded as a result of human intervention, the principle of letting-be may, on the face of it, seem to require that we step back and allow things to take their own course, even if this entails species loss or ecological damage. In this case however, as noted earlier, the principle of letting-be could degenerate into a rationale for neglect. Is there a third, synergistic way between outright interventionism and mere letting die? Such a way does exist, I believe, and it can be characterized as the way of environmental *healing*. Healing, in a synergistic sense, would involve not mechanistic intervention—the substitution of new parts or suites of species for old—but the reactivation of a system's own conative energies. Healing draws upon forces or powers already present within the existing state of things to restore the system in question to dynamic equilibrium. Healing represents a synergistic approach to human as well as to ecological illness and malaise. In the human case, it consists not in the prolongation of life by way of mechanical life-support systems in patients whose own conativity is terminally impaired, but rather in the strengthening of conativity—the boosting of the immune system, for instance—in cases where such strengthening is still achievable. In the case of ecosystems, healing might consist in the replenishment of exhausted soils or the removal of exotic organisms to enable the ecosystemic impulse towards biodiversification to be maintained. The wholesale "restoration" of an original suite of species would constitute interventionism rather than healing.[21]

It might be asked, however, whether exotic organisms, or feral species generally, can be removed from susceptible environments, or whether their impact on these environments can be diminished, without recourse to strategies that violate the spirit of letting-be. Can such removals or reductions be effected synergistically rather than in the typical dominate-and-control modality of environmental management? Synergistic strategies in this connection will presumably have to mesh the fate of exotics and ferals with the conativities of the ecosystem in which they are located. They will, in other words, have to utilize the resources comprised by exotics and ferals to service the ecosystem. When situations involving exotics and ferals are viewed in this light, it often turns out that removal is not required. As Tim Low reports, "[f]oreign plants—weeds and crops—now feed and shelter millions of native animals, and even a few native plants. Exotic animals—especially rats, mice and rabbits—feed millions of natives too. A typical bird of prey, parrot or orchard swallowtail now eats foreign food. Many species now rely largely on alien tucker. If Australia's foreign contingent vanished overnight, many ecosystems would be kicked into chaos."[22] "Environmental management" is not necessarily, from this point of view, a matter of trying to reinstate pristinely indigenous biotic regimes but rather of evaluating environments on a case-by-case basis, identifying the flows—food chains and disease vectors and catalysing factors, for instance—and opening them up or closing them off to one another in ways best calculated to serve the end of biodiversity. Where a given feral invasion is demonstrably destructive to a particular local environment and proves intractable in the face of local synergistic measures, the systemic frame of reference can be expanded to include human populations. It is these populations, after all, that are placing the greatest pressure on global ecological systems, and if vital needs of human populations can be satisfied by harvesting exotics or ferals—for food, for instance, or fertilizer— then to that extent exotics or ferals are reintegrated back into the larger system. They supply a demand that would have been made anyway, so that redeploying them to this end prevents further pressure being placed on the larger ecosystem. In other words, the problem of feral invasions can often be solved by us in the simplest of ways: *by eating the ferals.*

However, to propose this synergistic solution to the problem of feral invasions returns us to the discussion of economics. Environmentalism in a synergistic mode cannot always be grafted onto an economic system that is still organized along dominate-and-control lines. To implement the above synergistic solution to the problem of exotics and ferals in any systematic way would call for major adjustments to our economic arrangements. Our system of production and consumption is rooted in the same kind of agrarian civilization of which the abstractive mentality, which seeks to adapt the world to our needs rather than adapting our needs to the world, is an expression. The abstractive mentality, as outlined earlier, abstracts altogether from the actual in setting its goals: it erases the actual in favor of the abstract possible. It entertains abstract ends as *idées fixes*, which it pursues regardless of cost or context. Both production and consumption in modern societies follow this pattern. Agricultural centers or manufacturing plants are established on permanent sites to produce specific products that have generally originated abstractly in market researchers' imaginations and have then become fixed in consumers' expectations. Primary industry insists on producing lamb, for instance, in spite of the fact that the countryside is teeming with feral goats, rabbits, and camels; this *idée fixe* is then imparted to the consumer, who expects lamb for Sunday lunch and will not countenance the idea of roast feral.

Modern producers and consumers are in this sense still agrarian at heart: they decide what will be produced and what will be consumed well in advance of discovering what is actually on offer, what is already available in their local environment. They are *makers* rather than *finders*, preferring their own version of reality to reality as it is given. All the infrastructure of production reflects this outlook. Both production and consumption could however be geared along the lines of finding rather than making. Production infrastructure could be designed for assembly and disassembly and hence for mobility as well as for flexibility of output, and consumers could develop a taste for the given, in all its unpredictability, rather than for the ideally prescribed.

Of course, an economics of the given such as this would have to conform to the general or overarching principle of synergy if it were not to become merely another excuse for environmental ripoff. After all, the availability of native forests has not been overlooked by modern societies, and native forests have consequently been consumed to the point of obliteration. The same fate could await not only ferals but native wildlife if the ethos of utilizing the given were followed without caution and due regard for the larger principles of synergy and letting-be.

Politics in a synergistic mode. It was noted in the previous section that if everyone assumed an attitude of letting-be, then the consumerist motor of capitalism would stall and the progressivist thrust of modernity subside. Indeed, ideologies of oppression—oppression on grounds of sex, race, class, age, sexual preference, or species membership—would crumble in the face of a generalized respect for the conativity of things. But in reality it is not the case that everyone has assumed, or ever will assume, an attitude of letting-be. On the contrary, modern societies are profoundly committed to taking charge of things, to manipulating the world so that it serves sectorial human interests rather than ends of its own. Wouldn't following the principle of letting-be, in the context of this political reality, amount merely to leaving everything as it is, abandoning the world to those whose goal is to appropriate and exploit it? In other words, the principle of letting-be seems to afford no possibility for *resisting* the political status quo, where that status quo is a function of a systematic inversion of letting-be itself. In a political context then, the principle seems self-defeating: in deference to it we are required to step back and allow regimes of co-optation, which obstruct and divert the general unfolding of things, to prevail.

It is important to note here that the principle of letting-be does not apply to ideas, ideologies, or discourses in their own right. Our reason for letting things be is that they are imbued with a conativity of their own; left to themselves they take care of themselves and in taking care of themselves they promote the self-realization of the systems that constitute them. Clearly this is so only in the case of embodied things, things that are elements of the concrete, corporeal world. It makes no sense to ask of abstract things—ideas, ideologies, discourses—that they take care of themselves. But when ideas, ideologies, and discourses are operative in society—as institutions, customary practices, cultural attitudes—then they are implicated in real, embodied entities. In other words, as we find them in society, ideas, ideologies, and discourses are not merely attenuated abstract entities, but ride on the back of actual individual and collective conativities. In addressing discursive aspects of society then, we are engaging with these conativities, and in this sense we are indeed negotiating the concrete, corporeal given. The principle of letting-be accordingly comes into play.

So what is the advocate of letting-be to do in the face of institutions and practices that contradict her principle? Once again she must try to hitch a ride with the very forces that offend her, giving them their due as (possibly distorted) instances of conativity, but trying, by engagement, to induce them to flow towards a place of true conative increase rather than diminishment. So, for instance, confronted with sexist discourse, the advocate of letting-be will not go on the offensive but nor will she merely acquiesce. She will try to use sexism to transcend sexism. To the extent that sexism is legitimated by an ethos of masculine superiority, she might represent masculinity as an ideal of worthiness rather than of violence, so that men will measure up as most masculine, most manly, not when they are abusing women but when they are most respectful of them. Similarly with racism. Our advocate of letting-be might try to transform the ideal of white superiority into an ideal of justice, equality, and reason, the liberal virtues of the European enlightenment, so that people will never qualify as more white than when they are respecting the rights of others. Militaristic impulses can be harnessed to the goals of peace by converting military forces into peace-keeping forces, thereby putting courage, valor, and strategic acumen to good use. When conflicts between parties of different ideological or religious persuasion break out, one party can seek peaceful resolution by appealing to the ideological or religious terms of reference of the other. (So, for instance, in current conflicts between the modern West and certain strains of Islam, the West could find resources within the sacred literature of Islam itself to query the grounds of Islamic antagonism and enjoin Islamic good will.) Anthropocentric attitudes can be recruited to the cause of the environment via a demonstration that what sets humanity above and apart from the rest of life is our human capacity for awareness of metaphysical unity. In the very act of affirming our human superiority then, we are at the same time acknowledging our unity, our kinship, with all of Creation, and our consequent responsibility for it.

Faced with the devastating environmental and social impacts of corporate capitalism and contemporary global markets, the advocate of letting-be might search for the essence of capitalism and find it in the liberal tenet of freedom—the right of everyone to pursue their own good in their own way subject only to a minimal requirement that their doing so not extinguish the like right of others. She notices the isomorphism between this principle of freedom and her own principle of letting-be. Instead of opposing this freedom, out of disgust for the havoc it wreaks on the environment and on the fabric of society, she expands its scope: truly to follow through on liberalism, she points out, is to let *everything*, human and other-than-human alike, work out its own good in its own way—in other words, to let everything be. How is she to convince liberals that not only human beings but all things are entitled to work out their own good in their own way? She will have to persuade them to change their metaphysical premise. And how is she to accomplish this? By couching her argument within her opponents' terms of reference. If, as is generally the case, liberals' terms of reference are rationalist, then she must demonstrate rationally that a change of metaphysical premise is needed. She must out-reason, out-argue, the proponents of reason and argument.

The advocate of letting-be thus takes the world as she finds it—ecologically degraded, infested with ferals, rife with prejudicial attitudes, desecrated by commerce. She doesn't change the world. But by intelligently engaging with it as it is, rather than contradicting it, and by seeking synergistically to extend and enlarge the conativities she encounters there, she allows the world to change itself.

Synergy in this sense is, again, comparable to the Taoist notion of inaction, *wu wei*. Inaction, as was noted earlier, is not mere inactivity, but activity that is undertaken with rather than against the grain of conativity, whether this be the conativity of self or world. One who is committed to inaction in this sense seeks to overcome oppression, disturbance, and malaise not by confronting them head on, in the name of utopian norms, but by attuning and joining herself to ambient conativites, to the conative dynamics of self-increase. Although this synergistic modality can be articulated discursively—as it has been here—it can operate nondiscursively. It is called forth not by discursive deliberation but by encounter with the dynamics of a psychically activated world.

MODERNITY AND VOTIVITY

The ethos of letting-be rests on the metaphysical premise of panpsychism. As such it offers an alternative to modernity, which is, as was explained in chapter 1, premised on materialism: the project of modernity—of remaking the world according to our abstract specifications—rests on the materialist assumption that matter is sheer externality, devoid of its own informing telos, and therefore putty for us to shape to our own designs. Although letting-be offers an alternative to modernity, it does not coincide with *post*modernity, at least in the deconstructive sense thereof, since such postmodernity rests on an ostensible deconstruction of metaphysical premises per se. In fact of course the relativist outlook of deconstructionism serves to underwrite the materialism of modernity; by insisting on the entitlement of different cultures to live by their own metaphysical lights, deconstructionists imply that the world has no informing meaning or purpose of its own, thereby ruling out panpsychism and colluding with materialism: we can, again, do with the world as we will. However, the explicit—even if unrealized—intention of deconstructionism is to cut away the metaphysical premises of cultures. Clearly then the ethos of letting-be, as outlined here, can in no way be subsumed under this—prevailing—version of the postmodern.

But nor do I think that letting-be should be characterized as *counter-modern*, though this is how I have characterized it elsewhere.[23] To advocate countermodernity sounds unduly reactive; the countermodern would seem to have been set up in opposition to modernity, simply reversing the value structure of the modern, in something like the way this structure was reversed in eighteenth-century Romanticism and in the counterculture of the twentieth century. The ethos of letting-be however does not pit emotionality, sensuality, and instinct against reason, as the more popular forms of Romanticism and the counterculture did. Letting-be is perfectly comfortable with reason, so long as reason is exercised within the parameters of the given, and not used to appropriate, dominate, or reduce reality. Indeed, reason itself tells us that, relative to panpsychism, dialogical engagement and devotion, not reductive analysis, is the appropriate epistemological response, and letting-be rather than domination the appropriate existential modality. Reason then is not the problem, from the present point of view, as it was for countermodern positions such as Romanticism and the counterculture. Nor is metaphysics per se the problem, as it is for the deconstructive stream of postmodernism. The problem is the particular metaphysical premise of modernity, a premise that entrains a strict secularity and an inevitable instrumentalism with respect to the environment.

If that premise is replaced and panpsychism substituted for materialism, then a cultural tendency that is neither modern, postmodern, nor counter-modern is born. It could be described as *alter*-modern, in the sense of other-than-modern, a true alternative to modernity rather than an antithesis thereof. But thus to reference this position to modernity is, I think, misleading. It may be more helpful to characterize it, as it was characterized in chapter 1, as a tendency towards a *votary* culture, a culture whose fundamental attitude to the world is devotional. There are of course many cultures that are votary in tenor without being panpsychist: votivity may take theistic or non-theistic forms, the objects of devotion in each case being differently envisaged aspects of the Unseen. But the experience of modernity and latterly of postmodernity has compellingly brought to light the cultural contingency of different conceptions of the Unseen, leaving us doubtful of anything but the Seen, the mere, unprepossessing ground beneath our feet. It is this and this alone that can still be affirmed with any confidence. If we are to recover the votary attitude, subsequent to the experience of modernity, we shall have to find responsive presence within that ground; we shall have to find the wellspring of existence, the deepest sources of giving, of generation, of limitless generosity to which our gratitude and devotion are properly due, in the mere, indubitable matter on which we stand. We may have to pass, in other words, from our earlier devotion to ideal and imaginary manifestations of the Unseen, through a phase of nihilism, in which the votary impulse is abandoned and the basis of culture, the attitude of cherishing out of which all culture grows, forfeited. When we emerge from this tunnel however, we shall perhaps find ourselves in a new place of dedication—our dedication being this time, finally, to that humble, mysterious, protean ground beneath our feet, the all that is. The present project is precisely to effect such dedication, to outline a modus vivendi consistent with it, reintegrating human subjectivity and agency into the subjectivity and agency of this newly stirring, awakening world.

DISCOVERING THE TAO IN AUSTRALIA

It has been my experience that affinities exist between the broadly Taoist attitude and synergistic modalities of letting-be and certain fundamental characteristics of Aboriginal thought in Australia. It is not my place to comment here in any detail on these affinities nor to speculate that such affinities exist between the attitude of letting-be and the thinking of other indigenous peoples. Suffice it to say that the traditional cultures of Aboriginal Australia evince a powerful engagement with the given that ensures their continuity with their own past but also their flexibility in the face of an almost unimaginable scale of externally imposed change. For while not *craving* the possible and the ideal, they exhibit a genius for accommodating the new once it has become actual. One of the flashpoints in the evolution of my own thinking occurred when a nonindigenous friend who had married into an Aboriginal family in the far northwest of Australia told me about an elder there who included *motorboats* in his Dreaming stories. Years later I happened to find myself living for a while in the very community to which the old man—by then deceased—had belonged, and I was enchanted by the way in which the people in this community refused nothing. They accepted—though they never craved—anything and everything that drifted their way, all the trappings and junk of modern civilization. But in the process of accepting this tawdry stuff, they also uncannily Aboriginalized it, so that it assumed an entirely different significance in the context of their community from its intended significance within the framework of a capitalist culture. Somehow, through this affectionate trust and engagement with the given, the everyday was rendered numinously spiritual, and the spiritual unpretentiously everyday.

Murri Elder, Mary Graham, has declared that one of the foundational assumptions of Aboriginal thought is that spirit is real; another is that land is all there is.[24] That is to say, spirit has a status, in Aboriginal thought, as incontestable as that of energy and matter in Western thought; and, since there is no heaven and hell, and since theories and ideas, however dazzling, are not real, land is ultimately the only thing that exists. If land is expanded to encompass the concrete given—all that is actual in a physical sense—then I think that the attitude of letting-be follows from these twin premises: spirit animates the given rather than existing in the realm of the abstract, so we connect with spirit by engaging—and not unnecessarily interfering—with the given. By embracing the given even in its most adulterated forms, we reinhabit our own contemporary, mundane reality in the same profound way that traditional Aboriginal peoples inhabited their reality, the still edenic land.

Aboriginal peoples remained grounded in the real—rather than escaping into the ideal—by continually renewing their attunement to the wisdom that this peaceful old continent of Australia imparts to those who pay attention to it. I believe that my own early glimpses of this way of living came to me not in the first instance through explicit Aboriginal influences—though these influences later helped to bring it to consciousness—but through the opportunities for such attentiveness that were vouchsafed me as a child, as I played by the creek in the presence of crane, and in the spirit-field of the mysterious chateau, Mayfield, that had been left so unaccountably to "grow old." Born as we are into this intimately companionable land that has for so long been singing along, humming along, with its human inhabitants, non-Aboriginal Australians might also, if we collectively pause to feel the resonance of the endlessly poetic communiques that surround us, rediscover, in a contemporary context, some of the fundamental aspects of the native relation to the world.

Chapter 3

Becoming Native

The present global environmental malaise has come about, at least in part, according to the argument of the previous chapters, because we moderns, the people of the industrialized nations, no longer revere our world or engage communicatively with it. Over the last three hundred years or so, we have been taught to see the ground of being in materialist terms, as in itself void of significance and presence—as mere externality without an animating principle of its own. When we represent our world in this dualistic way, there is nothing that can be said against our parasitizing it and remolding it to the last degree: it is just lifeless clay, there for us to convert into things for our own convenience and diversion. This way of viewing the world removes any philosophical brake on consumerism and development. It also negates the possibility of truly being at home in the world. For from such a materialist perspective, all places, like all material objects, are interchangeable, since none is charged with any indwelling essence or presence. All places, like all things, can be converted into "property," to be acquired and discarded, traded and trashed, at will. For us to become emotionally attached to a particular house or neighborhood or tract of country is for us to project inappropriate significance onto something which is in itself uncaring and unknowing and unresponsive.

When a broadly panpsychist premise is adopted however, which is to say when an innerness is ascribed to things in addition to an outerness, then all things will be perceived as participating in a larger presence and purpose and will accordingly require something more of us. They will require, firstly, as explained in chapter 2, that we let them be, that we allow them to unfold towards their own ends, our interactions with them posing no obstruction to that essential unfolding. But as emanations of a potentially communicative and responsive world, they also require that we *engage* with them, that we not merely step back but that we invite them into relationship by committing to them and holding them dear. In chapter 2, "affirming the given" was read as affirming the actual, allowing the actual to unfold in its own way rather than intervening in favor of the ideal or the possible. But if we are to enter into relationship with the given then the given will have to be read not merely as the actual, but as that which is present to us. Affirming the given thus becomes a matter of engaging with world via its local modality, place. Engaging with the given in the sense of the local is the focus of the present chapter.

ENGAGING WITH THE GIVEN

Let's consider what follows from an ethos of engaging with the given. How does it pan out in everyday practice? The starting point for such an ethos is clearly to give one's own immediate world the benefit of the doubt: encourage it, say yes to it, whatever it contains. This means, firstly, standing loyally by one's own possessions or the objects in one's custody. If these happen to include a computer and car, for instance, be friendly with these machines. Don't turn away from them, but use them in the service of the rest of your immediate world—to enhance its beauty and improve its health. Keep your computer and car indefinitely. Don't trade them in for new models, unless this is truly necessary. Maintain them well. Shine them often. If you do have to part with them, try not to break faith with them—*give* them away, to someone who will, you hope, be as fond of them as you have been. Treat everything in your world with at least a touch of affection. If a particular artefact or technology is highly destructive in its purpose or effects, then you won't want to use it, ever, because it would harm other contents of this world that you treasure. But don't demonize it or vilify it. Adapt it to some other, positive use, and let it express the unique force of its being in that modified form. In this way, by reanimating artefacts, and gradually removing them from the market economy—the ultimate expression of disenchantment with world—and giving them the nonexchange status of gifts, of inalienable parts of the fabric of your life, you begin, again, to shift from consumerism, with its implied contempt for matter and its devastating consequences for the environment, towards a conserver ethos.

Meanwhile, if you possibly can, find a residence that you can occupy indefinitely, and when you do, commit to it. If you already own a house, perhaps you can decide that you will never sell it. Be devoted to your house. Let it know that it is yours for life, till death do you part: it is "family," it has its own people, and its destiny and identity are interwoven with theirs. Fill your house with life and beauty. In order to intensify its aura of being-a-home, an inhabited, hospitable place scooped out of neutral space by those who belong to it, encourage as many other beings as possible to make it home. Grow trees and plants in profusion, inside and out. Provide shelter and habitat for insects, birds, frogs, and other animals. Instead of trying, with barriers and chemical weaponry, to exclude all nonhuman life from your domestic space, share that space generously, adapting your house so that harmless wild creatures can cohabit with you: make a cave for bats under your eaves, and let spiders enjoy the corners of your rooms. Populate your house with contented companion animals. When they die, bury them in your yard, so that the soil itself is charged with memories. The more beings to whom your house is home, the more cherished it will be, and the more detailed and layered the cherishing will become. If you possibly can, grow food at home, because making your abode the source of your sustenance deepens your identification with it.

While you are committing to your house in this way, try to commit to the rest of your neighborhood. Make it your wider home, "owning" the houses and public buildings and streets, however drab or ugly they might be: this, after all, is the landscape of your life. It is through these streets that you have pursued your hopes and fled your disappointments: here is your grown child's primary school; there the house of your late doctor. On this road going down to the creek, where you walk your dog every week, is the house your great-grandfather built. You have a faded photograph of it on lockup day, sometime late in the nineteenth century. Around the corner is the store your grandfather ran, and over there is the park in which your parents walked, each evening, holding hands, for sixteen years. Here, alongside it, is the cemetery where you roamed in your gothic youth, looking for the grave of that same great-grandfather, keeping trysts in peppercorn groves, composing poems about roses. And it was along the tree-lined avenue at the edge of this cemetery that you pushed your baby son's pram to his creche. Layers and layers of significance accrete as our lives unfold in an environment of familiar things, significance that can for us never be reproduced in other settings.

As your personal history is stitched into it, your townscape becomes internal to you. When it does become internal to you, you will resist urban development, or at any rate development that begins with the razing of the given. For the cultivation of your sense of place calls for a certain degree of continuity—a certain respect for the given. This means that planners should not be permitted to succumb to planning hubris, erasing the old in favor of the new, however inspired and well intentioned, or even ecological, their vision of the new might be. Old existing structures and landforms need to be respected, and built on or modified rather than replaced. By existing in the world for long periods of time they have not only acquired meaning and character, a certain identity of their own, but have become interwoven with your destiny and the destinies of all the people who have known them. If they have been unhappy places, they can be redeemed. If they have been ugly, they can be made at least interesting, at best beautiful. Beauty is, after all, as much a function of meaning as of abstract aesthetics, and meaning takes time to grow. So when your city has become *your* place, you will let it change and grow, but organically, from within the shell of that which already exists.

Meanwhile, work to induce a similar commitment and sense of place in the other residents of your area, by cultivating community there, providing a focus for local affections and energy. And just as you did with your own house, make your neighborhood home to as many beings as possible, by abundant planting and provision of habitat. Notice, incidentally, how dead and forsaken are those places which are home to no beings at all—places of transience, utterly unclaimed, such as certain trafficways and car parks, especially underground ones. Such places, belonging to no one, not even insects, become sterile and dangerous twilight zones—scenarios for violence and crime. Bountiful places, by contrast, places brimming with life, home to myriads of little witnesses and abuzz with purposeful activity, have a certain naturally inhibiting effect on random malevolence. By means of street closures, food gardens, habitat plantings, and small-scale local amenities, reclaim and reinhabit as much of the anonymous, uncared-for space in your neighborhood as you possibly can.

Arrange, if possible, to have yourself buried either at home or nearby, in a site of personal significance. By virtue of your identification with this place you are ancestor to the inhabitants who will follow you: the presence of your remains will help to consecrate the site, deterring developers and enriching the spiritual texture of the area for your descendants—the next generation of custodians. Devise new forms of totemism, by declaring your child at birth a guardian of some local place or species, perhaps including place or species names among the child's given names.[1] Recover the poetry of place names, discarding the banal and arbitrary names that currently mar the landscapes of many colonial countries in favor of names that, growing out of significant features of place, reinforce the process of place making.[2] (I have in my possession a copy of an old Chinese map that includes such place names, in translation, as Where Horses Turn Back, Rock Which Points to the Sea, Cliff of the Love of Life, Heavenly Teapot Tower, Arch of Fairy Lu, and many others. To name a landscape in this way is already half way to singing it, "en-chanting" it, invoking it. Can we not invoke our own landscapes in this way, privately if the public naming authorities cannot be prevailed upon?)

As a result of your affectionate attention and commitment, your part of the city will soon begin to blossom. Places that had been ugly, desolate, and dangerous will, once you have made them truly yours, begin to heal, to mellow, and grow friendly and safe.

To commit to a particular place as one's own life-world is to signal one's faith that it harbors the sources of life, that life can be sustained there; it is to announce its potential sufficiency. This means not only greening its streets and open spaces, providing habitat for nonhuman species, and growing food for local people; it also means discovering the *power* of the place—synergizing with its potential sources of energy, such as sunlight, wind, and compost, rather than relying on external sources for one's needs. To emphasize the potential sufficiency of one's own place is not to deny the biospherical interdependence of places generally, but to point to the fact that each place has its own particular potencies and potentialities for giving and sustaining life. In this sense, commitment to place implies an ethos of self-sufficiency, an undertaking to adjust our energy requirements, as far as possible, to the capacities of the immediate and the local, rather than draining the world at large in the service of our appetites.

Such adapting of self to the immediately available, rather than exceeding the immediately available in order to adapt the world to self, may be generalized beyond the energy context: the sufficiency of the available can serve as a guiding principle for living. Such a principle directs us to allow the immediate and the local to dictate our choice of ends. So, to offer an obvious example, instead of selecting imported, out-of-season fruit from the supermarket, I might choose to eat whatever is available in local gardens. Or, to take a less obvious example, instead of electing to learn Latin, where this would involve traveling to a class on the other side of the city, I might ask my next-door neighbor, who was born in Italy, to help me brush up my youthful Italian. This would not only enhance my language skills, but increase and improve my communication with my neighbor. Or, seeking an outlet for my long-repressed churchgoing impulses perhaps, I might choose not to comb through the literature of the various denominations to find the one that most closely caters to my current convictions, but rather opt for the splendid gold-domed Russian Orthodox Church currently being hand built by the parishioners themselves on the banks of the nearby creek. In other words, instead of abstractly deciding what I want, and then scouring, and perhaps remaking, the world to find it, I look at what is already to hand and consider how my ends might be adapted to that.

The self of panpsychism then is an *emplaced* self. Place is a category already fostered by the principle of letting-be: a world in which things are allowed to grow old is one in which they start locally to take on one another's characters, to *cohere*. When things remain subject through time to the same physical forces—the same winds and rains, the same temperatures and atmospheric conditions, moisture and light and noise intensities, soil and microbial types, plant and animal impacts, industrial and traffic fallout—then co-local things start to exhibit thematic continuities. Under the influence of the same forces, different things become weathered and worn in similar ways. They start to look and feel as if they belong together, as if they are emanations of a single underlying theme.

This effect is strikingly evident—and we take it for granted—away from centers of human activity. In the bush, land figures and forms are pervasively cross-referenced. I remember being particularly gripped by this during a sunset walk to a granite ridge in the dry country around Hanging Rock last summer. All the forms were metamorphosing ethereally, hauntingly, into one another. Sticks lurking in the groundlitter alluded to snakes. Roos alluded to rocks and dead trees. The pristine whiteness of cockatoos answered to satin tree skin bared by peeling bark in amongst the scrub. Galahs were in tune with the pinky undertones of the grey ground itself, the sticks and sunlit granites. They picked up the rosy blush that underlights the sage greens, the olives and silver greys, rusty greys, of the entire countryside. A magpie rose vertically in a gully, a white cross against the twilit bush, speaking to blanched stumps jutting up among black tree shadows. This was not merely a matter of camouflage as an evolutionary strategy. Wherever things have had aeons to grow old together—as they have in the bush and even more so in the outback—*all* things, not merely organisms, fluidly partake of local essence: the rocks and ranges, the salt pans and breakaways, the vegetation and the wildlife, all wear one another's faces and forms, colors and expressions.

This effect is not confined to remote bushlands or the outback, however; it is evident too in ancient cities or hilltop villages—in old parts of Europe, for instance. Left to endure, things start to join hands with the things around them and embrace them, whatever they are; house and hillside, tractor and field, begin to assume each other's accents, to fall in step with the company they are keeping. Out of this progressive melding, *place* in an organic sense is born. By "place" I mean not merely a designated point in undifferentiated space, but a local modality of world. When things are allowed to cohere, through time, world is able to speak through them. Out of their emerging unity we begin to glimpse world itself as an *encompassing,* rather than something encompassed: it is not itself a thing nor is it a sum of things but it is rather the qualitative matrix out of which things take shape. Being thematic rather than substantival, this matrix evokes psyche rather than mere physicality; whenever this thematic unity or coherence becomes discernible, we do indeed become aware of place and find ourselves using expressions such as "spirit of place" or "power of place." We begin, in other words, to attune to *presence* in world, to the psychic aspect of our psychophysical reality.

When the world is allowed to grow old then, when things are retained, or left to unfold in their own way, the psychophysical nature of world starts to manifest through place. And it is through place that we begin to engage with the psychically activated face of world. If we commit to the things that surround us, allowing them to unfold in their own time, according to their own inner laws, then we ourselves become part of the unity, the cohering, of those things. The gap between things as objects and ourselves as subjects begins to close. We become implicated in things, and things become implicated in us. The place that constellates through this cohering becomes ours and we in turn become its.[3]

The absorption of place into ourselves occurs on both physical and psychic levels. Over time, we, like the other components of our place, are honed by the particular environmental impacts and forces that are characteristic of that place: our skin is textured by its particular intensity of sunlight and our imagination is suffused with the angles of that light; its gradients—its steeps and flats—are transcribed into our musculature; our posture is stooped or open-chested, our demeanor bound or free, depending on its temperatures and the extremity of its climate; our emotions are charged with its colors, our moods with its weathers, our spirit with its generosity or withholding.

In allowing ourselves to become interfused with place, we are opening ourselves to interfusion with world, and a psychoactive world will in time, and only in time, come to accept us, open its arms to receive us. Through a particular place, it agrees to become *our* world, attentive to us, attuned to us. We become its people. Through place the world claims its own. It can never receive the casual or expedient sojourner or stranger in such familiar fashion.[4] Only through reinhabitation do we awaken our world to our presence.

When our world is awakened in this way, through our attentiveness to the given, it invites us to engage communicatively with it. As we are absorbed into place, we are drawn imperceptibly, if we are alert, into conversation with it. We find greetings here on a fencepost, there on a rock by the creek. No, we are not (necessarily!) going mad; by entering into the fabric of this place we have slipped beneath the skin of the world and the world is starting to respond to us. At first it is just a "hello" here and a "yes, I know you" there, little synchronistic message sticks, decipherable only to ourselves, their meaning bodied forth in imagery uniquely derived from our own, often most private, lives. But gradually we find ourselves in an ongoing, utterly engrossing poetic dialogue. This is in no way comparable to the whispered prayer of theistic religion. It is not a matter of importuning an ethereal minder, asking for things and sulking when they are not granted, railing against perceived withholdings, entering into long arguments and explanations. It is more like a game of hide and seek, of seeking and finding—finding, often at moments least expected, a tender though always tantalizing riposte. No favors are granted here, no edicts offered that one can engrave on stone and pass onto others. ("The Tao that can be told is not the eternal Tao.") But there are sometimes surprises, overturnings of the presupposed, ironic little commentaries, nudgings when we have lost our way. Any message imparted is untransferable, since a rose, spoken to you, with the private set of associations garnered from your experiential depths, is likely to mean something entirely different from a rose spoken to me. This is the vocabulary of dreams, the poetic genius that lies at the root of language and mythic thought, the currency of a larger subjectival field.

Enfolded into place through poetic engagement in this way, the self is inescapably steeped in it. She speaks to it. It is her shelter, her sanctuary, her heart's home; it lines her path with poetry. She belongs to it and it to her. She is its *native*.

ON BEING NATIVE

In order to understand more fully the implications of the native condition and how it is entrained by panpsychism, let's consider in this section how the condition of the native self can be contrasted with that of the modern.

The Roman author and public servant, Claudian (370–405 A.D.), offers an early reflection on nativism in his poem "The Old Man of Verona:"

> This man has lived his life in his own fields.
> The house that saw him as a little lad
> Sees him an old man: leaning on his staff,
> On the same earth he crawled on, he will tell you
> The centuries that one low roof has seen.
> Fate has not dragged him through the brawling crowds,
> Nor ever, as a restless traveller,
> Has he drunk at unknown springs; no greed of gain
> Kept him a-quaking on the perilous seas.
> No trumpet sounded for him the attack,
> No lawsuit brought him to the raucous courts.
> In politics unskilled, knowing naught of the neighbouring town,
> His eye takes pleasure in a wider sky.
> The years he'll reckon in alternate crops
> And not by parliaments: spring has her flowers,
> Autumn her apples: so the year goes by.
> The same wide field that hides the setting sun
> Sees him return again;
> His light the measure of this plain man's day.

That massive oak he remembers a sapling once,
Yon grove of trees grew old along with him.
Verona further seems than India,
Lake Garda is as remote as the Red Sea.
Yet, strength indomitable and sinews firm,
The old man stands, a rock among his grandsons.
Let you go gadding, gape at furthest Spain:
You'll have seen life; but this old man has lived.[5]

Are we moderns in a similar condition to that of the worldly Claudian? While we delight in traveling extensively, adventuring, sampling other cultures, acquiring and accumulating artefacts and wealth, exercising power under the sophisticated cloak of legality, are we merely "seeing life," rather than, in some deeper sense, really living? If so, what is it about the experience of the old man of Verona that keeps him closer than cosmopolitan Romans and moderns to the true sources of life?

The old man of the poem is a native, born of and belonging to his own ancestral patch of country in the environs of Verona. Being native is an existential condition that imperial civilizations such as Rome, but even more particularly those of Europe in the modern era, tend to render obsolete. With their regimes of colonization and appropriation, such civilizations set both their own citizens and the peoples they subjugate in wholesale motion: the imperial citizens disperse throughout the empire, and in their countries of origin are inducted into new, mobile lifestyles via affluence; members of the subjugated populations are forcibly removed from their lands and sometimes transported to distant destinations at the will of their masters. The state of indigeneity becomes more and more attenuated amid the flux of peoples, cultures, and economies that imperial regimes, particularly those of modernity, entrain.

What, at a deeper level, does this vanishing state of indigeneity consist in, and what is the worldview that informs it? What is the cost of its loss? We know that natives can become deracinated and, in the space of a generation or two, turn into moderns. But can moderns become native again? Would this be a desirable end? How desirable is it, particularly, from the perspective of environmentalism? These are the questions that will occupy the remainder of this section.

"Native" is currently a heavily loaded word; deeply pejorative and romantic simultaneously, it is one of the quintessential designations of otherness, connoting a state of unreason, primitiveness, and closeness to nature that sets it in definitive contrast to European man's conception of himself as the rational master and director of nature.[6] But the word did not always bear this colonial loading. Derived from the Latin "natus," meaning "has been born," it originally referred simply to one born of a particular place. It is etymologically closely related to both "nature" and "nativity," and, like them, it antedated colonialism by centuries. It was cheerfully used by the English to refer to themselves in relation to their own land before it acquired its overtones of primitiveness, irrationality, superstitiousness—subhumanity. Can this concept be salvaged from beneath its colonial accretions, and rehabilitated as an identity that is in principle available to anyone who is prepared to renegotiate their metaphysical relationship with place and hence with world? By way of an evocation of the meaning of indigeneity, or the state of being native, that explains this metaphysical relationship, I shall try to show that this concept *can* be redeemed, and made available for use today.

What then, in essence, is it to be native? To describe a person as a native is not only to say of them that they were born in a particular place—since this after all can be said of everyone—but that they *belong* to that place, that they are made of its matter and imbued with its distinctive character. To be native is to have one's identity shaped by the place to which one belongs: one is a creature of its topography, its colors and textures, saps and juices, its moods, its ghosts and stories. As a native, one has one's taproot deep in a particular soil: one has grown in that soil, and continues to be informed and sustained by its essence. One is kin to all the other beings who arise out of and return to that patch of ground, and one draws one's substance and one's templates for meaning from it. The native is thus one born into a world that prefigures, predetermines, his being in every detail. He grows into the space that has been prepared for him, as a chick grows into its shell. He respects that space, never jeopardizing the perfect fit between himself and his world by taking radical initiatives or assuming hard-to-accommodate shapes of his own. The world as it is given affords material sufficiency, mythic inexhaustibility, and a rich vocabulary for both pragmatic and imaginative purposes.

A particular place, then, is an irreducible part of the identity of the native. To belong to place in this "internal" way however is already to bypass, to a significant degree, the dualistic premise of modernity.[7] For one cannot regard the identity of human beings as intertwined with the identity of places if one also regards human beings as set apart from the material world on account of some kind of mentalistic attribute the rest of reality categorically lacks. To experience oneself as part of the fabric of the world, in this deep metaphysical sense, is to experience the world as fundamentally continuous with one's own nature, rather than as an alien and lower realm of sheer mindless externality. The native is thus bound to experience his world as something like a wider psychophysical field within which his own subjectivity takes shape. For this reason nativism seems to be logically tied to panpsychism—to the kind of nondualistic worldview that attributes a dimension of subjectivity to all of matter.

Through the broadly intersubjective relation that the native enjoys with his homeplace, his nature is then, as has been explained, continuous with the world at large—he is of the world, or belongs to it, on account of belonging to a particular portion of it. In light of this intersubjective relation with place, the native's integration into his world might be perceived as analogous with the way in which humans generally—native and nonnative alike—become socialized into the human community. This is, of course, through intimate relations with particular human others. In modern societies, in which intersubjective relations with place are not accounted part of the process of identity formation and are thus either ignored, denied, or systematically severed, the self is no more integrated into the "psychic" fabric of the world than a self deprived of primary bonds with human others is integrated into the psychic fabric of humanity. Current psychoanalytic theory overlooks the alienation of the modern self from its metaphysical matrix. Identity formation is, from the basically Freudian viewpoint of psychoanalysis, entirely a function of the infant's psychosexual relations with primary human others. By ignoring our primordial relation to the world, and denying both the subjectival aspect of that world and its disposition to interact with us in a meaningful fashion, current psychoanalytic theory, from the viewpoint of nativism, induces in moderns a kind of metaphysical autism or psychopathy, an incapacity for affective connection with world. (See chapter 6.)

Etymology is suggestive of the broadly panpsychist foundations of indigeneity. Native. Nature. Nativity. If a native is one who is born of and belongs to a particular place, as flesh of its flesh and bone of its bone, then nature is the realm of natives, born beings, beings who belong to the great cycle of birth, death, and regeneration; to be a born being is also to be perishable and hence resigned to immanence, to reincorporation into matter, into primal flesh and bone. The native is resorbed into his birthplace. Yet in a religious (Christian) frame of reference, the word "nativity" signals the entry into nature, into the realm of the born, of one (the Christ) who is beyond mortality, one who has come from beyond space, beyond mere matter.

Out of this play of interpenetrating meanings we might, with a little creative license, distil a concept of the native as one who belongs to the realm of mortality, but whose taproot extends so deeply into his patch of ground that it reaches right through to the other side of matter. By remaining embedded in the substance of the world, he retains his originary connection with its psychic innerness or spiritual depths.

Let us contrast the native, understood in this way, with the modern. The modern individual is of course born, like other creatures, and is consequently mortal. But unlike the native he attempts, in part, to repudiate both his birth and his mortality. For through reason, and the sciences spawned by reason, he sees himself as capable of rebirthing himself, remaking himself according to his own chosen design; by the achievements of his intellect and will, moreover, he aspires to outlive corporeal death.[8] And although he, like other creatures, is necessarily born in a particular place, he is not of that place. Places generally are contingent to his identity. Enjoying the mobility and freedom from attachments that are synonymous with modernity, he is an habitual traveler, latterly a tourist, hungry for new terrain. He also typically moves his residence regularly, for social and professional reasons, and even if he happens for some reason to stay put, the property regimes of modern societies ensure that the character of the places that surround him will change dramatically and abruptly as a result of "development."

It is clear from these observations that the perspective of the modern is strictly materialist: matter is, for him, sheer externality, devoid of subjective interiority. Material particulars are distinguishable only by their external location and form, not by any internal or psychic principle that renders them present to themselves, either directly or as part of a greater subjectivity. Such particulars are disposable in the sense that in destroying them we are not depriving *them* of their existence—lacking self-presence they can neither be deprived nor gratified. If they share the same functional form, they are intersubstitutable, in a way that things that are present to themselves, whether directly or as part of a greater subjectivity, are not. Material particulars and places may thus, from this perspective, be considered as commodities, property, real estate, to be exchanged, traded up, or redeveloped at the first opportunity.

Far from the modern being a creature of the world then, an incarnation of its deepest themes, this world is *his* object, an ever-changing artefact of his passing whims. Since this artefactual reality belongs to him, he himself belongs to nothing. Prised away from primordial place, he is severed from world per se. Floating free, he experiences the world as a play of appearances, of surfaces that may be spliced and rearranged according to whim. He has no sense of the depth of matter, of its interiority, no inkling of the spirit that underlies the appearances.

The appearances themselves, robbed of their interiority, become scarcely distinguishable from ideas, with which the modern mind is full to the brim. Ignoring the given, except as a problem to be overcome, entranced with possibilities, the modern lives on an abstract plane. Since ideas lose their animating, recharging power the more familiar they become, abstract thought is intrinsically restless, forever in movement towards the next insight or breakthrough or unenvisaged horizon. Hence the modern's craving for novelty, his habit of listening to "the news" several times a day, and his intoxication with an already vast and rapidly expanding abstract or virtual world of representations, which is increasingly estranging him from any connection whatever with the concrete given. The modern relates to the world of matter not as a presence with its own integrity, but as a set of coordinates or building blocks for his own ever active imagination.

Extruded from relationship with the concrete world, unaware of the nurturing presence within matter, pursuing a mirage of alluring yet empty, uninhabited, and ever-changing images and abstractions, the camera-decked, laptop-lugging modern may, in the privacy of his individual psyche, struggle to escape his existential maroonment and seek to "make sense of things." He does so by summoning up yet more ideas—philosophies and religions that postulate a source of meaning and value beyond matter, outside the world. He may comfort himself with abstract ideas of transcendent entities or beings or forces, which, though inaccessible to experience, can be "believed in." Unless fleshed out in elaborate social customs and practices however, such beliefs have little sustaining power. This is evidenced by the fact that moderns who no longer participate in the major social institutions that have constellated around religious or other philosophical hypotheses tend to change their minds quite frequently, embracing new doctrines of salvation or redemption, converting to new faiths. It is the reliance on discursivity ensuing from a disengagement from matter that accounts for the characteristic commitment of modernity to the ever emerging new and the consequent discontinuity of modern societies with the past and their dissociation from tradition. Eventually however modern individuals are likely to give up the elusive search for transcendent meaning and settle instead for the secularism that is indeed the logical corollary of the modern condition.

The native, by contrast, being in and of the world, experiences no comparable existential estrangement. Spirituality is, for her, less a matter of belief than of direct experience. She *feels* the presences in particular objects or places. Oracular communications emanate from cracks in the rocks and from gaps in the clouds. Birds and other animals bring her messages. Her country rejoices when she returns home. This is not a spirituality of ideas, of explanatory hypotheses—though out of her direct experience she may speak on behalf of place or country in story and song. Since it is not a faith or system of beliefs, she cannot give it up, or at any rate not without leaving the country that daily speaks to her and through her. Her life, in situ, is saturated with spirituality, since in all her transactions she is in immediate contact with the spiritual depths of matter.

It may be objected that drawing the contrast between the native and the modern in this way begs the central question thrown up by the current wave of deconstructive thought—it may seem to assume what deconstructionists deny, namely that it is possible for human beings to engage directly with the real, as opposed to their own discursive constructions of the real. From a deconstructive point of view, the native's understanding of himself and the world is as abstract, as culturally mediated, as discursive, as that of the

modern. Although the native may indeed experience himself as intercon-
nected with the real, this experience is itself a function of his beliefs about
the world rather than of his actual relations with it. The native is living in his
own ideal construction of reality just as surely as the modern is.

In the face of this objection it has to be conceded that it is the—broadly
panpsychist—*beliefs* of the native that render him open to the possibility of
intersubjective contact with the world. These metaphysical beliefs are of
course as ideal or discursive as any others. However, such beliefs cannot of
themselves ensure that contact will occur. Beliefs can blinker or expand my
view; they can foreclose certain possibilities, and open up others. They enable
me to interpret the evidence of my senses, but they cannot predetermine
what that evidence will be—they cannot dictate how the world will behave. I
may subscribe to panpsychist principles, but this will not in itself ensure that
the world will respond to my communicative overtures in meaningful ways.
My panpsychist beliefs may simply turn out to be false. However, if the
world does engage in communicative exchanges with me, then I have experiences not available to the materialist. And it is such experiences, experiences
of intersubjective exchange, that, I am arguing here, shape the identity of the
native, an identity formed through communicative relation with homeplace.
So although the beliefs that render the native open to such intersubjectivity
are indeed ideal or constructed, the experience of intersubjective contact itself
is not so, for it requires not only the discursive amenability of the native but
the actual cooperation of the world.

The native, I am suggesting, experiences an aspect of the world that is
hidden to the materialist, and it is on account of being privy to this aspect of
reality that she is able to engage in a form of relationality not available to
the materialist—a form of relationality that extradiscursively structures her
identity, qua self-in-the-world, in the same kind of way that, according to
certain schools of psychoanalysis, intersubjective engagement with primary
human others prediscursively structures our social identity.[9] In both cases, it
is the fact of relationality, of communicative mutuality, itself, rather than
the discursive content of such communication, that structures subjectivity.
In this sense, while native identity indeed rests on, it is not reducible to, a
discursive dimension.

It is clear, I think, from the contrast I have drawn here between the
native and the modern that while the native's agency is limited, both geographically, to the place where she belongs, and spiritually, by her engagement with her world on its terms, the agency of the modern is
uncircumscribed, either geographically or spiritually. Since he belongs
nowhere, he considers himself free to exercise his agency anywhere and
everywhere, and since he denies the possibility of communicative engagement with the world, there are no spiritual constraints on his action upon it.

While a custodial ethos is clearly implicit in nativism, an exploitative ethos of "development," in its current economic sense, is a natural expression of the materialist perspective of modernity. It should be noted, however, that custodialism and development represent contrasting attitudes to *the given*, without regard to the form the given takes: the custodian is, as has already been noted, by no means exclusively concerned with the ecological, and nativism is accordingly not simply coextensive with ecologism or ecopolitics.

LIVING RATHER THAN HAVING A LIFE

Perhaps we can now appreciate some of the resonances of our poet Claudian's distinction between "seeing life" and "living." The modern, as the representative of the most extreme and encompassing of imperial civilizations, has become a spectator of life, a connoisseur, or at least a sampler, of different cultures and belief systems, which have for her been converted from genuinely inhabited forms of consciousness into a mere play of ideas, appearances, and representations, apprehended at an abstract level. The modern's sense of self depends upon which out of this range of beliefs and values she chooses to privilege, which she elects to build her life around. The particular beliefs and values out of which she forges her identity may be assembled by herself or prescribed by her society. Either way, her identity is at bottom an abstractly constructed one, a function of ideas or discourse, a collage of often mismatched fragments, continually subject to revision and review.[10] Although inevitably limited by empirical variables in a general way, it is not tied to particular concrete realities. The native, by contrast, has little choice as to who or what she is, because her identity is already predetermined by the metaphysical context of her birth. Ideas do not constitute the core of her sense of self. Her identity is rather a function of her actual relations with a particular place, a particular part of the psychophysical terrain of earth, and is thus rooted in reality. She is not a spectator of, but a participant in, the unfolding of the world. Where the modern observes the various manifestations of the life process—where she "sees life"—the native is herself a conduit for that process.

However, Claudian's distinction between "living" and "seeing life" perhaps fails fully to capture the distinction between the experience of the modern self and that of the native. The modern sets out not only to see life, but to "make a life for himself." He regards his life as a thing, a possession, a kind of narrative artefact, modeled on bits and pieces of the life stories of celebrities and others around him, as exciting or impressive as he can make it. He aspires not only to see life then but to "have a life," whereas the native, as Claudian notes, merely lives. However, while the life of the modern is always a patchwork that fails fully to cohere, the life of the native expresses an inner conativity that in turn participates in larger conativities that lend the native's life an organic momentum that carries her along towards ends beyond those of her own limited devising.

I can illustrate this distinction between the eclecticism of the modern's experience and the coherence of the native's by drawing on my own experience. For a long time, I was dogged by the feeling that I wasn't really living. It made no difference that I clearly "had a life"—work that many others regarded as interesting and worthwhile; creative writing projects; family and romantic roles and ties; friends I loved; even occasional out-of-the-way adventures. Whatever was happening in my life, it always felt as if *nothing* was happening—nothing was really moving or flowing of its own accord; I wasn't really living.

Consequently I spent a lot of time deep in doubt, psychoanalyzing my past, trying to ascertain when exactly it was that the drumbeat had stopped, that the sense of the Tao, once so strong, bearing me along on its swift current, had departed. A few years ago however I heard the stirrings of that deep pulse again, muffled and faltering, to be sure, but signaling the return of the feeling of life, of life that could carry me forward with its own momentum, instead of having to be reinvented, out of my own flagging will and limited imagination, day by day.

This return of a sense of really living seemed to occur as a result of my having a significant period free of paid work in which I decided to make my own neighborhood the site of my activism. The ecological ideals to which I had been committed in my work had hitherto seemed impossible to put into practice in the heart of the city. I had been waiting, for decades, for a chance to relocate myself to the country, to take up a lifestyle compatible with my dreams and convictions. In the meantime, I had searched among the innumerable urgent and compelling environmental issues that came to my attention daily for the one to which I could devote myself wholeheartedly; for a time it was rainforests, then uranium mining, then Tibet, and so on. But I had so little connection with the issues, and the effects of my actions were so negligible, it was hard to sustain commitment. So when this period of free time eddied into view, I decided to start just where I was, to focus my attention on the drab little precinct where I actually lived; I would try to care for it, to make it the site of an ecological way of life. It was undoubtedly a lost environmental cause, but it alone was mine. Little did I suspect that this attempt to reenchant my neighborhood would result in the reenchantment of my own life.

I started by enlisting as a weekend animal volunteer at my local environment park. This was a lonely and rather daunting affair, as at weekends there was no one else around to talk to but rats and the farm animals, who were distinctly bad tempered and uncooperative with their transient keepers. But in time this involvement led to other, more expansive and satisfying forms of participation, and the park has become for me a principal site of reinhabitation. (See Afterword.) Meanwhile, a dear friend presented me with a (supposedly!) miniature pig as a birthday surprise. The elemental presence of this eventually hippo-sized prima donna filled our home with radically nonhuman emanations and, by keeping us attuned to other-than-human perspectives and imperatives, freed us from the obsessive human-centeredness and reflexiveness of city life. Her presence also lent our backyard a distinctly rural ambience; it introduced a new range of raw and earthy sounds and smells into this hitherto rather ornamental space, and turned me into something of an urban farmer, hauling bales of straw and bags of feed about, mucking out the pen each morning, and trawling the neighborhood supermarkets for greenwaste, which the pig quickly converted into high-grade manure. As the scene of our pig's life, the backyard became a vortex of activity, of energic transfer and transformation. As the home of such a powerful being, the locus of all her needs, desires, and feelings, and the axis around which the weather and the birds and the seasons turned for her, it also became a site of richly layered psychic significance.

In the course of my wanderings along the local creek, I found a beautiful old market gardener who, with his ancient wooden wheelbarrow and 1957 tractor, still cultivated a couple of acres on a floodplain upstream. I was able to purchase enough vegetables from him each week to see us through to my next visit. The creek had long been "country" for me, and obtaining food from my own country, straight from the hands of a man who had worked that tranquil patch, with his family, for fifty years, gave new depth both to my relationship with the creek and to the business of eating. This was soulfood; it was the gift of my own country, and in eating it, I embodied my country, became substantially of it. This eating also bonded me to the man, my friend, who had grown the food, and knew and loved the country. (See chapter 7.)

Other activities included rescuing indigenous seedlings from development sites and replanting them in public spaces. I made an effort to patronize nearby businesses, facilities, and venues, and to take an interest in local initiatives and history. I joined action groups and wrote antidevelopment submissions. In the latter process, it became necessary to learn something of the workings of local government and planning procedures, a counterpart perhaps, in the contemporary urban context, to traditional indigenous knowledge of the factors that are salient to caring for country.

As a result of these and other activities, I discovered that my experience was starting to *cohere*—and this was an indescribably enchanting feeling, as if a long-lost elixir were bubbling up from archaic springs and bringing my arrested existence *to life*. It was then that I realized what had been amiss these many years. My life had become spatially dispersed and fragmented—work, leisure, activism, social life, family, the rhythms and requirements of my corporeal existence, all were relegated to separate locales and hence to separate experiential spheres or compartments. My family was scattered; my friends all lived in different parts of town and did not know one another; my food and clothing and other material requisites came, like my environmental causes, from anywhere and everywhere.

Since life had become broken up into so many discrete spatial compartments, it had also become disjointed in time, in the sense that activity in one sphere did not lead naturally into activity in another. It was therefore necessary to impose sequence by way of the calender and the diary. My time had to be plotted out in advance: a slab of days each month for work; separate slots, subject to availability, for appointments and engagements with different friends, members of the family, doctors and dentists, accountants and colleagues; times for language classes and tai chi sessions and political meetings, for shopping and cleaning and walking the dog. This arbitrary ordering of experience allowed for no *flow* of meaning or momentum from one activity to the next, from one day or year to the next. The continual "jump-cutting" from one activity or context to another gave rise to a sense of rush and breathlessness, of acute lack of time. (In a similar way, the jerky pace of a heavily spliced sequence of film creates an illusion of urgency or mania, while a camera that pans continuously generates a leisurely, even timeless, atmosphere.) The future being foreknown, spontaneous emergences and changes of direction were preempted; all possibilities of growth and development were foreclosed. Being fragmented, divided, parceled up in this way, my life had no dynamic or movement of its own—it was not a living thing, but something that had to be reassembled, reinvented, every day.

But now all this was starting to change. By reconstellating my existence around a particular place, I was bringing about the coalescence of the various spheres or compartments. Proximity ensures coherence: different activities undertaken in a given place interpermeate one another. My local activities and commitment to local sites had brought me into contact with local people. This meant that merely strolling down the street or to the shops was now a potentially social experience, so it was no longer so necessary to "put time aside" for social engagements: social interactions could erupt in the midst of mundane daily affairs. My contact with local people in turn put me in touch with local opportunities, issues, and possibilities, so that social activity could at any moment turn into work, activism, or food exchange, for instance. The various different parts of my life were in conversation with one another, a conversation that resulted in a rich layering of meaning in every part. It was no longer possible to compartmentalize experience, and hence it was no longer feasible to live according to the segmented, breathless logic of the diary. Time lost its choppiness, and started to flow long and smooth again, and my life, previously subject to the deadening control of will, reacquired an organic unity and force of its own. Activities, relationships, ends were now dynamically evolving minute by minute, day by day, and could not be prescribed. Each day was indeed a new day, though the unanticipated that it brought forth was not the exotic or imported newness that the modern craves, but a fresh unfolding of the inexhaustible richness of the given.

While the modern "sees life" then—busily ticking off innumerable predetermined destinations, acquisitions, appointments in itineraries, inventories, and diaries—yet is still somehow always short of time, short on life, the native lives in outstretched time that carries her along on its gentle curves to the greater ends that form in the confluence of the many local tributaries to the life of the world.

Perhaps the most serious deficit in the modern's experience however, from the present panpsychist perspective, is not so much its eclecticism as its construal of life as a possession of the self rather than as an aspect of the unfolding of world. When life is conceptualized as a possession, some lives are deemed more desirable than others. Individuals strive to make their lives better, richer, fuller than those of their fellows. They seek to "make the most of life" or "get more out of it." Those with lives that carry the "rich and full" tag are valorized at the expense of those whose lives are humdrum and empty.

From the perspective of the native however, one's life is not the property of one's self. To be alive is to be in the world, to witness it, engage with it, participate in its poetics. The measure of the richness of our lives is the richness of the world. The lives of all those who share the same world are of equal worth because the opportunities for dialogical engagement available to us are the same: we can all shine in the glory of the sunset, find sanctuary in the leaf shade of summer, surrender to the blunt-fingered tenderness of salt wind on our face. The poorer our world is, the poorer are we all. Modernity has foregrounded our individual *deeds*, the narrative structure of our personal experience, as if we exist on a stage, and life is the telling of a self-story.[11] Indeed modernity is glutted with self-stories: they pour out of literature and the media in torrents. But from a panpsychist perspective this glut is a symptom of the loss of the sense of really living, which is, simply, an opening into the presence of the world. Our deeds—the story stuff of our lives according to the modern conception—are, rather, merely our means to remaining on deck: it is necessary to act—to find food and shelter and social congress—if we are to continue to abide here. But this abiding is the real point of existence. Any action beyond this minimum is superfluous. The inexhaustible richness of reality is already given; it does not need to be invented, only embraced. We have only to engage with our world to inherit this bounty. The vessel of the engaged self is always already full, full of others, full of world. Neither emptiness nor aloneness is possible for it in any ultimate or existential sense. Engagement can take place even as one sits quietly on one's verandah gazing at birds in the sky. No great effort is required. But the result is something that no amount of success in the fast lane of life can entail: an inalienable plenitude.

The native then does not feel compelled to *do* anything; she does not strive to perform deeds that would flesh out a narrative in terms of which she could define her life. She is required only to secure the necessities for living, not to be busy, popular, successful, admired. Fulfilment consists in immersing herself in the world and conversing with it. The attitude of "getting the most out of life" is as crass, from this perspective, as it sounds. We get the most out of life by awakening to the world, to its vastness, its beauty, its endless communicativeness. The life of the individual is not so much narrative in structure as poetic: it is not a tale with a beginning and end but is rather constituted through *address*.

NATIVISM AS A FORM OF IDENTITY POLITICS

Part of the fruitfulness of nativism from an ecopolitical point of view is that it introduces an identity politics into the heart of environmentalism. This lends environmentalism the kind of urgency and energy that accrues to other social movements in which the emancipation or self-realization of a class of people is directly at stake—movements such as those against sexism, racism, or the denial of land rights. Radical ecopolitics, dedicated to the preservation of nonhuman life for its own sake, has tended to lack this energizing core, and perhaps this partly accounts for the miasma of boredom that has descended on environmentalism in recent years—the sense that, though important, environmentalism is a kind of societal chore, a bleak responsibility settling ever more heavily on the shoulders of younger and future generations. It also explains why eco-activists, motivated by pure ecological altruism or compassion, are peculiarly prone to burnout, since their efforts, even if successful, do not result in the kind of direct self-empowerment that has in the past rewarded the efforts of, say, feminists or black civil rights campaigners. Nativism, however, promises its practitioners emancipation from the meaninglessness of the modern condition. The meaning that it offers is not of the ideal kind, but is rather that which flows from connection with reality. This is a form of self-realization that many an anomic modern craves. In its pursuit, natives will defend their homeplace with the tenacity and passion that identity activists, such as feminists, defend themselves. They will in turn be recharged by the reconnection with the real that their efforts entail: through homeplace they plug into the sustaining energies and spiritual solace inherent in a psychically activated world.

These remarks about nativism as a form of identity politics immediately call for qualification on two counts. The first is that at least one strand of radical ecopolitics, viz deep ecology, has already offered its supporters an identity ideal to match their politics, viz the ideal of the ecological self. The second point is that identity politics, popular in the 1980s, was subjected to serious deconstruction in the 1990s. Is there then any justification for introducing a new genre of such politics at the present late stage?

Realization of ecological selfhood rested, according to deep ecologists such as Arne Naess, on recognition of the interconnectedness of all living things—on recognition of the fact that all beings are internally or logically related to other beings, and hence that the identity of any living being necessarily implicates that of others.[12] When we recognize this interconnectedness of self with wider and wider circles of being, then, according to deep ecologists, we no longer distinguish sharply between our own interests and those of the beings with whom we are intermeshed—their interests are seen as implicated in ours; defending them accordingly becomes a matter of self-defense.

The idea of the ecological self is obviously cognate in key respects with that of the native self. However the—crucial—difference is that the idea of the ecological self will remain, for most people in so-called developed societies, a perhaps beautiful but nevertheless definitely unlivable ideal. The greater part of the population of these societies lives in large cities, or on commercial agricultural lands, where original ecosystems have been dramatically modified or simplified, if they have not been outright demolished. Our selves are not in fact presently constituted within complex webs of ecological relations, at least at a local level, and many of the biological systems on which we depend are currently maintained not ecologically but artificially, with human intervention rather than ecological checks and balances sustaining production and other vital biological outcomes. (Food supply, for instance, is generally maintained by chemical fertilizers and pesticides, rather than by biological feedback loops.) So the ideal of the ecological self does not reflect the actual situation of most of us today. Nor is it achievable for most of us within the constraints of our actual lives: the prospect of returning as ferals to the forest is neither realistic nor appealing for the general public. The ideal of the native self, by contrast, is achievable by anyone, anywhere, provided they are in a position to commit to some particular place of residence. Since an identity politics can succeed only to the extent that the identity it promotes is achievable, the identity of the native self may provide a more viable basis for such a politics than does that of the ecological self.

Turning to the second point raised above, let us consider whether the problematization of identity in contemporary debates around issues such as sexism and racism vitiates the very possibility of identity politics. Under postmodern and postcolonial influences, feminist theory, for instance, underwent an "identity crisis" in the 1990s, questioning the very existence of woman as a

natural kind or class. Categories, such as that of *woman*, which impute a
common essence to a large class of individuals, are, from a deconstructive
point of view, politically suspect, serving to naturalize and legitimate the
oppression of such a group by rendering its members the same in respect of
certain characteristics that justify their oppression. So, for example, women
are defined as women in terms of certain reproductive tendencies that naturalize and legitimate their confinement to the private sphere; homogenizing categories of the colonized—categories such as those of blacks, savages, or
aborigines—are defined by way of dualistic contrasts with the colonizers: they
are constructed in terms of the irrational, the superstitious, the impulsive, the
childlike, the primitive. Whereas identity politics involves the reclamation and
revalorization of subjugated identities and throws up pride movements, such
as those of blacks and gays, and in the case of cultural feminism (which rehabilitated the traditional feminine), women, politics based on deconstruction
entails the rejection of essentialized identities, in favor of the plurality and difference elided by way of such constructs. If I can no longer be assimilated to
any particular discursive category, I cannot be systematically oppressed, nor
can my oppression, if it occurs, be naturalized and legitimated. If I resolutely
shrug off the constructed tags, woman, black, gay, in favor of more particularized indicators of identity, then I escape the discursive nets that would gather
me into various kinds of subordination.

In light of this powerful argument against identity politics, is there any
justification for reclaiming the category of native and building a new emanci-
patory movement upon it? Is native, in the present sense, as discursive a category as that of woman, for instance? While it is clear that all categories are
discursive in a trivial sense, inasmuch as they belong to our discourses, it is
open to question whether all are discursive in the operative deconstructive
sense of *fictive*—constructed to serve political and ideological ends. I have
elsewhere drawn a distinction between abstract and concrete forms of identity,[13] or discursive and energic forms,[14] and I would like to reinvoke that
contrast here. Abstract identity is based on identification with a discursive
ideal, whether the ideal is presented as an idea, such as that of woman, or as
a set of prescribed ideal behaviors. Concrete identity is the prediscursive relational dimension of identity formed through direct energic engagement with
other subjects: the self comes to know itself as subject, regardless of its contingent physical or cultural characteristics (such as gender, skin color, ethnicity), through the energic responses of particular others to it.

This contrast between abstract/discursive and concrete/energic forms or
dimensions of identity may be illustrated by way of the following pair of
cases. The identity of a child brought up in a small, mutualistic, face-to-face
community will be richly relational: her sense of self will be largely a function
of her positioning within the collectivity, and of the particular energic pat-

tern of her relations with its individual members. This child may or may not be aware, as she is growing up, that her people do in fact constitute a particular tribal or kinship group, let's call it the Black Swan clan, with a traditional culture of its own. If she later identifies as a Black Swan woman, it is not because she has identified with an abstract idea of Black Swan identity and culture, but because she has been constituted through her relations with the individuals who comprise the collectivity that happens to bear this name. However, another woman, who was as an infant removed from the same community and raised within another collectivity of different racial and cultural provenance, may one day discover her origins and try to reclaim her Black Swan identity. In her case, this identity will be abstract and discursive rather than concrete and energic, as it was for the first woman: the second woman will identify with an abstract idea of Black Swan identity and culture and try to recast herself in this image. In a sense this abstract identification is the final stamp of self-alienation effected by her removal from her own people. What is required of her if she is to begin truly to recover her birth identity is that she position herself physically within her birth community and seek energic reengagement with it.

Is the category of native, as I have defined it here, to be understood in an abstract/discursive or a concrete/energic sense? The colonial notion of the native, loaded with pejorative associations, was clearly abstract and discursive; it was an identity that the colonizers projected onto the colonized with a view to legitimating their colonization. But the notion of native that I am outlining here is of one who has been formed through intersubjective contact with a reanimated world. It is this contact itself that shapes native subjectivity. Qua discursive ideal, nativism directs us to seek the formative experience of such contact, for the sake of the real, extradiscursive restructuring of our subjectivity that it will entail. It is arguable that individuals in modern societies respond with such alacrity to the allure of identity politics precisely because the energic—and hence concrete—foundation of their identity is so thin. With only attenuated relations to one another and no anchoring relation to the world, they feel identityless and hence ripe for movements, such as feminism and black power, and more sinisterly, various forms of nationalism and fascism, that offer shiny new identity badges. Such abstract identities cannot, as I have already argued, assuage the problem however, because in the long term they only reinforce the modern individual's estrangement from the concrete. As an identity politics that regrounds people in relations with the concrete particularity of place, however, nativism does provide an authentic antidote to the excessive discursivity of modernity. In doing so it does not elide differences among those who identify as natives. Natives may be expected to differ from one another across communities and countries, since native identity is formed through intersubjective relations and energic

exchange with particular places. As different native populations are constituted by different places, their identities and cultures will be as distinct and
multiple as the places themselves. The category of native is thus not an
homogenizing one in any sense that might be relevant to the purpose of nat-
uralizing and legitimating oppression. Natives are identified in terms of their
relation to the world rather than in terms of informing attributes (such as
racial type, other anatomical features, costume, or specific cultural behaviors
or practices), which could visibly mark them as a class for subjugation.

NATIVISM AND ECOPOLITICS

The radical ecophilosophies that have emerged over the last twenty years—
particularly the many variants of deep ecology—have taken us some of the
way towards a reanimation of the world. They have taught us to recognize
the spirit moving in nonhuman creatures and in wild places and lands. They
have reminded us of our place in the greater scheme of life, and they have
enjoined us to consider other living things as our kin, or as parts of our
wider Self. Ecophilosophy has thereby encouraged us to fight for the rest of
the biosphere: it has called us out into the last remaining strongholds of
wildness—into the forests and swamps and aridlands—where we have made
our stand. We have become passionately protective of that "nature" beyond
our walls.

But this is as far as ecophilosophy has taken us to date. It has discovered
an inner principle—a principle of ensoulment—in wild things, living things,
and it has accordingly exhorted us to protect these things. It has also offered
us images of how we might live attuned to this inner principle in a world
consisting only of wild things, living things—a world of undisturbed
"nature." These are images drawn from hunter-gatherer and other tribal societies. Ecophilosophies such as deep ecology and bioregionalism explain to us
how, in such an ecologically pristine world, we could indeed belong; we
could truly be said to dwell in such a world, become native to it.
Bioregionalism in particular has explored the idea of becoming native to
place. However, in the bioregional context nativism has generally been
understood in strictly ecological terms—one belongs to the *ecosystems* within
which one is located, rather than to place per se, in its full materiality.[15] Such
a notion of nativism therefore has limited applicability in the modern city,
and even in the agricultural countryside, in which ecosystems have been
modified or replaced by human-designed mechanisms. Neither bioregionalism nor deep ecology has yet shown us how, in the world as it is, the "dis-
turbed" world of rampant urbanism and industrialism, we might live in
attunement with that inner principle. In other words, ecophilosophy has

offered us a *posture of opposition* to the contemporary world, but no true *praxis* for it, no way of living harmoniously in it.

Ecophilosophy is in this respect, I think, still incomplete. Deep ecology has achieved a certain depth of inquiry, but I think a further level of inquiry about the relation of humankind to the rest of reality is coming into view. Ecophilosophy has rightly invited us to resist the machines of modernity in defense of "nature," but at the same time it has left most of its followers still helplessly hooked up to the industries and technologies and modes of production of modern society in their everyday lives. There is an inconsistency here that undermines the ecological stance. In order to be consistent, ecophilosophy needs to complete or deepen the project of reanimation. It needs to take the final nondualist step and acknowledge an inner impulse or psychic principle, not only in the natural and biological order, but in the order of matter generally. Only when ensoulment is thus taken to its logical conclusion can we discover how to live attuned to soul in the world as it is, the world of cement, tar, and steel, of degradation and contamination, of the messes we have made.

To adopt a nondualist premise and become a native, particularly an urban native, in the present sense, is plainly to take a step beyond traditional environmentalism. Nativism involves an acquiescence in the concrete given, where this is alien to environmentalism, which valorizes ecological systems over the built or human-made environment. To the extent that the environmental project seeks to reinstate the ecological at the expense of the artefactual, it perpetuates the restless impulse at the heart of modernity—the urge to make the world over in accordance with human values and preferences. By yielding ourselves to the world as it is, however, accepting that this, and no other, is our world, full as it is of refuse and junk, we begin to make the transition from the modern mentality of management and control, which is at the root of the environmental problem, to the votary mentality of affirmation of the given. This way of affirmation is, I contend, a way to beat modernity, while conceding the inescapability of its effects—the cities, technologies, industries, the litter and junk it has spawned. For while modernity is the process of converting the hitherto sacred order of matter and place into commodities, cash, and property, our affirmation, forgiveness, preservation, and enhancement of the given converts commodities and property back into the sacred order. We shall also in this way reenter that order ourselves, as natives, recapturing its spirit within the mundane domain of our actual lives, rather than projecting it out into a romantic and atavistic space beyond the supposedly inevitable secularity and fallen-ness of the contemporary city.

It has been suggested here that nativism, adapted to the contemporary context, offers a deeper response to the challenge of modernity than do philosophies that are purely ecological in scope. Although the immediate outcomes of nativism may not always match our ecological aspirations, the attitude of the native truly subverts the modern contempt for matter that lies at the root of the present environmental crisis.

NATIVISM: FURTHER CONSIDERATIONS

As a response to the challenge of modernity, nativism unquestionably has depth, but as a practice it is still likely to raise many questions in the reader's mind. In this concluding section I would like briefly to address some of these questions, in the process staking out axes along which the ideas of nativism could be more fully developed.

Nativism and the Process of Reconciliation Between Colonizers and Colonized

As a white Australian, it is more than evident to me that I cannot become native to, and custodian for, my homeplace, however narrowly or widely I define that place, until my nonindigenous countrymen and women acknowledge the truth of our history here, since this is a major part of the truth of our land, a truth we must fully encompass if we are to lay claim to the status of native. To become native thus requires that we acknowledge the entire history of colonization, opening ourselves to all the regret and preparedness to compensate that such acknowledgment entrains. Nor can we assume the role of come-lately natives and custodians unless and until the original natives and custodians accept our presence here, and invite us to join them, as co-custodians rather than as conquerors. The original custodians can issue no such invitation, however, until we declare the wrong we have done them, and seek to make amends. If, after apologies and compensations, the original indigenes invite us to share their responsibilities as custodians, what deep knowledge of place they can offer us, they who have been engaging for aeons in the kind of communion that we moderns are only now rediscovering. But again, we cannot share that wisdom until the original inhabitants invite us to do so, and it cannot be hoped that they will invite us until we have admitted, and moved to rectify, to the degree that rectification is possible, the wrongs.[16]

Nativism and the Making of "a People"

In order to take care of their neighborhood, people have to cooperate and communicate with one another. Such caring for one's own place thus inevitably draws people together. Their deep investment in the place that they have collectively called up also inevitably binds them to others who are likewise invested therein—people who belong to my homeplace are my people. When I assume the name, "Freya of Brunswick," or identify as a Merri Creek woman, I feel an immediate affinity with others whose names or identities link them to my place. I want to meet the person who wrote BELOVED CREEK in large sprayed letters on the underside of the bridge, and the little band of troubadours who call themselves the Merri Creek Players. I want to know my tribe, those whose psyches are nourished by the same land-forms, the same ground, as mine. When we "take care of country," as indige-nous Australians say, then, whether that country falls in the inner city or the heart of the desert, community, by some kind of happy preestablished har-mony, tends to take care of itself.

Natives of a particular place share a common relational identity, what-ever their cultural and racial provenance. When we commit to a place, we become in due course the people of that place and belong to it, and hence to one another, whatever our initial differences. In time too the place inflects our different racial and cultural styles with its own subtle markers, bringing a richly differentiated coherence to our erstwhile heterogeneity. In these ways nativism unifies peoples without eliding differences.

For these reasons nativism cannot be charged with fostering racially or ethnically homogenous, closed communities that exclude, or refuse to assimilate, outsiders—migrants, refugees, dissidents, nonconformists. Yes, population size in nativist communities is limited by ecological parameters, since such communities are dedicated to the sufficiency of the given and therefore must find their livelihood largely within their own ecological com-pass while at the same time ensuring the integrity of their homeplace. But they are nevertheless essentially open communities. Newcomers find their place in them, not by fiat, by paper "rights" of citizenship, and the like, but by the actual, gradual process of becoming native, of becoming implicated, at the level of identity, in the place or land in question, and assuming a cus-todial attitude to it.

Nativism and Social Justice

If commitment to place enables people to achieve self-realization, as natives, and to escape the anomic condition of modernity, then it would appear that freedom to commit to place is a basic human freedom. Yet in modern soci-eties, many people lack such freedom. People cannot be assured of their tenure of a house or apartment, in capitalist economies, unless they are in a position to purchase it. Rented accommodation is subject to disposition by the owner. Nor may tenants be assured of finding new accommodation within the neighborhood they may have decided to make their own. Neighborhoods are subject to development and to the rise and fall of property markets, and an area that has been affordable in the past may not be so in the future. As an ideal then, native identity would seem to be accessible only to the relatively economically privileged.

Is the nativist ideal thereby vitiated? In my view, it is not. Rather, this objection from social justice brings to light a new fundamental human "right"—the right to homeplace, where this may be understood as a counterpart, for all peoples, of the land rights of indigenous peoples. From the viewpoint of nativism, every human being has the "right" to resist or overcome the existential alienation of modernity, and to preserve or restore her relation of belonging to the world through a particular place or set of places. (In putting the point this way, I do not wish to commit to an ethic or ontology of rights, but only to draw an analogy between the acknowledged—though generally not honored—entitlement of indigenous peoples to their ancestral lands, and a similar but so far unacknowledged entitlement of all peoples to a homeplace.) If a society is so structured as to deprive individuals of the possibility of retaining or reestablishing a homeplace, then to that extent the society in question is unjust, and in need of political reform.

Another objection to nativism from a social justice perspective is that, in affirming the sufficiency of the given, nativism condemns certain individuals to remaining in the straitened or derelict places to which an unjust society has consigned them, while condoning the monopolization of spacious, well-endowed places by those who currently enjoy the privilege of occupying them. This is a more serious objection than the previous one, because it brings out the point that nativism is a philosophy of sufficiency rather than equality. If a seemingly poor place has the potential to sustain life, materially, spiritually, and imaginatively, then it may be valued as highly as a better-appointed place, from a nativist point of view, since provided a place can support life, its value lies as much in its capacity to engage with us as in its more overt attractions. To appraise places purely in terms of their real estate values would be analogous, from a nativist perspective, to appraising marriage partners purely in terms of their looks and their dowries. Just as love and commitment allow individuals to blossom as spouses, whether they are initially rich or poor, attractive or plain, happy or sad, so love and commitment allow differently endowed sites to blossom as homeplaces. There are many examples of how the reinhabitation of neglected localities has rendered them colorful, vibrant, magnetic neighborhoods,[17] far richer, in an existential sense, than adjoining upmarket "addresses." (The danger then is that the sites revitalized by devoted, resourceful inhabitants become recolonized by capital—gentrified—and the natives are dispossessed all over again.) To say this, however, is not to suggest that people are obliged to commit to their homeplace at whatever cost to their physical and social well-being. Being grounded in the real may be a basic human good, but it is only one of a number of such goods, all of which must be weighed against one another in our attempts to achieve self-realization.

From the panpsychist viewpoint of nativism then, "wealth" is measured according to nonmaterialist as well as materialist yardsticks: homeplaces and possessions are valued in terms of the depth of their embeddedness in the fabric of our lives and their participation in the poetic order, rather than merely in terms of their "exchange value" in the market place. Such richness can only be won gradually, through time, as a result of our loyalty and attentiveness, a true "investment" of ourselves in things and places. It cannot be acquired and accumulated by the signing of checks, or other contractual forms of exchange, though it can sometimes be passed on, via gifts, to those who succeed us or cooperate with us as custodians of particular things and places. Loved places, whatever their initial worth and character, become rich places, charged with life and fertile with poetic significance. In light of this criterion of value, the ideal of material equality loses much of its point.[18]

The Native and the Journeyer

Does nativism imply an embargo on travel? Or, more accurately, will one whose identity is bound up with homeplace lose the impulse to seek out distant places? Will he, like the old man of Verona, be forever content with his own plot, forever content to see the sun rise over the same wide field on which it set? Clearly, for a contemporary native, whose consciousness and conscience is permeable to the global context, opportunities to recharge his network relationships via face-to-face meetings will be desirable, and gatherings may be arranged for this end, if they are within the means of the participants. But is travel in any wider, exploratory sense consistent with the ethos of nativism?

The first question to consider in this connection is that of nomadism. The nomad appears to present a contrast to the native, but insofar as the traditional nomad typically followed seasonal routes that were as familiar to him as homelands were to the traditional indigene, this contrast is actually more apparent than real. These routes in effect constituted linear homelands, and the nomad could assume as custodial a relation to them as did natives to their more bounded territories. However, insofar as nomadism is interpreted loosely, as connoting a merely wandering way of life, the question of its relation to nativism is more complex.

Evidently, the ethos of nativism is incompatible with travel in the touristic sense, where this is understood as involving the packaging or purchasing of certain prescribed geographical and cultural sights and sounds and "experiences" (the Eiffel Tower, Ayers Rock, a bullfight, a Japanese tea ceremony, an Aboriginal corroboree). Tourism is one of the paradigmatic pursuits of modernity, one of the principal ways in which the modern converts the psychophysical field of reality into a manifold of mere appearances, which can be duly accumulated, like possessions, and mentally encompassed. Having "seen it all," the modern feels larger than the world, and epistemically in charge of it, since he neither apprehends nor participates in its inexhaustible reality.

However, although the native is not a tourist, nor is he necessarily as entirely a homebody as the old man of Verona, even allowing for occasional sorties to cement alliances. Nativism today, I think, calls for complementation by a certain kind of free travel. This is because the native, dedicated to the familiar and the deeply known, also needs opportunities to experience the strange and the unknown, to discover the indifferent face of things. While the touristic mode of travel—of paying one's money to have one's expectations fulfilled, and the world dished up to order, a harmless potpourri of appearances—is antithetical to the spirit of nativism, there is a mode of travel consistent with this spirit. This is a mode of travel that might be described as *journeying*. Journeying involves a voyage into vulnerability, a doffing of one's habitual identity to become the stranger, open to serendipitous direction by the world, and to the self-appointment of one's destinations by themselves. It matters little, from this point of view, where one travels, but only how one does so. Indeed, perhaps the most challenging form of journeying is into the unknown dimensions of the deceptively familiar. To encounter the strangeness of the real in the midst of the everyday can be more unnerving than encountering it at a distant frontier.[19] (See chapter 7.) In any case, journeying in this way, in utmost humility, without expectation, open to revelation, one stands to discover those things about oneself, about one's own community and culture, that are hidden in daily life.

Such journeying, undertaken at critical points in one's life, with the attitude of a supplicant rather than of a spectator, is arguably only possible for one who has assumed the position of the native, for without the sense of existential security, of inalienable belonging to the world, that accrues from nativism, one might not be able to endure the vulnerability of journeying. It is perhaps by participating in the inner nature of the world, where such participation seems most achievable via the particularity of place, that one acquires the trust in things that enables one to surrender the precautions, plans, and itineraries that insulate the touristic modern from both danger and revelation.

Nativism and Liberalism

It is sometimes assumed that a society organized along nativist or bioregional lines would be illiberal—authoritarian—in the sense that it would predetermine the values and worldview to which its members must subscribe: the individual would have to share in the values and worldview of nativism or bioregionalism and adopt a compatible way of life. In liberal democracies, in contrast, individuals are (ideally) free to choose their own values, worldviews, and ways of life, provided their doing so does not curtail the like entitlement of others.[20]

As I have already explained in chapter 1 however, liberalism is deeply question-begging in this connection. Its espousal of moral and metaphysical pluralism is actually a function of its own prior metaphysical commitment to materialism and hence to mind/matter dualism. That is, it is only in light of the metaphysical premise that self is separate from world or place that it can be assumed that the good of the self is independent of the good of world or place. This latter assumption, in other words, grounds the assumption that the self can pursue its own good independently of the good of the world. According to the alternative premise, that of panpsychism, the good of self is inextricably tied to the good of world or place, and individuals must accordingly take responsibility for the care of their world or place. Liberals thus enjoin metaphysical and moral pluralism only because they have already, at the meta level, decided the metaphysical and moral issue. Liberalism accordingly emanates in a practice that corroborates dualism, not panpsychism. Societies cannot duck the issue of their metaphysical premise. To allow for ostensible metaphysical diversity is in fact to ensure outcomes consistent with certain metaphysical premises but inconsistent with others. To face the metaphysical issue squarely and, as a society, to commit to a search for metaphysical consensus raises questions of epistemology to which I can offer no answer here. Suffice it to say that this is a search—long since abandoned in the West—to which we must collectively rededicate ourselves if we are ultimately to secure the world and our place in it.

Relation between Sense of Place and Environmentalism

Much empirical work in geography, anthropology, and sociology confirms that in traditional societies, and even sometimes in certain strata of modern societies, homeplace is indeed implicated in personal or communal identity. Nativist tendencies, or tendencies towards cherishing a "sense of place," have, in other words, been quite widely identified by scholars across a range of fields.[21] However, there is little evidence that people's sense of belonging is directed to bioregions rather than to places in a more neutral sense. Yet from mere association with place per se, environmental implications seem not to follow. A person might relish sooty skies and the fires of industrial furnaces lighting up the night because this is the terrain of their childhood. They might accordingly fight to preserve industrial landscapes as heritage in spite of the degrading effect of such landscapes on the biotic environment. Unless one's homeplace is already an ecologically intact place then, the custodial implications of nativism do not seem necessarily to contribute to environmentalism.[22]

An initial rejoinder to this objection is that a thorough acquaintance with homeplace, such as would be expected of a native, would reveal the way that homeplace fits into and is informed by larger geographical and ecological contexts. Its viability as a homeplace will depend ultimately on the integrity of these larger contexts. In that sense a measure of ecological responsibility is intrinsic to reflective emplacement.

However, the main contribution of such emplacement to environmentalism has already been explained: rather than directly promoting ecological activism, identification with place undercuts the consumerist imperative of capitalism and provides foundations for a conserver psychology. In this sense nativist attitudes contribute to environmentalism even when they are focused on sites of little ecological significance.

The Nonlocality of Ecological Malaise

Many ecological problems are not localized but pervasive, even global, in extent. Hence they cannot be effectively tackled at a local level.[23] Global coordination of environmental management seems accordingly to be required.

As long as nativism is a minority ethos, communities organized along nativist lines will be unable to solve even their own ecological problems—insofar as these problems originate from outside their bioregions—let alone the ecological problems of the wider world. Even if nativism were universally adopted however, local custodial praxes would still need to be worked out by communities in consultation with one another, since local environments can be fully understood only against the background of larger ecospherical contexts. So while the custodial praxis of nativism will indeed contribute significantly to environmentalism, it will not obviate the need for broader-scale coordination of environmental effort in the medium and even long term. However, as I am about to explain, nativism need not be so defined that it is incompatible with globalism per se, though the forms of globalism with which it is compatible will need to be carefully specified.

Nativism in a Global Context

Contemporary communication and information technologies entail that nativism in the present day will differ significantly from nativism in certain of its premodern forms, such as the form in which Claudian found it personified in the old man of Verona. Modernity has created a new context for the local, one that cannot, and presumably ought not, be repudiated.

This new context is, of course, that of globalism. Globalism appears, on the face of it, to consist in the unilateral spread of the interests and influences of modern societies throughout the world. Instead of seeking to adapt and limit the needs of the emplaced self to the capacities of the immediately given, global capitalism ransacks the entire planet, both economically and culturally, to satisfy the demands of the free-floating modern self. Through tentacular strategies, facilitated by media and entertainment empires, dominant cultures extend their influence, and hence their markets, to the rest of the globe.

Globalism understood in this sense consists of the global hegemony of Western, or more latterly, American interests. It is the global imposition of a monoculture. But to this *unilateral* sense of globalism a *multilateral* sense can be contrasted. That is to say, globalism may be understood either as the unilateral spread of a singular dominant influence *or* as the multilateral interaction and interpermeation of local influences and hence as the mutual constitution of local cultures.[24] In the former, unilateral sense, globalism is clearly destructive of local economies and cultures. But in the latter, multilateral sense, globalism arguably furnishes an indispensible condition for positive forms of localism.

It is clear that nativist communities, with their commitment to the sufficiency of the given, would generally oppose economic regimes based on distribution of goods via global markets. They would insist on local production and consumption of the basic elements of subsistence and culture. Food, for instance, would be grown, gathered, and processed locally, ensuring freshness, distinctiveness, feasibility of conversion to organic methods, and minimization of transport and storage costs.[25] Energy would be obtained locally from renewable sources. Crafts would be cultivated regionally for the sake of their contribution to local character and identity. But each region could perhaps also develop its own manufacturing speciality, in which sophisticated technologies, centralized forms of management, and economies of scale were deployed. Such manufacture at the more specialized end of the industrial spectrum would allow entry for regional groupings into cross-regional markets. The exchanges of specialized products that would thereby be permitted would afford continued access for local communities to a wide range of sophisticated items, such as medical technologies, that could not generally be produced locally. More importantly, such cross-regional economic groupings could assist in safeguarding regional security. The increase in cross-regional and international trade in the latter part of the twentieth century witnessed dramatic new possibilities for world order based on multilateral economic agreements and sanctions rather than on militarism, and to this extent they perhaps represented an historical and environmental advance that would best be maintained in the face of localist devolution. To abandon multilateral trade altogether would be to abandon the economic glue for international law and a legally constituted world order. This would in turn leave localist communities and cultures unprotected in the face of larger powers.[26]

Culturally speaking, globalism is of course a function of new communication technologies. While certain of these technologies, such as television and cinema, afford unilateral electronic access of hegemonic influences to vulnerable cultures, others, such as the internet, allow these cultures to engage in multilateral electronic exchange among themselves. Top-down, unilateral communication is of course destructive of on-the-ground, local cultures. But multilateral communications induce a healthy local-level awareness of the cultural differentiation of the global. This awareness will ensure that attachment to the local will not degenerate into the narrow-minded partiality and parochialism, xenophobia and exclusionary (us/them) mindset that has often in the past characterized the mentality of the insular village, region, or clan. By maintaining the global array of places, peoples, and cultures in view, multilateral communications enable natives to remain mindful that their own local scenarios are but one manifestation of the variegated possibilities of the planet. Such natives are thus not tempted to mistake the preciousness of these scenarios to them for outright superiority—for a degree of preciousness that other places, peoples, and cultures lack.

Having the capacity to locate themselves within a greater scheme of peoples and places also enables natives to know themselves better, to understand the true character of their homeplace in comparison with others, and its role in the relational fabric of the planetary environment. Being mindful of the indefinite differentiation and interconnectedness of the global, they are less likely to take the hallmarks of their own scenarios as the yardstick for other scenarios, where it is this myopic tendency to universalize one's local norms and values that generates all manner of parochial intolerance and devolutionary mayhem. Such awareness of a world of differences beyond one's native borders is best maintained not merely by way of electronic windows onto other peoples and places, but by way of communicative *exchange* with them. Their responsiveness will ensure that one remains attuned to their inner reality and dynamism, so that they do not assume the aspect merely of picturesque or exotic media images or charades (as colonized cultures typically did for the colonizers).

The native is of course *disposed* to forge communication networks with other communities of natives, and with the wider world generally, because the consciousness of the native, though rooted in place, is ecological. That is to say, through her attentive participation in the life processes of her own homeplace, she will have discovered its implicatedness in a biosherical field of ecological relations that inform and determine the particularities of its character. In turning in upon her place then, she is simultaneously turning out to the matrix of external relations through which her own place is sustained. Since culture, for the native, grows out of and distills the essence of place, culture will necessarily express this interleaved nature: it will take its forms from the local but at the same time draw sustenance from the nourishing influences that flow into the local from the perimeters of homeplace.

The native's communication with natives elsewhere, which is so greatly facilitated by multilateral electronic mediation, may include exchanges of knowledge, arts, and moral and political lore. These cultural exchange networks may also be mobilized for political purposes when the need arises—as when the homeplaces of native allies are threatened by development. Transnational alliances of custodians, organized via the internet, allow for effective forms of (synergistically orchestrated) resistance to hegemonic globalism when this is required. In this sense too then multilateral communications are a necessary condition for a viable localism, since without such communications a nativist regime would offer no proportional political resistance to corporate excess.

The global—in the sense of multilateral—cultural context afforded by modernity has thus ensured that a truly benign, open, and politically efficacious form of nativism can now be reliably practiced. This is an ecological form of nativism not premised on ignorance of other cultures, or hostility to their intrusions, or helplessness in the face of their aggression, but on appreciation of the indefinite differentiation of the global and on access to its unlimited possibilities for solidarity. Within this global frame, the native celebrates the uniqueness and authenticity, but not any supposed superiority, of his own particularity. He understands that the uniqueness and authenticity of his own local culture is partly a function of its dialogue with other local cultures, of its porousness to them.[27]

Part 2
Ground Studies

Chapter 4

Julia's Farm: Fertility

I had long wanted to see in the new millennium in the company of my friend, Julia Bell. For ten years Julia and I had been dreaming of taking a camel trek, either down the Canning Stock Route or across the Nullabor Plain. During that time Julia had indeed become a cameleer. She had acquired a number of camels and moved from her home in the hills of Perth to a property in a remote area of southeastern Western Australia. As the decade wore on, we started hatching plans for a millennial trek up to the Central deserts. Julia now had the camels, the experience, and the equipment, but she also had the farm, which included an enormous menagerie in addition to the camels. As millennial fever began to grip the rest of the globe, it became clear that Julia would not be able to absent herself from her establishment. I was myself by this time feeling that perhaps I had left it a bit late for becoming a cameleer. So we started thinking in terms of a week in the desert over the New Year's Eve period. Even this dwindled to a couple of days. Nevertheless, determined that we would at least greet the millennial dawn itself in a suitably millennial setting, I boarded the train late in December for the arduous thirty-five-hundred-kilometer sit-up journey from my home in Melbourne to Kalgoorlie, and thence to Ravensthorpe.

Even on the very eve of the new year there was still uncertainty as to whether we would be able to take leave of the farm. But if there is one thing I have learned about pilgrimages, it is that there are never any assurances that the quest will succeed, right up until the very last minute. Sure enough however, sunset saw us pelting down the road to the coast in a classic battered utility, with Dingo the dog and Digger the joey, noses to the glass, along for the ride. In the very last light, we crossed a sandbar at the foot of a solitary mountain—such a mountain! spray-wrapped from the wild sea beating at its gates, it looked like the citified abode of all kinds of spirit folk—and entered a primeval world of windswept coastal plains and turreted ranges. The plains were clad in low coastal flora, intricate, diverse, and much of it, as I was to discover the following day, in flower.

It was very dark when we found a cove in which to camp, so we just laid out mattresses and blankets on the tray of the utility. After Julia had tucked herself up I wandered down to the beach to linger with what remained of our century. Snuggled inside a white blanket I sat on the white sand and looked out over a white tumult between black headlands. It was nice to sit alone and tiny among the vast starfields, lost for a while among the centuries, on a shore that had not changed for thousands of years. There was no light of human habitation in sight because no human habitation existed for scores of miles and the Southern Ocean was lonely clear to Antarctica. Sadly I said farewell to the twentieth century, to our time, the time that, for better or for worse, we had all shared.

We arose at first light and I raced up to higher ground and was just in time to see the sun rising out of the ocean. It was a lemony dawn, with the sun gold and biblically rayed, lighting up the waters between two black shoulders of coast. I had a sense of heavenly trumpets sounding as the light spread over the land. There, where the surf beats out the passage of time on the beach, and the sun rises in such triumphal splendor every day, I offered greetings to this uncertain stranger, the twenty-first century.

Such an access of sublime sentiment could not fail, of course, to attract a comment or two from the other end of things. Even food for the soul returns ultimately, after all, to shit. So during the night, while Julia and I had been sleeping in the back of the ute, Dingo, locked in the cabin, felt he had no recourse but to relieve himself behind the seat, and then, inevitably, his discreet deposit had been padded all over my jacket and bag and the other things in the cabin. Later in the morning, responding to the same call, I wandered down to a rocky knoll standing out to sea, joined by a landbridge to the main coast. I was looking, on the stony ground, for a place to crouch, and I spied a nice shoaly patch at the edge of some bushes. I started digging with a stone. The earth was surprisingly soft, even moist. I soon realized that I was in fact digging into shit and toilet paper in an advanced stage of decomposition! In all these miles of deserted coastline I had homed in on a few centimeters of ground favored by another of my kind! The message was clear: you may be a child of the galaxy—the role in which I had fondly cast myself the previous evening—but only in the same sense that a dog sitting alone on a beach is a puppy of the galaxy. You too view the world through the filter of your species' needs and functions. No unmediated encounter with the universe for you! Still, it was a gentle reminder. The unmanifest "universe" still talks to us, after all, through the manifest one. It is just important to recall, now and then, that the reality that does the talking is ultimately unmanifest.

Back at Julia's farm, the "holiness" of "shit" is very much in evidence. A sense that the precious, the sacred, is not merely effortlessly granted but must be *created* alchemically through transmutation of abased, unwanted elements is at the core of Julia's vision. Hers is a place built from the discarded, the despised, the rejected. Leftovers, hand-me-downs, retrievings from the tip, the op shop, the side of the road are eagerly sought and received by her, and the orphaned, the runts, the surplus-to-requirements are taken in. All these "fallen," animate and inanimate alike, are set on course again, given a new lease of life and a part to play in creating a uniquely sanctuarial domain, a domain of forgiveness, of the cherishing of all matter.

When Julia arrived here, seven years ago, she found a fibro miner's shack sitting amid decades' accumulation of rubbish on a sixty-acre partly cleared paddock just beyond the edge of town. There was electricity and town water, the latter a great asset in this arid country. She set to work with her own hands. With the help of her many local friends, her son when he came to stay, and more recently her partner, Rob, she has embarked on an epic project of place making.

Now luxuriant flowers bloom at the front of the house, all grown of course from cuttings and bulbs that have been passed from hand to hand. Pennyroyal thrives unchecked around the ponds, and hundreds of bees—from Julia's hives—are drawn to its little purple blooms. A young citrus grove is struggling to take root, and Julia asks me to pee around the trees rather than in the toilet—the trees need the nitrogen. There are also a couple of large vegetable plots in which the soil has been enriched not only by the copious amounts of compost and manure available from the farm, but by the digging in of roadkills. Innumerable roos and rabbits and birds picked up from the roadside have been given solemn burial here, as well as sheep that have died on neighboring farms from causes—such as snakebite or cancer—that make them unsuitable for dog meat.

The home site is full of pens and cages. A large wire enclosure has been built against the back wall of the house for two disabled galahs. As I wash clothes at the laundry trough I am studied by two pink faces looking quizzically in at me through the window from their specially provided window shelf. Another cage has been attached around the corner of the house, on the west wall. This is the residence of a carpet python. A miniature window can be opened into this cage too from inside the house to give the python entry into ... Julia's bedroom! This is where the python crawls when nights are cold—into Julia's bed for warmth. It had been grumpy and off-color for a few days before I arrived, but all was explained when a freshly sloughed skin was found in its cage. Julia hopes to attract lots more pythons to the home-site, to mop up the (innumerable) other snakes, and of course the mice. There are runs and pens of all kinds for ducks and geese and chooks in various different family arrangements. An old turkey, whom I knew when Julia still lived in Perth, had recently died, at the age of eighteen years. On the other side of the house are yards for pigs, Dexter cows, goats and the inevitable black sheep. Adjacent to the main poultry runs is the camel stockade, where eight camels amble in from their paddock at sunset to feed and bed down—and to rumble all night like beasts from the jungle depths! I'm scared of their hugeness, the pillow-sized feet with which they can lash out not only to the rear but also to the front! But I enjoy patting their nuzzly heads when they are on the other side of the fence. Julia has never used force or aggression in training them, which is apparently unusual among cameleers, here and in India too.

Into this little bastion of redemption, tiny refugees from civilization are moving of their own accord. Under the wide front veranda, in among potted moonflowers and waxflowers and hanging bits of plough and harness and untold salvaged paraphernalia, are a number of hanging baskets. From the largest of these, flanking the front path, trail thick tresses of the dainty-leafed "chain of hearts." Into the depths of one of the baskets, a pair of spotted pardalotes has excavated a tunnel-nest. Julia has shone a torch down the tunnel and discovered two eggs. There are now three pairs of this normally shy but pretty bird—yellow breasted and red streaked with painted white dots on its back—looking for nesting sites around the house. We can hear their call—just a single crystal gong—and see them at the windows throughout the day.

From mid-morning to dusk the front veranda is occupied by blowflies. The air there is dark with them, swarming, vibrating, droning. This creates a heaven for the large "motorbike" frogs, which sit under the foliage of the potted plants and on rafters and suspended logs, their mouths wide open, simply waiting for flies to stumble in. There are dozens, possibly hundreds of them, lined up along every available roost, looking like tarnished bronze buddhas. Up close they are leopard-marked. Julia tells me they are spotted-thighed tree frogs (Litoria cyclorhynchus). While frogs of all kinds are fast retreating even in this remote region, as they are in most parts of the world, they are flocking to Julia's farm. The word is out and the party is on. At other times of the year other species are apparently here in force, including pobblebonks. Once Julia even unearthed a turtle frog—a strange little cartoonlike creature, which I have only seen in books; it is a mere blob with four rudimentary protrusions for legs and a bulge, with black eyes, for a head.

With flies in such abundance, there is also of course a good supply of cobweb under the veranda. This encourages willywagtails to settle there, since they use the old webs to seal their nests. The loud, multilayered hum of the blowflies is quite hypnotic and would serve well as a meditation aid in a Buddhist temple. I don't find out the types of spiders frequenting this meditation hall, but golden orb spiders are establishing colonies on old rubbish sites elsewhere on the property. *She* is long and oval shaped, and hangs in the middle of a great complex of linked webs. *He* is much smaller and hovers at the margins of the condominium. I never do see them in their golden garb, but I do see lots of Christmas spiders, with tiny rhinoceros horns and armored bodies painted like Venetian glass beads.

The resacralizing intention is explicit everywhere. Around the yard Goddess figures (including lots of discarded Our Ladies) and Buddha heads peep from altars made of old bits of farm machinery and whale jawbones. Prayers and philosophical maxims are everywhere inscribed, in gilded letters, on doors and window frames and archways.

In the center of the home paddock lies the animal cemetery. This is where Julia herself hopes to be buried. Many a time have I rung Julia to find her tearfully in the midst of nursing a dying animal. Whether it is a birthing camel, a snake-bitten dog, or a run-over wallaby, this is where the one who has come to grief is laid. There are inscriptions over the graves, touching little meditations on those whose remains further sanctify the ground. A large shrine presides over the cemetery, a six-foot-high grotto built of quartz crystal and shimmering pink tourmaline and housing a blue-robed Mary with her foot on a serpent. (I hope she will protect Julia from the ever-present risk of snakebite!) In another part of the cemetery a feeding tray fashioned from an old ploughshare is set up; this is where dead mice from traps inside the house are laid each day for carnivorous birds. In another corner again stands a sign bearing just a single word scrawled with a gold-painted finger: FORGIVENESS.

The philosophy that is finding expression in this place is not merely a prosaic one of "recycling." It is not merely a how-to-do-more-with-less philosophy of thrift and self-reliance. It is much deeper than this. It is a philosophy of reclamation, resurrection, and renewal—where these are, I think, at the heart of the notion of *fertility*. Yes, it is this archaic principle—that of fertility—that is the animating principle here. The farm is a temple to fertility and Julia is a fertility priestess. But she is a priestess who intuitively understands that the scope of fertility includes not only living things but all of matter. The worship of fertility entails a practice of "recycling" at every level of life—the forgiveness of the degraded, the readoption of the rejected, the reclamation of the discarded. It is only from the perspective of such encompassing forgiveness that we can truly affirm the given and that the new can find its authentic form from within the shell of the old.

What has happened to the principle of fertility—so central to the organization of archaic societies—under the contemporary conditions of modernity? It has vanished from view. The very word "fertility" is scarcely heard. There is "fertilizer" in agriculture, but this is just a powder, one among many chemical powders, mechanistically applied to crops to cause them to grow. There is "fertility control" in animals and humans, consisting again of mechanical or chemical interventions to limit reproduction. And there are "fertility clinics," where those suffering from infertility undergo interventions that aim to induce conception. But as a template, as the very pattern for the conduct of life at both personal and social levels, fertility has sunken into oblivion.[1]

Some of the import of the old fertility principle was absorbed into the Christian tradition through the Jesus story. Fertility myths were descent myths, in which an earth or grain goddess undertook a dangerous journey to the Underworld, the realm of darkness and death, in order to bring the gift of new life back to the land of the living. The spiritual dimension of these myths was already well understood in pagan contexts: the descent was not only the journey of crops back into the soil in winter and their reemergence in spring but the journey of the soul into mortification in order to achieve its own full flowering: all aspects of life, unwanted as well as wanted, are part of life's sacred unity and must therefore be accepted, forgiven, if the spirit is to grow.

Fertility cults thus revolved around sacrifice as the condition for rebirth: the individual was sacrificed physically, through death, to provide the material matrix for a new life which, while no longer the original individual's, would nevertheless represent the continuation of her story; and individuals were encouraged to embrace suffering, spiritually, in their own persons in order to consent consciously to the terms of life and thereby achieve a deeper experience of living.

Christianity takes up the latter, spiritual thread of the fertility myth, but discards the former, physical thread. Jesus' life may be read as a descent. An emanation of God, Christ made the journey from the spirit realms of heaven down into this mortal "underworld" to suffer and die on a cross in darkness of spirit and flesh, from thence to ascend again to heaven to rejoin his father. (The parallels with the Demeter and Persephone myth could hardly be more evident.) Although Jesus' entire life is a descent, this descent and the subsequent ascent are acted out symbolically via the crucifixion and the resurrection, where these symbolic events are memorialized at Easter, the traditional fertility festival named for the egg goddess, Oestra. Despite the insistent parallels however, the purpose of the Christian myth remains resolutely "spiritual": Jesus descended and ascended again in order to win for us individual rebirth on a purely spiritual (i.e. disembodied) individual level. He forgave us our sins, which is to say, he reconciled us to our deficiencies and miseries, and thereby enabled us to love life more wholeheartedly. Forgiveness thus retains its central role in the Christian reworking of the fertility myths. But Christian forgiveness does not extend to death: while the need for spiritual sacrifice is upheld, Christianity balks at the necessity for individuals to make the final physical sacrifice, namely death. Jesus promises his followers eternal life. Through his sacrifice, they will be "saved." No one else need ever die. The age-old wisdom that life is a gift that endures only as long as it is passed on is here compromised. Jesus offers the individual a "spiritualized" escape clause from the cycle of birth, death, and regeneration. Via this device of "spiritualization," the individual is invited to introject the great cycle, to situate it within himself rather than situating himself within it.

So while the Christian notion of forgiveness does indeed capture a profound aspect of the fertility principle, and while the roots of the Christian Mystery of resurrection are deeply entwined with the Eleusinian Mystery of rebirth, the link between Christianity and fertility is nevertheless broken at a crucial juncture. Through the refusal of Christianity to sacrifice the individual for the sake of life in a larger sense, value shifts, historically, from the renewal of the world to the fate of the individual.

The "spiritualization" of the fertility myth in Christianity also renders its message abstract and hence open to mediation and disputation. The principle of fertility in itself is so easily understood. Any child can see that a crop must return to the soil if a new crop is to sprout, that new life springs from the death of the old. This is a tangible truth. As long as our understanding of life is fitted to this tangible template, we cannot go wrong. But Jesus' message of divine love is complex and speculative. Its point, even at the spiritual level, is easily missed, as history so eloquently testifies.

In any case, under the conditions of late modernity, even the attenuated "spiritualized" message of forgiveness that Christianity offers has been largely lost from society. The decree that the "first shall be last and the last shall be first" has given way to a credo that the last are "losers," and that for that very reason they deserve the hand that fate has dealt them. Success, by whatever means, justifies itself. This is the yardstick by which individuals and states are currently measured. Success consists in vanquishing poverty, discomfort, obscurity, humiliation, shame, pain, and ultimately perhaps, death itself. Forgiveness, in the sense of accommodation of weakness, failure, and adversity, is definitely *out*; triumphalism, in the sense of rewriting the terms of life to suit oneself, is *in*.

This defiance of the terms of life reflects the fact that in the modern era civilization is no longer organized around the organic principle of fertility but rather around the manufacturing one of production. Whereas organic processes are continuous and cyclic, new forms emerging continuously out of those that precede them, manufacturing processes involve a hiatus, a point at which old forms are melted down and matter is reduced to an undifferentiated state, a state in which it retains none of the traces, none of the rich and poetic story, of its metamorphoses. Out of this bare substrate, new things are fashioned, their form derived not from their own histories—since they have none—but from the imagination of the manufacturers. It is through such processes that modern societies have hijacked reality, overriding its inherent logic of unfolding and forcing it to conform to abstract human designs and fantasies instead.

What is this logic of unfolding, this logic of fertility that is inherent in a world left to its own devices? In the processes underlying fertility, the germ of the new takes shape in the depths of the already given and preserves the essence, the "spirit," of the given. The already given then grows old and decomposes into the mulch from which the new will grow, but the new carries the essence, the preview derived from that which preceded it, into the future. Continuity of form is thus preserved through time and change. The new springs forth afresh, again and again, but always to the drumbeat of its predecessors.

This continuity of form lies at the heart of fertility. Fertility affords a thread of storied or poetic identity linking past to future, an identity in which all living things, and ultimately things in general, share as long as conditions of fertility prevail. Is it important, we might wonder, that such a thread hold? Would a world in which the thread unraveled support life? Could such a world exist at all?

Let's consider for a moment how such a world might begin—is beginning—to come about. Agents under the direction of abstractive thought (such as ourselves) might commandeer the life process, reproducing existing life forms in test tubes from laboratory materials and engineering new or modified life forms to suit their own purposes. In such a scenario, life, including the life that feeds life, viz food, becomes the province of manufacture, built from inanimate elements according to ever-changing designs. The authors of these designs might live in plastic domes and mix their own atmosphere, distil their own water, and so on. Confronted with "limitations" in themselves, they reengineer their own nature to ensure that they achieve their goals. They drive their planet, and the other moons and planets in their solar system, along trajectories plotted to suit their own ends, producing seasons and lengths of day and night to order. Everything manifest in their environment, at least at the macrolevel, is harnessed to their particular intentionality.

Such a world would be largely devoid of storied or poetic integrity. The things that formed its contents would not embody the history of their predecessors nor would they pass on their own history to their successors. There would thus be no narrative threads linking past to future. Since it is through these branching lines of narrative transmission that the identities of coexisting things come to be narratively or poetically intertwined, the contents of such a world at any given moment would be narratively unconnected: there would be no greater story tying individuals together. In the absence of such a greater story, a story that does not consist in the self-referencing deeds of individual actors but rather in an overarching order to which all things belong and within which each thing finds its meaning, such a world would have nothing to communicate to us. There would be no Way that it could reveal to us, no cycles or patterns to which it could enjoin us to align ourselves. With nothing to say, no meaning of its own, no wisdom to impart as to the proper living of life, such a reality could not function as a *speaking* world. It seems idle then to impute a subjectival dimension to it. The "psyche" in panpsychism thus appears to depend upon the preservation of the thread of storied or poetic continuity that is at the heart of the principle of fertility. Fertility in this sense entails much more than the perpetuation of life. It is the principle that expresses the poetic integrity of existence and hence the psychic dimension of reality.

We might even wonder whether a world deprived of its poetic integrity could function as a *world* at all. If continuity of form were ruptured to the point that reality consisted in nothing more than a sequence of momentary states unconnected at the level of form—now this, now that—then there would appear to be no grounds for considering it to be the same reality from one moment to the next; it would fail to preserve its own unity through time. But surely, it might be protested, the bare laws of physics suffice to preserve material continuity if not continuity of form, where material continuity would suffice to preserve sameness through the vicissitudes of differentiation. The form of the world might vary randomly from moment to moment, but the fact that it is in any given instance the same matter that is assuming different forms secures material coherence and continuity. Such material coherence and continuity is sufficient for worldhood. Perhaps. But what underpins this continuity, this cohering, at the purely material level?[2] Why does the center hold and space and time and their contents not break into pieces? Why *are* there laws of physics that ensure a *uni*verse, a cosmos rather than chaos? Might this not be because reality is indeed a *psycho*physical field, and while nonconnectivity of form between past and future physical states and among the physical elements of the present might perhaps be deemed imaginable, nonconnectivity of form between past and future *psychic* states and among present experiences is simply not imaginable at all: some continuity of form or narrative connectivity must obtain for psyche to exist and hence for psychic states to occur at all. Bare continuity and coherence at the physical level may thus be a function, ultimately, of the irreducibly *psycho*physical nature of reality, and of the fact that narrative continuity is requisite for psychic existence. In other words, unless the universe admitted of a psychic dimension, a dimension to which narrative continuity was intrinsic, there would be nothing to ensure that it was a *uni*verse at all—there would be nothing to hold the laws of physics in place.

Admittedly this latter argument and the previous one are highly speculative, and I am in no way insisting on them here. My aim is merely to suggest that the principle of fertility expresses a dynamic of preservation of sameness through differentiation that is integral to psychic existence but may also be necessary to secure the lawlikeness and hence the coherence of the physical manifold. In other words, this argument implies that the universe is, as the ancients intuited, necessarily organized around the principle of fertility and necessarily partakes of the nature of psyche.

If fertility is indeed an expression of the fundamental dynamic of reality, then of course we cannot undermine this principle in any ultimate way. We can only disrupt it in our own local environment. In doing so, we condemn ourselves to living against the grain of things, missing the point of existence, a point which would become evident to us were we to participate in the narrative unfolding of world that fertility entrains.

In the context of modernity, civilization is, as I have remarked, no longer organized around the organic principle of fertility but rather around the industrial principle of production or manufacture. Manufacture follows the logic of consumption rather than of fertility. Although consumption is a modality integral to natural systems, within those systems its logic is subordinate to the principle of fertility. The scope of the principle of fertility encompasses both organisms and the environments that sustain them: both the organism and its environment must be fertile if reproduction is to be achieved. Fertility in an organism pertains to the capacity of the organism to replicate itself genetically. Fertility in the environment pertains to the capacity of that environment to sustain the growth of organisms, providing nutrients for them to consume. The presence of nutrients is secured by the return of the by-products of consumption, and ultimately the return of the organisms themselves, to their environment, and by the effect of biological processes on this "waste." Consumption is thus a strand in the cycles involved in reproduction. In consumption however, there is no preservation of poetic or narrative continuity. The formal integrity of the given is destroyed: plants, for instance, are ingested and converted into undifferentiated liquids or pastes in which nothing of the plants' story is preserved; these liquids or pastes are then either incorporated into the substantival identity of the consumer or excreted as "waste." In itself then, the process of consumption fails to preserve the thread of identity from past to future. But when consumption is integrated into cycles of reproduction, the thread is rewoven: consumption enables the organism to attain maturity and hence to reproduce, thereby perpetuating the thread of identity; the by-products of consumption, including the body of the organism at death, supply the nourishing matrix for such reproduction.

Production or manufacture in modern societies however follows the logic of a consumption process cut loose from cycles of reproduction. In manufacture, the already given is seized and pounded into undifferentiated substrates which are then molded into forms dictated by human imagination. When the things thus produced have served the purpose for which they were intended, they are thrown away. They do not "seed," with their form, new products, nor are they typically converted in their turn into undifferentiated substrates for the production of further articles. Admittedly, under current ideologies of sustainability, such industrial "recycling" is increasingly being practiced. But even if manufacture succeeded in closing the resource loop through recycling, it would still entirely fail to capture the spirit of fertility, for it would remain the case that no narrative continuity would obtain between one generation of artefacts and the next.

At every level—from the biological through the material to the psychological—human life can be conducted according to the template of either fertility or production. The conduct of life in modern societies currently follows the pattern of production. Biological processes are broken down into their mechanical elements and then redesigned as far as possible to suit human ends. The production of material items proceeds according to the logic already outlined. And the human self repudiates its givenness and aims instead to remake itself, physically and psychically, to match its abstract image of itself. (If a person has dark hair, she will dye it blonde. If she is old, she will have a facelift. If she is timid, she will take a course in assertiveness training. If she has feminine traits, she will revise her "performance" of gender. If her personality is out of date, she will undergo therapy to change that personality!) The very idea of givenness in any domain is in fact repudiated in the chic idiom of contemporary cultural studies, in which the *production* of things and selves, indeed of the world at large, de novo, is the rule.

When the conduct of life is allowed to follow the pattern of fertility, however, the givenness of things is not only acknowledged but protected. In the realm of horticulture and animal husbandry, we resume time-honored organic practices, such as composting and free ranging, that ensure that the stories of living things are perpetuated. And while we of course adjust the scale of manufacture to the requirements of sustainability, we revision manufacture itself. Instead of grinding existing things down into substrates from which entirely new things can be fashioned, as if from a blank slate, we preserve the "spirit" of existing things in the new things we elicit from them. New houses are built from within the shell of existing houses. New clothes are stitched together from fragments of old. Such recycling of the given into the emergent is not undertaken merely for the sake of sparing further inroads into ecosystems, but out of appreciation for the poetic integrity of existence.

When manufacture follows the principle of fertility then we will have built a world in which every thing, artefactual as well as natural, retains its own story, its unique place in the poetic unfolding of the world, and all things are in conversation, "in story," with the things around them—just as things are in the "state of nature."

When we acquire the habit of this poetic perspective, this appreciation that it is in the story of things, in their poetic recapitulation of their antecedents, that the key to ongoing existence lies, then practices of sustainability at an ecological level will be second nature to us. Unless we can grasp this metaphysical dimension of fertility however, practices of ecological sustainability will remain ad hoc tack-ons to the deeper presuppositions of our culture, and hence themselves difficult to sustain.

At the deepest level, of course, the principle of fertility is applicable to the inner life of the self. The self dedicated to the principle of fertility honors its own givenness. It does not subscribe to the ideal of perfectibility but embraces its own failures, defects, and limitations. Since it embraces the fallibilities not only of itself but of everyone, its self-acceptance does not degenerate into an excuse for the ill use of others. The self dedicated to the principle of fertility honors her own givenness because that givenness harbors the "spirits" of those from whom she has sprung. To try to erase this givenness in favor of some socially prescribed ideal is to obliterate the traces, the faces, of her antecedents within her; one's large ears or crooked smile, for instance, are the very things that hold one "in story," in conversation, with one's forebears. To try to ameliorate such features is to cut oneself loose from the larger narrative.

This is not to say that selves must not strive to develop their capacities or seek healing for their wounds. Their *potential* however is a specific and limited rather than unlimited component of their givenness. To respect one's givenness is thus not to ignore one's potential, or damage to that potential, but nor does acknowledging one's potential involve a denial of one's givenness. The psyche of a child deprived of opportunities or traumatized early in life may lose the original course of its unfolding. Remedial or healing processes of potentiation or repotentiation may then be required to enable it to return to that course in later life. This however is not a matter of cutting and pasting the psyche to match arbitrary norms imposed from without, but rather of enabling it to recover its own unique place within the larger story.

At Julia's farm one is greeted at every turn with fresh evidence of a profound affection for the given, an affection for the story, the fragment of the greater poem, that is held within each concrete particular. Everywhere an intuitive rapport with the deep metaphysics of fertility is evident. Indeed, the property is for Julia a metaphysical exercise. Years ago she studied philosophy at universities in Perth (which is when I first met her). She likes to say now that she is "doing philosophy." Other people claim to be "doing philosophy" when they are reading and writing philosophical books and articles. Julia's "doing" is much more complex: it is both an application of certain principles and an active elaboration of them. Her farm in fact represents a new kind of collaborative and counterdualistic "text" in which certain principles are set in motion and the world itself, as collaborator, draws out their inexhaustible implications.

The pedagogical intent of the farm is also explicit. Visitors from far and wide drop in for a chat, and Julia, ever in the grip of a new development or discovery in the drama of the farm, is not shy about sharing her excitement. During my stay an older couple, Bunty and Margie, call in for a yarn. Margie has brought a rice pudding; Bunty soon disappears under the bonnet of Julia's car. Julia takes Margie in among the chains of hearts to show her the pardalotes' tunnel. Pardalotes are zipping about busily on nest business. Margie has lived in the area all her life, but has not heard of pardalotes, even though she has probably seen them often. But suddenly pardalotes burst into salience for her. She will henceforth be alive to the poetry that is pardalote existence. She says wistfully, as she is leaving laden with fresh milk and eggs, "One day, Julia, I want you to sit down and tell me just exactly what philosophy is!"

Another day a friend from Esperance calls, a lovely, serious man, on whom the rural crisis has however exacted a heavy toll. He is just recovering from a major depression. He sits in Julia's book-lined cave of a living room, among the curios and old china, the cases of bones and specimens and examples of the taxidermist's art, and I can't help feeling that he is receiving here exactly the medicine he seeks: meaning. Not the kind of meaning afforded by an abstract creed, plucked from some egomaniac's overheated brain, but the meanings, the stories, of things themselves, here set out so eloquently for the telling. Two of Julia's friends in Ravensthorpe, a doctor and a beekeeper, have given up their careers, under the influence of Julia's unique "text," and gone off to study philosophy—so far with joyous results!

Towards the end of my stay we take a trip to a nearby mine site worked by another friend of Julia's. This is where Julia obtained the crystal quartz and tourmaline for the grotto in her cemetery. There are no shafts here, just dynamited pits surrounded by piles of sand filled with shattered fragments of crystallized pink and green. Pink and green! Everywhere, here and in the east of the continent, the dominant themes of the bush. Mauves and roses and bruised pinks; sage and jade and olive greens, sometimes even lemon and lime greens. Pink tips, pink veins, pink stems, pink bunches and frills. And here now, these pinks and greens permeate the very rocks, interspersed with leaves of mica, as the pinks and greens of eucalypts are shot with silver in the sun. The crystal glimmers and the mica gives off thousands of points of diamond light in the scrub. Julia tells me how the whole place becomes a fairy-land of unearthly lights under a full moon. We wander around picking up keepsakes from the treasure strewn so thickly and carelessly on the ground. The crystal is "waste." The object of the operation is tantalite, a functional kind of metal used in medicine. This beautiful "waste" seems a fitting image to carry away from my visit.

The day before I leave I go for a last ramble in the bush. Walking back into a white sunset I have a view of the farm from the track at the rear. The feathery grasses are picked out by the low light, each plume shining silver-white. The house is such a humble little shack, yet with so much going on around it—paddocks full of animals, gardens and plantings, cages and yards—it holds the center like a manor in a medieval tapestry. Everything is shining. The pigs lying on the red ground have silver linings. So do the goats and sheep and cows. The goslings are balls of silver gauze as they dash across the yard. Julia comes out of the house with washing over her arm—the rags that serve as nappies for Digger, the joey—and her red hair, tangled into a long plait, catches a medieval halo. *Everything* wears a medieval halo here. Nothing—no rusted gate or broken bottle or bush rat—is left out of this pagan heaven, this moment of transfiguration in which all things participate in the course of their journey to regeneration.

Chapter 5

Hamilton Downs: Philosophy in the Field . . . of Being

PHILOSOPHY IN THE CONTEXT OF MODERNITY

If the roots of the environmental crisis are entwined, as has been suggested in earlier chapters, with the philosophical roots of Western civilization itself, then any search for the fundamental antidote to environmental holocaust might need to begin not in front of bulldozers or under police batons at antiglobalization rallies, but in the philosophy classrooms of contemporary Western universities. There is a quiet malaise in these classrooms that is obscurely—but deeply—tied to the crises in the forests, oceans, soils, and other habitats of our beleaguered planet.

What is this malaise that has passed virtually unremarked in Western societies? Philosophy as a practice within the academy has become a strangely attenuated and narrow concern. Philosophers today are middle-class professionals leading nine-to-five office lives, cultivating their own small turf of specialized thinking, a turf rarely visited or registered by outsiders. As an educational tool, contemporary analytical philosophy is little more than a training in critical thinking. As an area of professional inquiry, it dedicates itself to the flensing of preexisting texts. In this sense it might be ascribed the niche of scavenger in the ecology of ideas, cleaning away rubbish, confusion, rot, and excess from the bones of theory. This is an important role but not a glamorous one, and analytical philosophers are by and large unassuming figures, keeping their heads down and chomping stoically through the conceptual detritus of a civilization in the throes of informational explosion. Their poststructural colleagues are less stoical, more expansive in their own right, but their central project—that of deconstruction—is also largely phagocytic in nature, seeking out ideological contaminants in our discursive systems and subjecting them to techniques of dissolution.

I do not doubt for a moment that this kind of "underlaboring," to which the seventeenth century English philosopher, John Locke, adverted, is valid and worthy work. But is it all that philosophy could be, should be? What of the questions that were constitutive of philosophy at its origins, questions about the nature of reality, the scope and limits of knowledge, the ends of human life? Doesn't philosophy still have something of its own to say in answer to these? True, a purely critical practice—slicing through obscurity, exposing humbug and wishful thinking, critiquing common sense, science, theory of all kinds—leaves us in a better position to answer such questions and achieve authenticity in our thought. In this sense the skeptical practice of contemporary philosophers does constitute at least a *preparation* for answering the foundational questions. Living by the sword of doubt then, spurning the false comforts, the expediencies and complacencies, of ideology, is properly integral to the pursuit of philosophy. And to some extent this skeptical orientation explains the reluctance of analytical philosophers to accept the "situatedness" of their thought, its cultural and historical specificity and contingency. Philosophers aim precisely to "stand outside" the belief systems of their own cultures, subjecting these systems to logical scrutiny. But can one live by doubt alone? Hardly. To doubt everything is in the end to miss the truth—of the nature of reality, the possibilities of knowledge, the telos of life—as surely as believing everything does.

But what is the philosopher to believe? How, after clearing away all the "rubbish," is she to find answers to her foundational questions? Is she to reenter culture and satisfy herself with the relativities of her place and time? Or can she maintain her original aspiration to make do with nothing less than truth?

Notice, in this connection, that the foundational questions of the philosopher's discipline—the questions of metaphysics, epistemology, and value theory—are interlinked. Complex dialectical relations obtain among them. Finding answers to any of them will depend, to a certain extent, on finding answers to all of them. However, if any of these questions can claim a degree of priority, it is, I believe, the metaphysical one: epistemological and normative possibilities are plainly circumscribed by metaphysical premises. For example, the possibilities of knowing are determined, initially, by the constitution of the individual subject or self, and the constitution of such a self is implicated in the constitution of the wider reality to which it belongs. In other words, philosophers who, in Cartesian fashion, take as the starting point for all their researches the givenness of the human subject typically build certain metaphysical assumptions into their conception of the subject.

The subject is, from their point of view, already set apart from world rather than necessarily, intrinsically, implicated in it. Western philosophers take this givenness of the human subject as self-evident, forgetting that cultures exist—indigenous ones, for instance—in which entirely different presuppositions concerning the subject are current. From many indigenous perspectives, the self, and hence the subject, is always already an emanation of land, of country, of world. Within such an initial frame, it is the subjectivity of the world that is given, and the human subject has to discover itself within that primordial matrix. The relativity of what can be taken as self-evident in this connection demonstrates, I think, that metaphysical decisions have always already been made before we define our epistemological program; metaphysics, in other words, enjoys a certain logical priority.

Equally, identification of the proper ends of human life depends upon a prior grasp of the ends, if any, of creation as a whole: if creation is unfolding towards ends of its own, and if we are, ontologically speaking, part of that process of unfolding, then our proper ends will be referenced to its—our ends will be tributary to a larger telos. If, on the other hand, creation is without its own intrinsic telos, then we will presumably have to discover the telos of human life in a purely self-referential fashion.

To a certain extent then, and to simplify our present inquiry, we can limit the question of whether and how the philosopher is to arrive at foundational beliefs to the question of whether and how she is to arrive at a metaphysical premise. Can she acquire the basic grasp of the nature of reality that would provide a ground for further philosophical venturings?

The "method of doubt" that is so definitive of academic philosophy is of course complemented, in contemporary classrooms, with a reconstructive method: existing discourses are reduced to their elements and certain of these elements are then selected and reassembled into hopefully sounder, more comprehensive and more fully explanatory discursive structures. These structures are the hypotheses or theories proffered by philosophers. In this sense philosophy borrows its premises from preexisting knowledges or areas of inquiry. If the ultimate aim of philosophy is, however, to provide satisfactory answers to its foundational questions—questions that in principle bear on our deepest destiny, the very flourishing or otherwise of the human species— can philosophy necessarily trust premises thus derived from other disciplines? For no other discipline combines the various foundational aims of philosophy. Science seeks understanding of the nature of reality, but the kind of understanding it seeks disregards the normative entailments of its metaphysical presuppositions and is not testable in terms of those entailments. Religion seeks normative understanding—answers to the question of how to live—but does so in a way that omits any credible account of empirical reality. So the findings of these two major spheres of inquiry will not necessarily furnish premises that can serve the ultimate ends of philosophy. Philosophy needs a theory of reality with functional normative implications and a normative theory that meshes with a functional theory of reality.

While the findings of either science or religion or both may be relevant to the philosopher's inquiries, then, they may not prove sufficient. The philosopher might need to develop "experimental" methods of her own. What could these methods be? What kind of experience, other than the empirical modalities of science and the introspective modalities of religion, could conceivably afford access to the fundamental nature of reality? To answer this question it is necessary to look beyond the historical parameters of philosophy and consider a possibility that has been more or less excluded from the speculative thought of the West from the start. The possibility in question is of course that matter itself is "alive" and potentially communicative. To adopt such a view would be to introduce the possibility of a new, dialogical method of inquiry: instead of the resolutely monological method of traditional philosophy, in which humanity asks itself what is the nature of the world, this reanimation of reality would open up the possibility of humanity directing its foundational question to the world itself.

It needs to be reiterated that, in importing such a (broadly panpsychist) premise, we would be doing so, initially, in a purely provisional way, for the sake of the method that it would make available to us. If experimentation with this method yielded no useful results, the method, and the premise from which it derives, could be abandoned. If the method confirmed the premise however, which is to say if seeking to engage the world in dialogue did indeed elicit its response, then that method would be likely to open up further horizons for metaphysical discovery.

Before detailing how a dialogical method might work in practice, let's consider why this method has been for the most part systematically ignored, even as a possibility, throughout the history of Western philosophy. Why, in other words, has the view of matter from which the dialogical method derives more or less dropped from the purview of the Western mind? To explain this is important because exclusion of panpsychism has been integral to the self-constitution of philosophy thus far. To introduce a panpsychist horizon might be significantly to redefine the scope and form of philosophical practice.

THE ORIGINS OF PHILOSPHY IN THE SEPARATION
OF SELF FROM WORLD

Why then has the practice of philosophy seemingly rested on the systematic exclusion of a particular metaphysical possibility, the possibility that I have been characterizing as panpsychist? Why indeed did philosophy coincide, at its origins, with a particular metaphysical stance? The original presocratic philosophers—Thales, Anaximander, Heraclitus and Democritus, for instance—may be seen as extricating themselves from the panpsychist consciousness in which pre-philosophical Greece was wrapped. In their various ways they attempted to naturalize the spiritual dimensions of reality that had until then been represented anthropomorphically, via mythology. For Thales the underlying animating principle was water; for Anaximander it was air; for Heraclitus, fire; for Democritus, atoms. In their naturalized form, these underlying forces of animation were increasingly divested of any subjectival dimension, any quality of felt interiority, such as human beings experience. However such a quality may be described—as soul, spirit, mentality, life force—it was this, together with its correlate, the quality of agency, that these thinkers began to evacuate from the natural world.

In thus turning away from animism—from an "ensouled" view of world—the early philosophers were, as I have remarked, turning away from the anthropomorphism of the pre-philosophical cosmologies of mythology. But the significance of anthropomorphic terms of reference in this context is ambiguous. In prephilosophical cultures the personification of natural phenomena undoubtedly represented a tacit avowal of panpsychism, of an outlook that accorded the world a life and personality of its own. Since human personality is the readiest model of personality available to us, it is natural that such cultures would have represented a panpsychist world in terms of human personality, without this implying that such anthropomorphisms were intended literally. In cultures in which other metaphors or models of subjectivity are available, panpsychism may be represented in nonanthropomorphic terms. On the other hand, the mythopoetics of prephilosophical cosmologies might also have arisen from a failure to distinguish self from world and a consequent disposition to see the world as an extension of self. In this case the cosmologies in question would indeed count as instances of anthropomorphic projection rather than as poetic intimations of the subjectivality of reality.

In the animistic cultures in which philosophy originated, anthropomorphism as a vehicle for panpsychism and anthropomorphism as a habit of psychic projection were probably intermingled. In turning away from animism, the presocratic philosophers seem to have been both breaking the hold of a panpsychist world over them and breaking free from the habit of anthropomorphic projection. In any event, philosophy was born in this moment of disengagement from world, of retreat from *participation mystique*, a participation which may in part have resulted from a psychic failure to achieve an adequate degree of individuation, but might also have been a function of a panpsychist apprehension that the world is a subjectival presence capable of dialogical engagement with us. In seeking to transcend the habit of anthro-pomorphic projection then, the presocratics also suppressed the panpsychist possibilities with which it was entwined. In doing so they may not merely have been attempting to disarticulate the human from the nonhuman but also to win outright human sovereignty over the nonhuman, by breaking out of the grip of an omnipotent and all-enfolding reality.

The later history of philosophy attests to the latter motivation. For as I have remarked, panpsychism figures quite marginally in the subsequent annals of the Western tradition.[1] The pendulum of metaphysical thought has typically swung between the poles of two positions which equally withhold subjectival presence from the world, namely transcendental idealism and materialism. From the viewpoint of idealism, the world is nothing but a manifold of "appearances" manifest to a transcendent but nonetheless still humanlike subjectivity. This world is not an existent, let alone a subjectival presence, in its own right. From the viewpoint of materialism, on the other hand, the independent reality of the world is indeed conceded, but subjecti-val presence is denied to it. In this sense, materialism and idealism are ulti-mately two sides of the same view, a view that arrogates all subjectivity and agency to a human (or humanlike) locus. Let us dub this view "human-cen-tered psychism." Idealism and materialism are twin faces of human-centered psychism. The true converse of this position is panpsychism.

Since the advent of science in the seventeenth century, the *materialist* face of human-centered psychism has been increasingly in the ascendant. Not only philosophy, but Western civilization as a whole, has come to rest on this materialist premise. Throughout the history of philosophy, and even more especially in the modern period, the claims of panpsychism have been in recession and this is no longer for want of nonanthropomorphic concep-tual resources with which to represent it. One might therefore with some reason conclude that the possibility of panpsychism truly constitutes a blind spot of Western philosophy. One might furthermore conclude that philoso-phy has been an expression, and a primary tool, of a struggle for human sov-ereignty that began with the Ionians and continues, not merely unabated but with increased insistence, to the present day.

In the original moment—the moment of disengagement, of retreat from unreflective participation in a reality understood as animated with its own informing telos—the world became our "object." Hence, simultaneously, the possibility of "knowledge" was born. That is to say, speculative questions about the nature of reality—its structure, its purpose, its intelligibility—came into being at the very moment we ceased to be active participants therein. We became knowers, thinkers, embarked on a monological practice of obser-vation, speculation, theoretical construction, where before we had simply experienced, relatively immediately, the nature of our world and our relation to it. At the moment our participative relation to reality was severed, which is to say, at the moment we ceased to be immersed in the subjectival field of the world, we began to ask ourselves what this world was. Indeed, our capacity to ask this question, to seek to "know the world," was henceforth regarded as the distinctive vocation of humanity, a humanity that had come into focus for itself via its disengagement from its matrix. The presupposition of such knowing—the conversion of world into object, the confiscation of its subjectivity—was forgotten, relegated to unsayability.

The monological approach of the ancients has been carried over into the main historical stream of philosophy and from thence into science and the bloodstream of Western civilization. It is currently resulting in ever-tightening circles of self-referentiality in modern societies. Increasingly we consult our theories about the world rather than turning our attention to the world itself.[2] Even observation, the bedrock of science, is receding as a practice. The reality of materiality is increasingly backgrounded. Our discursive self-absorption is spiraling. We chase the tails of our texts, picking out our own footsteps in a realm of anthropogenic abstractions, passing the ball of ideas from hand to hand, never lifting our eyes to the land that stretches outside our office walls. In the context of Western civilization, matter as an independent presence is now discounted. Materiality is subordinated to human ends and stamped with human intentions. We are shaped not by nature but by discursive patterns and forces. Physicality exists merely to underpin the "nous-sphere," the great mantle of ideality that now overlays the biosphere. Humanity appears to have more than won its bid for sovereignty.

And what are the consequences of this obsessive *anthropocentrism* that is now shading into a veritable *logocentrism* unprecedented in the annals of human history and reflected in the attenuated abstractions and insubstantial scholastics of present-day philosophy? The biosphere, the ontosphere, neglected and silenced for centuries, is unraveling. The land that we ignore, except as raw material for the actualization of our own designs, is coming undone. Our monological outpourings have yeilded neither the basic metaphysical insight nor the basic affinity needed to sustain our world. The environmental record may with some justification then be taken as testimony to the fact that the presocratics, and the civilization they inaugurated, got it wrong. A form of inquiry that leads its followers and their world towards extinction cannot have found adequate answers to its foundational questions.

It seems crucial then that the possibility of recovering a panpsychist premise for our civilization be acknowledged and the tenability of such a premise explored. But, we may well ask, is philosophy the appropriate vehicle for such a recovery? If philosophy was indeed born in the breach that opened between ourselves and our world—in that dualizing moment in which the world became an object for our contemplation—could philosophy reincorporate the possibility of panpsychism? Or is philosophy dualistic to its core, so that attempts to reconfigure it along dialogical lines are categorically doomed? Is there any way in which an intersubjective approach can combine with the traditional philosophical ideal of objective inquiry without producing cognitive deadlock?

To answer these questions, let's start by prefiguring, as far as possible, the dialogical practice that a philosophy premised on panpsychism would employ. How would we make ourselves available for dialogical exchange with world, with a view to asking it directly the metaphysical questions we have for centuries been discussing among ourselves? The conditions for such a dialogical practice are as yet largely unknown. Protocols for addressing the world and semantical codes for framing our questions cannot be entirely prefigured in a priori fashion, but must rather be determined by trial and error in the field. Possibilities in this connection might be suggested by the rich ceremonial and ritual traditions of preexisting cultures premised on panpsychism.

But resort to "the field" is perhaps most salient as the starting point for our dialogical endeavor. We must be prepared to leave the office, step outside the academy walls and be available for encounter with reality in the raw. This involves, as far as I can tell, dispensing with the excessive discursive preoccupations and distractions of Western civilization and placing oneself in material contexts whose integrity has not been entirely compromised by subordination to abstractive ends. Thus stationed, one opens oneself to possible communiques, which might perhaps take the form of synchronistic occurrences in one's environment or significant dreams. "Dwelling in place" in this way, attentive to the subtleties and complexities of other-than-human story lines, the revelatory potentialities of place, of country, of world, might begin to manifest.

PHILOSOPHY IN THE FIELD: A CASE STUDY

To provide at least the flavor of the kind of dialogical practice I have in mind here, let me draw from my own store of philosophical excursions "into the field." I have undertaken most of these excursions either alone or with one or two other persons. They have usually involved setting up for a considerable period in a significant place, often but by no means always in an outback location. But dialogical engagement seems also to be achievable via organized gatherings.

One such gathering I have attended was in Central Australia. It was styled a colloquium, and it was broadly philosophical in intent, though the thirty or so academics who attended were interdisciplinary in background. The theme of the conference was "sense of place," and although participants were each asked to submit a paper in advance, the focus of the gathering itself was intended to be experiential. The organizers of the conference—Craig San Roque, a Jungian psychoanalyst resident in Alice Springs, and John Cameron, a social ecologist from the University of Western Sydney—envisaged the event as a "coming into country."[3] The participants would stay on a remote former station named Hamilton Downs for five days, during which time they would be "introduced" to country by indigenous custodians and invited to engage in a variety of potentially dialogical activities. The form of these activities was not preconceived, but devised daily by a group of facilitators (including myself) who steered the event by whatever stars happened to be rising or setting in the collective psyche and environmental ambience at the time.

It was easy to feel cynical about the prospects for such an event. Wasn't it bordering on the kitsch and touristic in its conception? Perhaps. But anyone who came to Hamilton Downs with this expectation was, as it turned out, in for a rude surprise. The power of this colloquium was elemental, and it rearranged the lives of many of the participants for months and years to come. This demonstrated, to me at any rate, that protocols for dialogical engagement with world—in this case with country—are necessary and also perhaps sufficient. No special mystical aptitude or pious demeanor was required for "things to happen." It was enough, it seemed, that no one was making money from the event, that traditional custodians were present, that participants were already inducted into a receptive frame of mind by their own reflective writings on place, and that the process of engagement was sensitively orchestrated in response to the actual dynamics, in the moment, of all the parties to the encounter, including country.

I have not the space here to detail all that took place over those days or the extraordinary consequences of that gathering in the lives of participants. But let me convey just a little of the sequence that transpired.

Upon our arrival at Hamilton Downs we were delighted to find that it was a classic old homestead, set close to a dry rocky creekbed and looking out towards a pink range. A high windmill and palm stood to the front of the cluster of buildings. The country around the homestead was "sweet," meaning fertile, according to local ethnobotanist, Peter Latz; this was women's country. The ranges were dry and infertile, men's country.

During the first couple of days a lot of local people visited the site. There were talks by custodians, artists, Central Australian identities. There was all the negotiation of interpersonal space, the tentativeness and confusion natural in a group of relative strangers coming together in an isolated environment. Only by the third day was the main action ready to begin. At the suggestion of the facilitating group, the men and women broke up into separate camps to develop "stories of place" woven out of their own personal stories and dreams and perceptions of the place in which we found ourselves. The idea was that each group would present its stories to the assembled gathering around the campfire that evening.

We women sat at the spot we had selected in the creekbed, within sight of the homestead, through the day. We spent the time getting to know one another, exchanging whatever seemed appropriate and significant to us. There was resistance in our group to developing a presentation, or even a story of place, for the evening's show, and it was decided that we would simply invite the men to join us, in silence, around a tree in the middle of the riverbed. We were accordingly utterly unprepared for the action-packed performance the men had in store for us. After dinner, when we returned to the riverbed, we found an enormous campfire already alight, and soon the men were in the throes of their story. There were frogs with giant phalluses and jet-fighter totems. We were dive-bombed by crows; there was vomiting and killing, crashes and shootings, and much allusion to hanky-panky in local Aboriginal idioms. It was all incredibly energetic, like stories written by schoolboys, and by its end the whole firelit space was littered with the dead. How astonishing—and touching—it was to see all these senior academics charging about in this fashion, throwing themselves into the thing as absolutely as we women had chosen to refrain.

In the face of this generosity of spirit, I felt very nervous when our turn came around. Would our noncompliance be read as standoffishness, sullenness? But how could we ever have matched the manic outpouring of the men in any case, even in the opposite direction? Of course, what we had "planned," by default, did just that: it was as yin as the men's offering was yang. One of our number led us in a circle around the fire, speaking skillfully, the men following the women. Out into the dark we padded, then settled in the sand around the white trunk of a great old gum. We sat there, mute and at a loss, but, in spite of our reticence, or rather because of it, a whole beautiful performance proceeded to unfold. The camp cooks, two inspired young acrobats, Nathan and Jonathan, appeared unbidden in the center of the circle, playing haunted bush sax and rainsticks. Still playing, Jonathan slithered up the tree like a possum, or a serpent. Lightning, which till then had been flickering around the horizon, now kicked in, flooding the whole scene at intervals with momentary flashes. The entire scenario could scarcely have been a more perfect, or lyrical, counterpoint to the men's offering. Yet this, our "presentation," was largely inadvertent, and the men's, as it turned out, was the result of all kinds of conflict and dissension. So who was in charge here? One could not escape the conclusion that *it was the land that was holding the script.*

This kind of orchestration by the land happened consistently, almost continuously, throughout those days at Hamilton Downs. It happened at a personal level. I found myself repeatedly in scenarios in which the most significant gestalts of my life were being played out, and symbolically resolved, before my eyes. I was gently called to take the steps I previously could not take. And I could see the same thing happening to those around me. The orchestration happened at the collective level also. The "script" for the gathering itself continued to unfold with breathtaking poetic accuracy and inventiveness. The experience was uncanny, seemingly miraculous though of course eminently natural. It was also ineffably companionable. We were not alone. We were in the presence of the world, and the world was speaking, to each of us separately and to all of us together. Only a cosmos could devise a script so complex that it could coordinate all our disparate, infinitely layered story lines, truth lines, into a story line, a truth line, that encompassed us all, country included. All we had to do was leave gaps in our own scripts, gaps that this speaking world could fill.

I have, as I mentioned, spent a fair bit of time in the outback, but I have rarely witnessed or experienced a more collaborative engagement with reality than was evident at Hamilton Downs. It felt to me as if one were riding something alive out there, a dragon, a great serpent, a current of energy. It would not necessarily carry one to where one wanted to go, but with a little steering, a little reining in, it would keep one moving, in process, evolving. To my mind it was the Tao. Out in that archaic world, the Tao was a bucking, plunging presence, wild but trustworthy, as real as a desert river in full flood, no longer a mere idea.

Hamilton Downs was perhaps, then, an instance of the dialogical method, rendered all the more powerful because exercized collectively rather than individually. But, it might be asked, did country in this instance really offer any answer to foundational metaphysical questions? Did the multilayered script that unfolded at Hamilton Downs offer any kind of insight into the nature of the universe, insight that could be translated into properly philosophical terms?

I would offer two initial reflections in this connection. The first is that when one asks the world a metaphysical question, one does not expect a reply along the lines of "e=mc²" or "reality is a reflection of the Form of the Good." One does not expect a *universal* pronouncement of any kind. One expects to be addressed in particularistic terms. This is because the world must speak, if it speaks at all, in the poetic language of particulars. It speaks through *this* landscape, through *these* individual women and men, through the tangled psychic terrain of *this* gathering, and through images borrowed from the seekers' personal frames of reference. Perhaps this is also why, when one asks the world a metaphysical question, it so often seems to turn the beam of one's inquiry back onto oneself, to highlight the wounded core out of which the question comes. *You want to know about the nature of reality?* it seems to say. *Well, here, look at this. Before I can give you answers you'll have to refine your questions. Let's look at the secrets in the heart of the one who asks.* So when the world speaks, it seems to want to talk, not in the first instance about metaphysics, but about oneself, about individual men and women, about country, about fear and suffering, the joys and trials of animals and people— about the same things that concern *us*.[4] But of course in taking this interest it is offering a metaphysical revelation of the highest order, namely that the world *does* speak, that it is a communicative presence capable of engaging responsively with its creatures. This in itself is a full-blown answer to our foundational metaphysical question, a rich starting point for further philosophical venturings.[5]

My second point is that many of the findings that come to light in the field may turn out to be not for public consumption. This is not only because they might be referenced to intimate aspects of the field worker's life but more importantly because the field worker might come to feel that divulging such findings would amount to a betrayal of the world's confidences: the revelations vouchsafed to me might in the end be just between the world and me. In this respect they might be comparable to the "business" transacted by indigenous cultures, or to esoteric traditions such as those of the early Pythagoreans or the later alchemists. In such traditions, esoteric knowledge was indeed passed on, but not in the essentially exoteric form of the written text, which can in principle be read by all. Revelations vouchsafed to me by country may perhaps be properly communicated only via reenactment of the message addressed to me, a reenactment that preserves the narrative and poetic particularity of the original message and observes strict ceremonial protocols. Reenactment should perhaps, moreover, be performed in the presence of country itself, so that country can participate in the process of transmission, changing or redirecting elements of the narrative in response to the dynamics of the new communicative situation. Gaps will be left in the choreography of any such performance to allow for the interventions, the speakings, of other-than-human parties. In this way such knowledge might never become solidified, insulated from the particularity of those for whom it is intended; it may never be communicable simply to anyone, anywhere. It might rather remain essentially knowledge in situ, a communicative exchange between particular subjects and particular country.[6]

The issue of "secrecy" then—so alien to the epistemological mindset of modernity, which has been forged in the crucible of literacy, and which insists, with ever-increasing assurance, on the supremacy of the text—might reemerge. Knowledge is no longer a monological affair but the product of intersubjective negotiation, of potentially intimate encounter with world. But again, even if the philosopher finds new constraints on the transparency of her testimony, the fact of the intersubjective encounter itself is a rich new starting point for philosophical reflection.

But still, we might ask, in what sense are the insights gained by such intersubjective negotiation *philosophical*? How, if at all, do they differ from the kind of insights that traditional indigenous peoples gained from their ceremonial and spiritual practices? Any answer to this question of course depends on our definition of philosophy. Is philosophy defined by its foundational questions or by its traditional methods? In other words, is knowledge philosophical if it throws light on the foundational questions, those of metaphysics, epistemology, or value theory, or is it philosophical if it is acquired via processes of analysis and argumentation? If the former definition is assumed, then aspects of indigenous knowledge—those pertaining to metaphysics, for instance—are eminently philosophical. If the latter definition is assumed, then philosophy is a function of particular historically constituted and culturally specific modalities, and insights acquired through intersubjective negotiation will not qualify as philosophical.

If the former, larger definition of philosophy is adopted here, then insights garnered by the dialogical method can indeed be counted philosophical. However, there is no reason why these insights should not be further processed by the methods that have traditionally been constitutive of philosophy in the West. That is, if the world itself does indeed proffer answers to our metaphysical questions then there is no reason why we should not reflect on these answers. Indeed, it would seem that we have every reason to seek to render those answers intelligible in the light of the rest of our experience, where doing so may involve inferring to general propositions consistent with the particularistic and esoteric nature of the actual speakings.

In other words, the approach outlined here may be described as philosophical in both content and form: it seeks answers, via a dialogical method, to foundational questions of philosophy, and it subjects the findings of this dialogical inquiry to both interpretation and critical analysis. These interpretations and analyses remain perpetually open to doubt. We might, after all, be deluded or simply mistaken in our account of our experience. As philosophers we retain our right to reject the panpsychist hypothesis itself and any or all of our readings of purported panpsychist revelations. We are not in the business of exchanging reason for faith. Nor are we sacrificing our hard-won human individuation: our engagement with world is a matter of mutualism, not mystical merger. In this sense the panpsychist consciousness of the philosopher is still provisional, still reflective, and hence essentially and always in process; it is held differently from the panpsychist consciousness of the prephilosophical Ionian or the unreflective pagan. It is thus possible and indeed necessary, I think, to retain our old skeptical edge and expectation of open-endedness even as we embark on a new chapter in the adventure of consciousness.

In conclusion, once the philosopher has embarked on philosophy in this new key, she will never be the same again. She will, for a start, be increasingly reluctant to return to the office. Her sources of insight are now beyond the walls.[7] She is drawn to places of revelation. Just as her inquiries are now conducted in a dialogical mode, so she finds that teaching can likewise be conducted in partnership with world: she is disposed to teach in place, mediating the wisdom of a communicative world through the particularities of a given place. The metatext of her message is indeed that wisdom is not the province of human thought alone, but of human consciousness in conversation with world. In order to optimize her receptivity to possible communiques, she will find herself in flight from the distractions of a materialist civilization. Her way of life will become materially simplified. Absorbed in her subtle concourse with a larger, responsive world, she will be inattentive to the crass blandishments of a consumer society. In time she may no longer fit the respectable mold of the middle-class professional, but may find herself reverting to the ancient mode of the sage, roaming the countryside or dwelling in place, constituting in her very person a challenge to the complacencies of middle-class somnolence, whether that of the professional or that of the dedicated consumer. Alive to oracular signals and poetic emanations, mightn't she evolve into the kind of figure who, "flashing-eyed and floating-haired," could point the way out of modern insentience? Weave a circle round her thrice indeed, for where might she lure us? Into the embrace that, as moderns, we have taken such trouble to flee? Isn't this embrace—that dissolves our discursive blinders and enables us to hear the imperatives to which we have for so long blocked our ears—the embrace of the real? Where will these imperatives lead, if not underground, into a cathedral of innerness vaster by far than the plain theatres of existence we can at present conceive?

Chapter 6

The White Heron: Grace and the Native Self

In the late nineteenth century, American writer Sarah Orne Jewett published a story entitled "A White Heron." Jewett was a writer of place. She lived all her life in New England, and lovingly chronicled the landscape, people, and mores of that region. Her work was admired in her time but has now been relegated to the minor register—a common fate for writers who focus their gaze on the concrete and particular, eschewing the grand themes that infatuate the modern mind. Jewett's work may be seen, in fact, as a study of the phenomenon of *inhabitation*. She offers detailed and always wryly affectionate portraits of people who belong *in place*, people whose character and manners follow the contours of their place as surely as the shape of a pea is molded to the contours of its pod. She writes particularly of old people (hardly a favorite preoccupation of modernity) usually old women (what could be more unpopular?) and usually in the context of their houses. This is presumably because the fit between person and place is perfected with advancing age. She once remarked to author Willa Cather that "her head was full of dear old houses and dear old women, and that when an old house and an old woman came together in her brain with a click, she knew that a story was under way."[1]

Jewett herself never married but lived happily with an older female companion for most of her life. Judging from her biographies and her wide correspondence, she was a remarkably cheerful soul, successful but modest, content to devote her highly accomplished art to the delineation of the small world so dear to her. Her attitudes were in many ways profoundly counter-modern, indeed votary. What reputation still remains to her rests largely on two works: a novel entitled *The Country of the Pointed Firs* and the short story "The White Heron."

"The White Heron" is simple but resonant, with something of the gem cut of Hans Christian Anderson's fairy tales. It tells of a shy, pale child, Sylvia, who is given up at the age of eight by an impoverished family in an industrial town to be raised by a country grandmother. The grandmother is also poor, but with fresh milk, eggs, and vegetables and freedom to run, the child loses her apathy and at last begins to thrive. Through her close communion with the wild birds and animals of the fields and woods surrounding the house, she finds an unselfconscious fulfilment and feels "as if she never had been alive at all until she came to live at the farm."

One day a handsome young man appears on the scene. He is carrying a gun. The little girl meets him when she is out in the woods. He asks where he can find accommodation for the night. She is tongue-tied, but leads him back to her grandmother's house. The young man stays. He is of course charming. Self-assured and worldly, his manners towards Sylvy and her grandmother are upper class but gallant. He is here in the backwoods hunting. But he is not an ordinary sportsman. No, he is an ornithological collector, and he is searching for a specimen of the rare white heron. He has heard that one has been seen hereabouts. Although she says nothing as the young man announces his mission, Sylvy has indeed encountered the bird. The young man looks closely at her, and suspecting her secret, promises money— money beyond Sylvia's and her grandmother's dreams—and, more importantly, his esteem and favor, if she will lead him to it.

Sylvia spends the next day in the company of the young man. As they roam the woods together, he passes on all kinds of interesting information about birds to her, while at the same time shooting many of the objects of his obsession. Although she "would have liked him vastly better without his gun," Sylvy is nevertheless increasingly enchanted by the young man. She longs to aid him in his quest and later in the day she hatches a secret plan.

At the farther edge of the woods, where the land is highest, there is a great pine tree that towers over the rest of the trees, "the last of its generation," a relic of the primal forests. Sylvy reasons that from the top of this giant she would be able to take in the countryside for miles around, and would easily spot the nest of the white heron in one of the lower treetops. She will do it! She lies awake all night and before dawn steals out of her grandmother's house. The climb is exceedingly dangerous and demanding, stretching the little girl beyond her limits, but the tree shelters her, holding the winds away and enabling her to reach the top. As the golden disk of the sun appears, she gazes out over the woods and marshes, clear to the sea beyond, and sure enough she catches the white spot of the heron rising "like a single floating feather" from the birches and hemlocks at the marsh's edge.

Indeed, the heron makes straight for the great pine, and alights on a branch not far from Sylvy's, where he calls back to his mate on her nest and preens his feathers for the new day.

Sylvy has the heron's secret now, and hurries back to her grandmother's house. She longs so desperately to bask in the glow of the young man's atten-tion—to *exist* for him. Although she has been mute before him she now has in her custody the object of his heart's desire. But what is this? As she runs, tousled with her adventure, up to the door where her grandmother and the young sportsman stand expectantly, she cannot speak! "What is it that sud-denly forbids her and makes her dumb? Has she been nine years growing, and now, when the great world for the first time puts out a hand to her, must she thrust it aside for a bird's sake? The murmur of the pine's green branches is in her ears, she remembers how the white heron came flying through the golden air and how they watched the sea and the morning together, and Sylvia cannot speak; she cannot tell the heron's secret and give its life away." It is as if, via the revelation of the white heron, the world has claimed her conclusively as its own. Later in the day Sylvy watches sadly as the young man goes away "disappointed," emptyhanded.

The story of the white heron perhaps offers a key to a deeper psychology of inhabitation. Born into a family that could not support her, physically or emotionally, the child has little opportunity for establishing a bond with a "primary other," until she is sent to the country. Then the world itself, ren-dered finite and particular through place, becomes the responsive subject that awakens her subjectivity. In psychoanalytic terms, her primary *cathexis* is not to a human parent but to the world itself, as particularized in place. Via innumerable dialogical encounters in the woods—particularly with birds, to whose voices she listens with "a heart that beat(s) fast with pleasure"—the world signals to her that it has indeed received her, that she now belongs to it. (That she is to belong to the woods in this way is of course foreshadowed by her name.) Through engagement with her new homeplace the child's life force, the potentiation that flows from intersubjective contact, is activated. She needs little else in order to flourish. She does not think of herself as being *this* or *that* way, as pretty or plain, clever or slow, poor or genteel, as someone of whom mummy is proud or in whom the family might be disap-pointed. She has little in the way of a discursive sense of identity. She simply *is* by virtue of her daily encounter with the communicative world around her.

Then the boy walks into her life. He is *this*, he is *that*. He has an articu-lated, discursive identity: he is confident, worldly, schooled in social arts and manners. He has projects, ends, ambitions and is capable of concealment and pretense in pursuit of them. Sylvia feels her discursive nullity as she stands under his appraising eye. She has never before had to adapt her sense of self to the requirements of human others. Since she has never really mattered to human others, she has never felt the force of their expectations. She has never had to define herself according to their abstract specifications: "If you want my approval you will have to do this, act like that, think the way I think, follow this code, fashion, religion, occupation, football team...." But suddenly there is someone whose approval she desparately wants. And what does he ask of her? Nothing less than her very self: he asks that she sever her bond with the world in whose embrace she has sprung so gladly to life.

There is a great deal at stake in this meeting between socialized city boy and shy female wild-child. In it psychology and metaphysics are mixed, and the outcome will have profound implications for sexuality and gender. More importantly, the way the meeting turns out will ultimately decide whether we *inhabit* our world or objectify and subdue it. But in order to understand *why* so much hangs in the balance at this juncture, we perhaps need to back-track a way, and examine the notion of cathexis together with certain correl-ative notions.

In psychoanalytic theory, *cathexis* is the term that denotes the orectic charge that a particular object possesses for a subject: the subject focuses orectic attention on the object in question and becomes psychically invested in it in consequence. *Orexis* designates a state of desire, where the desire in question may be understood appetitively, socially, or spiritually—it is simply longing per se, literally "stretching out for" or "stretching out after."[2] When the state of desire is not merely appetitive in nature, but is desire for engag-ment with another subject, then orexis takes the form of *eros*. "Eros," as I am using the term, denotes the longing for *intersubjective contact*.[3]

I propose here to adapt the general notion of cathexis to a somewhat more specific usage, defining as the *primary cathexis* that initial psychic reach-ing out whereby an infant, or proto-subject, seeks to establish an intersubjec-tive bond with one who is primally present to it. It is via this bond, or primal psychic investment in another, that the infant comes fully into being as a sub-ject.[4] Only through contact with another subject does it feel the finitude, the boundaries, and hence the reality, of its own existence. When a subject cathects to another subject in this way, its psychic energies are activated and begin to flow outward. This activation is experienced by the subject as poten-tiation. The particular rhythms and patterns of this flow towards the other are the expression of the self's energic essence. They are the rhythms and patterns that will determine the self's unique dance with the universe. The erotic impulse to reach out to other subjects, to find *synergistic* rapport with them, is, according to the present view, foundational to psychic existence.[5]

A subject that is denied the opportunity to achieve such a primary cathexis will suffer orectic arrest: unawakened to its own subjectivity it will, as soon as its behavior is no longer a function of purely instinctual drives, fail to sustain the psychic will to reach out to world. Such a subject cannot thrive.

It is, in a literal sense, "an-orectic," lacking in desire per se. Little Sylvy was precisely in such an an-orectic condition before she was relocated to the country. The narrator notes not only that it seemed to Sylvia "that she had never been alive at all before she came to live at the farm," but also that she remembered "with wistful compassion a wretched dry geranium that belonged to a town neighbor." Sylvia clearly perceived the starved plant as a metaphor for her own psychic condition.

To whom or what the primary cathexis is made, however, matters. That to which the self originally reaches out and in which it makes its primary psychic investment must be in some sense an encompassing and enabling other, one which can awaken the self to its own subjectivity. Although it is assumed in psychoanalytic theory that the infant typically cathects to its mother, there is in principle no reason why cathexis to a different other—human or even, from a panpsychist perspective, nonhuman—might not occur. The only requirement is that the emerging subject discover itself in the responses of another. While it is implausible to suppose that cathexis could occur with the nonhuman when the latter is present only in the form of a being of limited responsiveness, such as an insect or a frog, it is entirely plausible that the communicative world itself, particularized via land or place, could serve as primary nonhuman other.

When the primal psychic investment of the infant is in a human other, then the original erotic impulse will presumably, as Freud believed, be sexually tinged, since intersubjectivity between persons always harbors sexual possibilities. If such investment is in a human individual of the opposite sex, then, assuming a heterosexual social milieu, the erotic impulse is likely to be strongly sexualized from its moment of origin. In this case, "reaching out" to others, seeking intersubjective contact with them, will always, for the subject in question, involve a sexual dimension. If the psychic investment of the infant is in a nonhuman other, however, then eros will not be sexualized at its origin. There will be a flow of energy outwards, an impulse and capacity to engage, which is not primarily sexual in its form of expression.

If the cathexis is to a human individual, and that individual is, as is typically the case, the parent or primary caretaker of the infant in question, then further complications ensue. For the parent is normally the agent of the child's socialization. The child's erotic aspirations will be acknowledged and reciprocated only to the extent that the child conforms to a complex set of norms and expectations imposed by the parent, both on the parent's own behalf and on behalf of society. In this case, the pattern of the child's outward-bound energy is met with innumerable resistances—the flow of its energy is rerouted to match the parent's agenda. The parent imposes her own sense of timing, level of need, and pattern of relating on the encounter; synergy is not achieved. The child submits to this co-optation of its erotic impulse because of the force of the cathexis. It *must* strive for intersubjective contact, as best it can, even if it has to sacrifice its energic integrity in doing so. In this sense, cathecting to a parent results in the suppression, the "killing," of the child's original psychic essence, its energic identity, and the replacement of that energic identity by a discursive one: the child no longer experiences its selfhood through the flow of its impulses towards others but discovers itself discursively, through the perceptions of others and the categories they impose on it—through its abstract social "acceptability."

Establishing a primary intersubjective bond with a parent who is also an agent of socialization tends then both to sexualize eros and to sadistify it from the start: the primal erotic impulse of the subject—to make contact with another subjectivity—involves the child both in a sexually tinged interaction and in the "killing" of its own energic integrity. It has to submit to the sacrifice of its "wildness," the unique rhythm of its energic outflow, in order to secure the necessary bond. The later sexuality of a person who has made such a cathexis will involve a reenactment of that cathexis: their sexuality will be modeled on a relationship with one for whom the price of love was a "killing" of the original identity of the child. In sex then such a person will seek to "kill" in the other, or have "killed" in themselves, all that is truly original or wild in the erotic impulse. "Killing," in this sense, is sexualized. When psychic "killing" is thus sexualized, it is difficult to insulate killing in a literal sense—especially the killing of wild things—from such sexualization.[6]

If the primary intersubjective bond of the infant is with the nonhuman world however, then the erotic impulse is neither sexualized nor sadistified at its point of origin, since the other in this case is neither sexed, at least in any sense that is humanly relevant, nor responsible for the child's socialization. Subsequently to or simultaneously with this cathexis to the nonhuman world, the subject may be socialized by human caretakers, but since she has not cathected to them the strictures they impose on her behavior may be accepted by her without her internalizing them. That is to say, she may accept these strictures without feeling that she must adjust her psychic organization to the discursive requirements of the caretaker. She can, in other words, alter her overt behavior in accordance with social expectations, without suppressing and reprograming her inner being. She will in this case retain, as her primary sense of self, that particular constellation of out-reaching psychic energies with which she was born. Discursive layers of identity may be contingently overlaid on this energic foundation, but they will not replace it. Erotic relations with human persons will then follow the (synergistic) pattern of her original relation with world, and sexual relations will be a subset of her erotic relations. Sexual relations will accordingly be primarily synergistic relations of intersubjectivity rather than relations that involve the "killing" of the capacity for synergy.

It is worth noting that whether the primary psychic investment of an individual is in the human or the nonhuman is largely determined by cultural factors. In cultures of materialism, the animistic tendencies of young children will be discouraged, trivialized, and overridden: the child will be exhaustively engaged by the mother or other primary caretaker, and its interest in the nonhuman will be redirected either into mere fantasy or into overtly instrumental channels. Only a child who has a strong innate orientation towards the nonhuman and who is not psychically engaged by a human other is at all likely to cathect to world in such a culture. Even then the chance of their doing so will depend on circumstances: the child must be situated in an environment that provides opportunities for dialogical exchange. If Sylvia had not been relocated to the child-friendly environment of the country, where she had opportunities to roam at large and encounter the land for herself, she would not have made a cathexis at all, and would never have come to life. On the other hand, in cultures premised on panpsychism, the young child is ceremonially introduced to homeplace or country and its cathexis thereto is likely to be deliberately facilitated and fostered by the entire community. Its socialization is also typically at least partially postponed to a later stage of childhood: the child is given a long rein and thus permitted to experience and express its energic essence relatively freely in its earlier years.[7]

Returning now to the meeting between the self-assured young man and the shy female wild-child, it is possible to view this meeting as one between an individual whose original self has long since been "killed" via his cathexis to a human agent of socialization, probably his mother, and another whose original self is still intact as a result of her cathexis to a responsive world. The boy's sense of his own identity is abstract and mediately rather than immediately grasped ("I am this, I am that . . ."). This accounts for his sense of his own station, his complacent enjoyment of his social superiority in the face of rude country folk. But the price of such discursive identity is the primordial "killing" of all that was truly original in himself—his innate rhythm and pace and pattern of engaging with the energies surrounding him. This "killing" imperative—upshot of his primary cathexis to an agent of socialization—now informs his entire orientation to the world: "killing" has become entangled, in his psyche, with primal eros. As a result of his conventional cathexis to mother, primal eros has been sexualized as well as sadistified, so that sexuality also for him revolves around a convoluted sadistic logic of "killing" and "being killed."[8]

Such an analysis of identity formation in relation to world is alien to contemporary psychoanalysis because Freud and his followers were theorizing from an unavowed metaphysical premise, the materialist premise of modernity per se, namely that the nonhuman world lacks a subjectival dimension and is incapable of standing in a responsive or communicative relation to us. Such a world can accordingly be nothing but inert background to psychodynamics. When this premise is replaced by a panpsychist one, the world, rendered particular through place, is recognized as an active force in psychodynamics, and its potential role in human identity formation—with all the consequences not only for identity but for basic metaphysical attitudes that this implies—is acknowledged.

The consequences of acknowledging place as a potential primary other, through investment in which a subject may be brought into psychic being, extend not only to sexuality but to gender. To appreciate this, let's consider what would happen in later life to the little girl who refuses to allow the killing of the white heron. What kind of woman would Sylvia grow up to be, and would there be a place for her in modern society? The short answer to these questions is, I fear, that she would be *unclassifiable* in terms of modern categories of sexuality and gender, and would therefore fit into modern social systems only with the greatest difficulty.

A longer answer to these questions calls for some preparatory remarks concerning the psychogenesis of gender identity. These remarks are only pointers to a theory of gender. My present concern is not to develop a theory of either sexuality or gender per se, but to demonstrate the difference that is made to theories of sexuality and gender by a revision of our metaphysical premises.[9] Our understanding of sexuality and gender is in turn a key to our understanding of the modern (sadistic) attitude to reality.

My remarks concerning the psychogenesis of gender rest on two assumptions. Firstly, the sex of any particular individual is biologically given. The human species, like all other animal species, is sexually dimorphic. Only male sex organs and female sex organs exist. Some individuals may possess both male and female organs, and some organs may be deformed or dysfunctional, but no individual possesses reproductive organs that are neither male nor female, because there are no such organs. Sex, in this sense, is dictated by the requirements of reproduction and is biologically determined.[10] (This is not of course to say that the sex of an individual cannot be biologically adjusted, male to female or vice versa.) The second assumption is that both sexuality—in the sense of sexual functioning and orientation—and gender are far from biologically given. They are determined wholly or at least largely by psychogenetic and cognitive/cultural factors.

The sexual functioning and orientation of an individual is generally laid down in childhood, and will depend on how other members of the child's family or wider community respond to her early erotic impulses. Her sexuality will depend on how the object of the child's cathexis—if it is human—responds to these impulses. In a generally heterosexual social milieu, a mother is likely to respond differently according to whether the erotic impulses directed at her emanate from a male or a female child. She is likely to reinforce the sexualization of male eros and discourage the sexualization of female eros.[11] But these psychodynamics are infinitely variable. The salient point in the present connection is that once a sexual orientation has been established, the child is more or less committed, consciously and unconsciously, to a particular gender path: her gender traits are dictated by the discursive requirements of the desired sex. If her orientation is heterosexual, she will attempt to make herself attractive to members of the heterosexual male class, or a subset thereof. If her orientation is homosexual, she will mold herself to the desires of the class of lesbians, or a subset thereof. A similar adjustment to the expectations of others will be required of men. (Note that on this account of gender, a homosexual orientation entails a distinct correlative gender. Subgenders might also be differentiated along similar lines.) Individuals whose erotic energies have been sexualized at their point of origin via cathexis to a human parent or caretaker have no option but to mold their identity in accordance with the desires of those they themselves desire. Their very existence, as subjects, is at stake, since it is through their sexuality that their out-reaching energies—the energies that connect them to reality—are activated.

Those whose primary intersubjective bond is with the world under some other-than-human aspect thereof, however, are under less psychic pressure to measure up to the discursive requirements of a particular set of human others. Their psychic energies are already activated via their engagement with land or place—they are already psychically functioning in erotic mode and experiencing the potentiating effects of synergistic concourse with everything around them. They may indeed need to cultivate certain "occult" powers in order to sustain and deepen this engagement—the power to induce a response from the world, to enhance dialogue with it, to read the signs through which it "speaks." They have to understand how to make themselves "attractive" to the universe! But such "attractiveness" is likely to be a function of energic adjustment rather than conformity to a discursive ideal: the subject engages the universe by "dancing" with it rather than by merely adopting the discursive persona of shaman, mystic, sage, witch, or whatever.

How is this "ontic" orientation of one who has come into subjecthood via their relation with the other-than-human, and whose erotic impulse has accordingly not been sexualized at its point of origin, expressed at the level of sexuality? Presumably sexual orientation is established in this instance in much the same way as it is for those who have come into subjecthood via their relation with the human; namely by way of the responses of family or community members to the sexual behavior of the individual in question, though this developmental process is likely to occur later in individuals who have cathected to the other-than-human than in those who have cathected to the human. The difference is that sexual orientation will not, in the case of those who have cathected to the nonhuman, commit the subject irrevocably to a particular gender identity. This is because the subject's very existence as a subject—her sense of her self—does not depend on sexual acceptance by other humans. Her sense of her existence is grounded in an energic relation with a responsive world rather than in a set of discursive ideals socially imposed upon her. Sexuality thus does not have the same existential importance for her as it does for those in whom eros has been sexualized at its origin. Not only is her sense of her own existence not dependent on her sexual identity but her basic social orientation is erotic rather than sexual, and sexual relations constitute for her a substream of her erotic life.

Nevertheless, given the usual structuring of families within many traditional and modern societies, an individual's sexuality is likely to be central to her happiness. For that reason one whose primary psychic investment is in the other-than-human will seek to assume, as a discursive overlay to her basically energic identity, the traits that match the requirements of those whom she sexually desires. To the extent that these traits revolve around the sadomasochistic dynamics of "killing," however, one who has cathected to the other-than-human is in a bind. She cannot assume such traits, since "killing" is alien to her own psychodynamics. In sex, as in the rest of her erotic life, she seeks to join her own rhythms to those of others, rather than subordinating theirs to discursive imperatives. The dynamics of power, of domination and subjugation, so deeply embedded in the psyches of those who have cathected to an agent of socialization and so central to the construction of femininity and masculinity in modern societies, are an unknown quantity to her; she comes to understand them, if at all, as an external observer. She may be disadvantaged by this "innocence" in her sexual interactions with others.

For this reason, and also because the discursive traits that are definitive of the various genders have never, in her case, been internalized by the force of an original cathexis, one whose primary psychic bonding is to the other-than-human will never appear to others as a "real" woman or lesbian or whatever. She just *plays* at being such. Unlike those who have cathected to the human, she never submits to discursive appropriation—she never really believes in identity definitions per se. She will avoid overidentification with institutions, professions, groups, constituencies of any kind, and, to preserve her discursive indeterminacy, she will tend to situate herself *between* different social worlds. Although she concedes that social approval is required if one is to function effectively in society, the yardstick against which she measures herself is ultimately independent of social expectations. In the eyes of those who cannot conceive of a yardstick that exceeds the social, she appears strangely halfhearted in her social endeavors, maverick, less than fully committed to success, to winning the approval of her peers. The one tag she does embrace wholeheartedly is her identification with a particular place or land. This is because she intuits that her bond with this place or land is the energic ground of her identity.

Individuals who have achieved subjecthood via the other-than-human rather than via the human and whose identity has accordingly followed the energic rather than the discursive path are of course natives. They belong to place at the most fundamental psychic level. When a particular individual in a modern context happens, by disposition or accident, to have cathected to place rather than to a primary human other, I propose to refer to her as a *medial*, to mark her difference, particularly at the level of gender, from other members of modern societies. In the case of medials, as I have explained, identity has followed the energic rather than the discursive path: the original pattern of their energy outflow is still the basis for their sense of self.[12]

The term "medial" is selected in this connection for several reasons, each pertaining to the preference of medials for zones of betweenness. Firstly, although a medial may identify, somewhat halfheartedly and at a superficial level, as masculine, feminine, lesbian, gay, or bisexual, he or she does not really fit any of these categories, on account of the fact that these categories are, in nonpanpsychist cultures, generally constructed around the dynamics of "killing." In this sense the medial is situated *between* the other genders. Secondly, with their reluctance to commit to discursive tags generally, medials also mediate between different spheres in society: they are likely to keep feet in different camps, maintaining something of a marginal status in the various camps with which they are associated and bringing the perspective of other camps to each. Thirdly and finally, medials are constantly in transit between the human and other-than-human communicative domains, and again bring the perspective of the latter to the former. Since the other-than-human is necessarily imbued, for them, with a subjectival dimension—since it is a responsive, speaking presence—their communication with it appears, to nonmedials, to partake of the occult, the supernatural, the spiritual. In this sense the medial is in a position to mediate for secular society with the hidden faces of reality. In consequence she may be acknowledged as a medium or healer, hailed as a guru, spurned as a witch, or dismissed as a nutcase, depending on the social milieu in which she happens to find herself. She may engage with the other-than-human wisely or unwisely, skillfully or unskillfully, superstitiously or in a genuinely spiritual manner. Her medial status is not in itself a guarantee of any kind of wisdom or enlightenment.

According to the present account then, the child, Sylvia, would have grown into a medial. Since the category of medial did not exist in her society however, she would very likely have had difficulty both in understanding herself and in being understood by others. At best she would have had to carve out for herself a singular social niche. (If she had continued to belong to the rural poor, Sylvia might have become a herbalist and local healer. The heroine of Jewett's best known novel, *The Country of the Pointed Firs*, assumes just such a role in her community. If she had risen a little on the social scale, she might have become an artist or writer, like Jewett herself.) In any case, Jewett recognizes the difficulty. The story ends with a reflective question mark. Sylvy does not forget the young man. Are birds better friends than their hunter might have been? The child is privy to the "gifts and graces" of the woodlands, but will these sustain her? Is she marked out for loneliness? The same question hangs over those in contemporary Western societies who have, either by disposition or by some accident of circumstances, originally cathected to the nonhuman rather than to a human other.

Yet such cathexis is, as I hope already to have shown, a key to the psychology of reinhabitation. One who has cathected to the world through place already feels that they belong to that place, and, through that place, to the wider world. Inhabitation is thus their natural modus vivendi. Although the possibility of cathexis to place is not even recognized in the context of modernity, it would appear to be the psychological norm within many indigenous societies whose cultures rest on a panpsychist premise. In such societies, identity is, according to innumerable testimonials, grounded first and foremost in living land, country, homeplace. While I have reserved the special term "medial" for individuals in modern societies who achieve subjecthood through place, no such special term is required for those who, as a matter of course, cathect to country in indigenous societies; they are simply natives. An individual's identity, in such societies, is not in the first instance a discursive construct, a function of a system of social approvals and disapprovals, but an energy which follows its own original pattern, a pattern inherited from the energic contours of the place, the land, to which the individual belongs. Having originally cathected to world rather than exclusively to a human other, such an individual is fundamentally an erotic self: eros has not been compromised in the originary moment by the requirements of socialization. The discursive templates imposed on the self in the course of socialization lie lightly over the surface of the psyche rather than cutting deep into its energic structure. Nor has eros been sexualized at its point of origin. The child is already erotically engaged with reality when opportunities for the sexual expression of eros present themselves. Accordingly, when sexual expression is achieved, it will conform to the dynamics of eros already established in the psyche rather than to the punitive or sadomasochistic dynamics of socialization.[13] In other words, sexuality is not the primary conduit of energic being in societies resting on a panpsychist premise. Nor is the exclusive allegiance of individuals belonging to such societies to culture, let alone to civilization; it is not, in other words, to a discursive system but to reality—to country, land, homeplace. This is the commitment locked fast in the individual unconscious by the force of original cathexis.

The commitment to country rather than to any discursive system binds the native to her countrymen and women and makes them, all together, a people. A discursive system—a culture—emerges as the expression of this shared commitment, but it is not itself the original object of the commitment. That is to say, it is not in the first instance a culture that binds such a people together, but their country, even though culture is a facilitating factor in actualizing commitment to country. Through their culture, natives seek, collectively, ever to improve their psychic fit, ever to elaborate and expand their embodied dialogue, with the animate ground of their being.

When an individual or a people acts, consciously or unconsciously, from a panpsychist premise—which is to say, when they are actualized, at the deepest level of self, through synergism with a psychically activated world— then their basic modus vivendi will be entirely different from that of an individual or a people acting from a materialist premise. From the viewpoint of a materialist premise, the human self in society is all there is, psychologically speaking. The individual subject has no alternative but to find itself in relation to other human subjects who are simultaneously instruments of a discursive system for the creation of social order. Materialism thus imposes an anthropocentric horizon on identity formation: cathexis is bound to be to a human other who is likely to be an agent of socialization. Such a cathexis results in the killing of the energic self. From the killing of the energic self, two trains of consequence flow. These are as follows.

Firstly, when the energic self is suppressed, a discursive self is substituted for it. The discursive self is built out of the (positive and negative) perceptions of (human) others: it derives its sense of its own existence from a *self-image* or self-*story* constructed out of those perceptions. The self-image or -story in question must have a basically positive cast if the self is to feel any confidence and pleasure in itself. A negative reflection of itself will cause anxiety (loss of confidence) and depression (anhedonia). The basic stance of the discursive self is thus one of approval seeking. It can win the approval of others either by conforming to their discursive prescriptions—being *this* kind of person, or *that*—or by manipulating their responses to it. To manipulate others successfully requires that one exercise power over them. Such power to manipulate may take many forms, from flattery or charm through popularity or fame to the exertion of influence or outright coercive force. The discursive self is thus simultaneously a slave to others and a would-be tyrant over them. Its own initial depotentiation leads to a modus vivendi that revolves around both social conformism and the exercise of power.

The second train of consquence that flows from the original killing of the energic self is the one already traced: when its inherent elan has been suppressed, the self is compelled to act out this suppression in its relations with others. It has to block or plug others' energic spontaneity, kill their wildness, in order to compensate for and naturalize its own loss. This sadistic impulse informs the self's attitude both to human others and to the world at large, with the result that sexuality, in particular—as a last refuge of spontaneity in human interaction—is sadistified, and the natural environment is violated, stripped of life.[14]

Clearly these two trains of consequence converge in the materialist self, the self whose identity rests on a premise that can brook no cathexis with the other-than-human world. The power-seeking imperative of the discursive self and the sadistic impulse of the killer self both combine with the bruteness and blindness that is the basic modality of the materialist self. The result is a devastatingly insensitive modus vivendi designed to subordinate reality to the psychological needs of a subject primally depotentiated by its psychological estrangement from the ground of its being.

The contrast with the modus vivendi of the native self, whose identity rests on a panpsychist premise, could not be more complete. Having invested herself psychically in the responsive ground of her being—her country— rather than in a human agent of socialization, the native self is not energically compromised at her moment of origin. Her impulse towards erotic engagement remains her constitutive modality, a modality addressed to reality at large as much as to human others. The native self is thus an erotic self. Still wild in herself, she is not disposed to destroy wildness in the outer world, either in the natural environment or in human others: sexuality, for instance, is for her a substream of eros, not sadistified but adapted to the end of intersubjective engagement.

The native self is plenitudinous in essence. Her core consists of a nourishing fount, an inexhaustible outflow, rather than the energic black hole, or nullity, that lies at the center of the discursive self. The native is thus not dependent on the perceptions and judgments of others for her sense of her own existence. True, she does rely on energic engagement with others for her ongoing potentiation, but engagement can be with the ground of being, with country, as well as with persons. So while the discursive self is a dependent self, forced to seek power over others to ensure her own existence, the native self is psychically and socially relatively independent: simply by *being* in the world she is already potentiated, already filled with the charge of her own reality. It is precisely this independence which confers on the native the freedom to engage with human others for the sake of engagement itself, rather than for the sake of reinforcement of her own self-image.

If the discursive self, resting on a materialist premise and psychically divorced from world, from country, is ultimately a driven and driving self, the hallmark of the native self is *grace*. The discursive self relies on external testimonials to her existence: not only the perceptions of others but also monuments and memorials—material transformations of the status quo that afford visible evidence of the self's presence. The native self, by contrast, dwells within the parameters of the given. She looks for no testimonials to her existence—no obituaries or biographies—nor does she seek to recast the earth in her own image. She stands in the calyx of an inexhaustibly deep and poetic reality that opens its petals around her. She breasts these layered energies, gently launching herself on their swells and swirls, attuning herself to the inner rhythm, the pulse, of their unfurling, letting that pulse lift her and carry her forward. She adjusts her own inner curvature to that of the world, and in gratitude she lets the waves plot her course.

Moderns know what they want and they move in for the kill to get it. They elbow their way forward, determined to reach their destination. They jostle for center stage, competing for the limelight of approval. The native meanwhile irresolutely eddies here and there, tarries at the edges, lingers in the background. She may be ignored as a contender, passed over in discussion, slighted as a friend, sacrificed on the altar of others' self-interest. But somehow she evades capture. She eludes extinction. It is her very graciousness in the face of those who kill to achieve their ends that places her beyond the reach of their predation. For although the killers may have charm, brilliance, influence, and ultimately even brute force at their disposal, they sense the hollowness at their core relative to the plenitudinous presence, the ease of being, of the gracious.

The predators march all over the planet, planting flags and endless rows of chimney stacks, bulldozing highways through every last mountain fastness, crisscrossing the skies with jetstreams and blinking satellites. Yet still there is a sense in which, amid all the bluster, the sound and fury, they are never really *there* at all. The natives watch, mute and wide-eyed, as the armies of modernity march by, but at the end of the day, when those armies have expended themselves and smoke is rising over the ruins, it is they, the natives, who will still be there, sifting through the litter and making their campfires among the wreckage. For although they do not contend, the natives have their own ways of withstanding regimes of killing. These are Taoist strategies, the strategies of the surf rider who navigates the shifting gradients, negotiates the king waves, of life's dangerous field. The surf riders prudently make way for those who adopt the self-imposing modus operandi of the motorboat, who ignore currents and tides and cut straight lines from *A* to *B*. But the natives know that those who are driven and who drive will meet their inevitable demise when the tiny power of their motors is finally quenched in the inexhaustible field of night.

Part 3

Views from the Ground

Chapter 7

The Merri Creek: To the Source
of the Given

Have you ever had an experience but still, at the end, been unable fully to *imagine* it, to hold it, all in one piece, in your imagination—to *grasp* what has happened to you? This is how I felt after my pilgrimage to the headwaters of the Merri Creek. Memories of the separate days of the journey were fresh, but the poetic significance of the journey as a whole eluded me, even as I burned, bright as a biblical bush, with its afterlight.

Where did it begin? Where does any pilgrimage begin? At the dawn of personal time, I suppose, in earliest life, in those one or two images which, as Albert Camus put it, first open childhood's heart. Creeks were already charged with this kind of primal significance for me. A small creek without a name had wound through the back of the farmlet on which I was raised. I had no idea where it came from or where it went, but it was always full of news from upstream, especially after heavy rains, when inflated carcasses of sheep and other animals would float past or pile up against the barbed wires that were here and there strung across its course. These tidings from places that were entirely unknown to me, yet to which I felt mysteriously connected as part of the wider world that the creek created for me, were always tremendously exciting, and I was even more thrilled when the creek would "break its banks" (how I loved that expression!) and rise up to cover the bottom of our paddocks. What a cold but exhilarating elementalism I felt when I paddled, sometimes up to my knees, in that muddy water that the creek had laid, against the accepted order of things, under fences and gates and across pastures, making the familiar landscape strange. Of course, it was not long before this elementalism was taken in hand, and the bed of the creek bulldozed out and straightened. Although I was only seven years old at the time, I know I was shocked at the effects of this bulldozing, transforming the creek from easygoing meanderer, so at home in its well-worn, overgrown channel, to raw clay excavation, straight sided and steep. Still, the billy buttons and watercress grew back, the tadpoles and cranes returned—though there were no more rumors of eels after that—and the creek continued to bring gossip from upstream, and even to break its banks from time to time. My fascinated love for it continued unabated. The creek was not like a paddock or rock or other land form—it *did* things, it *told* things—it was busy and talkative and full of surprises. It was, above all, companionable.[1]

After my family moved from this rural fringe of Melbourne to the inner city, that rural area was rezoned heavy industrial and the creek channel was fully "upgraded" into a concrete drain. No more watercress and billy buttons now. My attention however was by this time turning from creeks to other things, and it was not long before I had relocated to London. I remained there for ten years, with nothing but a distant, rarely glimpsed Thames for fluvial company. (I remember however my sense of enchantment when I obtained a map of the old Thames river system. Most of the tributaries in the inner London catchment still existed but had been converted into underground sewers. Some of the streets still bore the names of the waterways they had supplanted. Fleet Street, for instance, followed the course of the old River Fleet.) It was not until I was in my late twenties that I returned to Melbourne, and settled in inner city Brunswick East, not far from where my parents still lived.

That was twenty years ago. It was a couple of years later, when we acquired our first dog, that I discovered the Merri Creek, which formed the eastern boundary of the municipality. My early memories of this urban creek are blurred. It grew into my consciousness gradually, imperceptibly, as I walked our mad bull terrier along its banks, and watched the transformations occurring there. From an utterly degraded and neglected little gutter, winding past the backs of factories and under flyovers, choked with fennel and blackberry, it was returning to life. Under the auspices of its Friends (Friends of the Merri Creek) and its heroic Committee (the Merri Creek Management Committee), which was coordinating the efforts of local councils and community groups to revegetate the urban reaches, native trees and shrubs were reappearing, and with this the native birds, long since driven from their old grounds, were coming home. Gradually a bicycle path was laid, from the mouth of the creek at the Yarra River to the lake at Coburg, and eventually right through to the outer northern suburbs. At the same time, as factories looked for cheaper real estate on the edge of town, community projects moved in on the scraps of degraded "wasteland" the factories left behind. An amazingly colorful landscape started to cohere along the banks. Walkers and riders on the bike path were greeted by the windmills and African grasshut rooftops of CERES (the environment park in Brunswick East), the Aboriginal flag of the Caring Place, and the gold spires and domes of the Russian Orthodox Church, which the parishioners were building with their own hands over many years. There was an old market garden, still under cultivation, and reestablished swamps and grasslands, and one could pass under the newly cleared arches of bluestone bridges that would look at home in the villages of Old Europe.

Ironically, here, where the cause was already lost, where urbo-industrialism had already had its way, and ripped the innards out of the land, one could find solace and hope for the future. In this small valley, the engines of "development" that were overtaking the rest of the world were grinding into reverse. While elsewhere, everywhere, cities were expanding, reaching ever further out into the countryside, devouring farms and towns and rural landscapes, the bush was here sending a tentacle back into the city, nature was recuperating its old haunts and, like shoots breaking through concrete, creative forms of new life were springing up. It was often actually a relief for me to return from the country, where so many pristine beauties were yet to fall, to this place that had already been gutted and smashed, but was now in the process of recovering a new, readjusted wholeness. It had swallowed, or been swallowed by, modernity but had reemerged, transformed, as a new kind of place, a place in which a new balance had been struck between human and other-than-human elements. As I watched this process taking place, the creek gradually became, over the years, my place, my "country," in something like the Aboriginal sense of that word, and it has sustained me, as it has many other local people, through these times in which our world is being vandalized beneath our eyes.

It was natural then that I should wonder about the Merri's upper reaches. Where the bike path ended, at Mahoneys Road, the watercourse wended off into terrain that was quite unknown to me, most of it privately owned. I had driven up north of Melbourne to look for the creek a couple of times, and gazed at it from rural roadcrossings, slightly disoriented but also excited at encountering my little friend in such untrammeled guise. But roadcrossings were few and far between, only four or five of them on the creek's entire seventy-kilometer passage down from the Great Dividing Range to the edge of Melbourne. So its story remained closed to me, a mystery. When a young friend, Maya, who shared my attachment to the creek, said she would join me if I undertook the journey to its headwaters, the wheels of pilgrimage began to turn.

As the idea took shape, it became clear that such an expedition would entail preparations on a scale comparable to those required for more conventional pilgrimages, to India or China, for instance. The project became something more political—an exercise in the politics of repossession and reinhabitation—when we learned that the then state government had put back on the drawing board old plans for a freeway extension along a part of the Merri valley.

Maya and I were at this point joined by a third member of the expedition, Cinnamon, who, like Maya, worked at CERES. Together these two turned the first stage of the Walk into a community event, tying it to the spring Kingfisher Festival (we would walk to meet the first kingfishers flying down the valley to their summer breeding grounds) and to the CERES education program (we would set off on World Habitat Day). They organized a launch, and invited hundreds of schoolchildren to join us for short intervals over the first two days. Kind friends and fellow creek devotees agreed to act as our support crew, bringing food and gear out to appointed stopovers at each day's end. In these and other ways, many people entered into the spirit of our undertaking and helped to bring it to realization. I came to think that such wider participation is part of the essence of pilgrimage, that the pilgrim carries in her backpack not merely her own longings but those of many others, to lay at the doorstep of the sacred destination.

While Cinnamon and Maya were organizing the public side of things, I embarked on a series of reconnoitering trips into the uplands, chatting with local people, setting up stopovers, writing letters to landowners. I had already discovered that another, little known world still existed intact just off the Hume highway, forty minutes from the city center, under a patchy overlay of subdivisions and commuter farmlets—a world of bush pubs, pastoral holdings, and old homesteads. Somehow I could not imagine reaching this strangely preserved remnant of colonial days simply by stepping out my front door and ambling upstream. Could such romance really be within such easy reach? Was it really as much a part of my own world as the hideous industrial imperium that lined the highway? If it was within walking distance of home, then surely it was! But at this stage I could scarcely believe that these worlds could be bridged in this way by my own feet. So I could not really imagine our journey.

There was also something slightly frightening in this as-yet-unimaginable prospect. The task we had set ourselves was simply to follow the creek wherever it led—through suburbs and industrial zones and rubbish dumps, under bypasses, beside highways, along the edge of quarries, across bull paddocks and acres of gorse and briar, as well as through any scenes of natural beauty that happened to present themselves. Although the journey was small in scale, and would take us through no wilderness zones nor to any guidebook destinations, it offered the kind of uncertainty that made it feel like a true adventure. For when all frontiers have been tamed and developed, when all exotic tribes and species have been winkled out of their hidden crannies and firmly tagged, where after all can one look for the wild, the unknown? When all natural wonders have been scientifically investigated, and all ancient monuments have become tourist attractions, where can one seek the numinous, the sacred? In a world contracted by motor travel and telecommunications, how can one experience vastness?

Do we have any choice, ultimately, but to turn back to the familiar, to the world we have so rapidly and hungrily made over to our own design? When we examine it again, won't we find cracks in its ordinariness, with strangeness, dangers, and distances showing through? Don't we find the wild in the unnamed, the unmapped? And where are the unnamed, the unmapped, if not everywhere, in everything that has not yet been deemed salient? Dimensions of salience change. As new ones come into view, old ones recede, tip over the far edge of the past into oblivion. Isn't the unknown forever replenishing itself in this way? Are not wildness and numinosity inexhaustible? "The Tao that can be named is not the eternal Tao. The name that can be named is not the eternal name." From this point of view, pilgrimage, as the quest for the unnamed—not to conquer but simply to encounter it, face to face—must be perennial, though reinvented anew by every age. As for distance, what is it but a function of our modes of transmission and travel? To find vastness, haven't we only to set out from our home at the foot of city towers, and in the course of one day's march watch those towers shrink to dwarf dimensions and then disappear? Can one really cover such distances on foot in the space of a single day? This is vastness!

I didn't actually grasp this fully then. But I had had a whiff of the mystery at the heart of the mundane. People seek mystery in the exotic. Every second person one meets these days seems to have toured Outer Mongolia or studied Tibetan scrolls at an anchorage in the Himalayas or been lowered in a cage to meet a white shark face to face in the ocean depths. But when these experiences are commercially preconceived and prearranged, unconnected with the seeker's daily life by a filigree of real relationships, how authentic are they? Can mystery be prepackaged? Can someone else's blueprint become your adventure? Doesn't the mysterious, this place of transcendent encounter and discovery, lie at the edge or at the source of what is already meaningful for us? Doesn't it lie on the other side of the given? And don't we have to be our own guides in seeking out this other side, since only we can identify "the given" in our own lives, and find our way to its edges or its source?[2]

So it was that, on the morning of 7 October, World Habitat Day, Maya, Cinnamon and I met at the confluence of the Merri and the Yarra River. Hundreds of children from nearby primary schools joined us as we strolled along the bicycle path in radiant sunshine towards the environment park. Maya gave them the pitch about our walking to the hills to meet the first kingfishers as they arrived from northern Australia. For seven days we would walk, she said, and the children's eyes widened, as the creek suddenly stretched out beckoningly in their minds. At CERES a sendoff awaited us, with well-wishers and children and speakers from the Creek Committee, the Gould League, and Friends of the Merri, all hoping that our pilgrimage would help, in some way, to protect and bless this much-adored creek. Then off we set again, with our jaunty little cavalcade, and no sooner were we out of CERES' gate than a group of children spied the first—and, as it turned out, possibly last—kingfisher of our journey, called up, no doubt, by the "kingfisher boogy" that had just been sung and danced, midst squeals and excited kingfisher tweetings, at the CERES cafe.

Through the luminous blossom and foliage of early spring we made our way up past the Caring Place, the golden church, the now scarcely used vellodrome, replanted grasslands and swamps, to the old market garden. My friend, Joe, who has worked those few acres with his family for fifty years, but now does so on his own with his wooden wheelbarrow and 1957 tractor, was harvesting chicory and spinach as we passed. Standing in the cool shade of trees that overhang a battered gate, by a large stone trough in which he washes freshly picked bundles of greens, Joe often brings to my mind the old peasant couple at the end of Goethe's *Faust*. In their hut under the linden trees, holding out against the "developer," the master of man and nature that Faust in his last years had become, they were the thorn in the flesh of Faustian pride. "Yon aged couple ought to yeild," Faust mutters. "The lindens still I have to gain, / The clustering trees above the weald / Mock and destroy my wide domain."[3] Old Baucis and Philemon were mown down to make way for the next two hundred years, but at the end of it all, here is Joe, hemmed in by town houses, yes, but still standing, digging, harvesting in his own field! How it pacifies my mind to come to this shady spot from time to time, with my basket over my arm, to buy vegetables direct from Joe's weathered hand!

After taking a snap of Joe we continued on along the path, past pigeon lofts, ducks sunbasking in meadows of buttercups, a waterhole where I once saw a giant longneck turtle perched on a post, up to Coburg Lake. Once there, with plenty of time to spare, we camped under a peppercorn overlooking a rocky playground of pools, small cliffs, and beaches just upstream from the lake. This was a black-duck runway, and watching the ducks plying back and forth across the little amphitheater, their nut browns blending in so rightly with the fawns and buffs of the rocks, splashed with red bottlebrush and streaked with blond wattle, the whole scene took on the aspect of a place out of time. Here just a sliver of a past world of black-duck dreamings had somehow slipped out from behind the facade of the present. "easy to imagine that this might be / their Melbourne home and increase center," observed John Anderson, seer of the invisible within the visible and creek minstrel extraordinaire. "Nothing more beautiful than the glad charge," he goes on, "of duck through galleries of red gum—but / here in their absence the cliffs lend that / vista that paces and fledges each dip, makes / the history of that flight visible."[4] (Oh, that Anderson could have been with us on our journey to see the black duck make their glad charge through the red gums that still actually exist further upstream! But sadly, with so much seeing still ahead of him, he has himself passed into the unseen. Nevertheless, I think of him all the way to the creek's rising.) Ducks and rocks seemed to be the main things on the Merri's mind here, as Anderson would have agreed: it is not for nothing that the creek is called the Merri Merri, as we find out ever more graphically as we proceed.[5]

We cooked a meal that night at the confluence of a storm drain and the main channel, and slept in a scout hall, having been provisioned by my friend, Len, the first member of our trusty support team. The next morning dawned as resplendent as the previous one. We walked springily up the tunnel of willow and ash past Heartbreak House. (This is an old leadlit weatherboard standing in an acre of stone-terraced grounds, with a ruined swimming pool, pines and cypresses, and rambling sheds. I had first discovered it by peeking through a gap in its long, shambling back fence and finding myself inside a veritable Daphne Du Maurier dreamscape. But I had named it Heartbreak House because a friend of mine had come within a whisker of purchasing it, for the purpose of setting up an urban ecocommunity. At the time that it slipped through our fingers I had, in my imagination, already moved in, and my mind was full of pictures of myself with my arms around sheep amid fruit trees and windmills. To walk past the old place still opens up in me little crevasses of loss.) We followed the path past backyard vineyards and vegetable patches, warehouse walls and drive-in screens, to where the valley widened out into a teeming tangle of introduced vegetation. A rather agreeable air of fecund neglect prevailed here, though we did notice that, with the disappearance of native brush, the number and variety of birds dramatically declined. We were due to meet a group of children from a school named St. Joseph the Worker in Reservoir, and we arrived at our rendezvous with a couple of hours to spare. The map showed a Buddhist temple adjoining the creek nearby, though it was nowise visible from the track. We decided to climb out of the valley to investigate.

Away from the creek the streets were lined with light industrial and automotive workshops. The entire neighborhood had the bleak, still-unlived-in feel of outer suburbs, the buildings punishing to the eye and the truck traffic and wind tunnels battering to the other senses. Imagine our astonishment then, when out of this harshness a dazzling white colossus, Kwan Yin, Chinese goddess of compassion, reared up, serenely forgiving the desolation surrounding her. She stood, fourteen meters high, complete with neon haloes, in the grounds of an old primary school converted now into the Vietnamese temple shown on our map. Concrete lotuses bloomed in the pond in which she was set, and an open-air altar was placed before her. We were stunned by this apparition. I myself was not only stunned but touched, because Kwan Yin, the "female Buddha," happens to be my own hearth deity, though I had no inkling of her Vietnamese connection.

There was a monk in saffron robes beside the altar in conversation with some other Vietnamese folk, and they all smiled as we stood at the front fence, gaping. The smiles broadened when Maya recognized one of the men in the party as Van, a worm farmer from CERES, who was, as it turned out, showing some relatives the Buddhist venues of Melbourne. We were warmly invited in then, and guided around buildings and grounds. As rough and raw as it was on the outside, the school had been transformed within into a series of colorful shrines and meditation halls, each one devoted to a different ethnic buddha or deity. The main business of deities and devotees alike seemed to be care of the souls of the recently departed, of whom there were numerous small photographs set around altars. Offerings of fresh flowers and fruit were also arrayed in abundance. Outside, the long scruffy schoolyard led down to the creek, but a little way back from the goddess, set over against the side fence, was another sculpture garden, in the shade of an old white gum. It was named the Deer Park, "where Buddha first spoke of Dharma to five brothers," according to the sign painted on the adjacent palings; the white figures of Buddha and the five brothers, larger than life, sat in a peaceful, dappled circle, surrounded by old school benches with sayings, in both English and Vietnamese, such as "Deluding passions are inexhaustible" and "Buddha's way is supreme. I vow to attain it," inscribed in gold letters on their backs.

As I was noting down some of the inscriptions, the resident monk came up for a chat. His name was, incredibly, courtesy of his master in Vietnam, Dao.[6] I told him, as far as language permitted, of my own devotion to the Tao, and he remarked on the closeness of Taoism to Buddhism, especially of course to zen. We nattered pleasantly about the ineffability of Enlightenment ("the Way that can be named is not the eternal Way"), and also about what it meant to be a monk or nun in a modern context. It meant attaining happiness, he said, not in a temporary or relative fashion, but absolutely, noncontingently. Had he himself attained this, I asked, and he paused, and beamed, and still paused, and then said, not like the Buddha, but yes. He certainly gave an appearance of immense cheerfulness, though he was clearly overburdened with duties, ministering to an entire Vietnamese community, organizing ceremonies and large festivals, with only one brother to assist. But I wondered to what extent his good cheer derived precisely from this, this being needed and loved by so many people. Could the happiness be realized without the sangha, the community—by someone living lonely and unloved in a rented room, for instance? But given the sangha, would one need the dharma at all—or rather, is dharma ultimately just the training that is needed for maintaining sangha? Whatever the answers to these questions, for a beatific monk named Dao to manifest right at the start of one's Taoist journey, out of the very teeth of industrial disenchantment, was upliftingly auspicious.

After a picnic lunch under an oak sapling next to the Deer Garden, to the accompaniment of pop music from the corrugated iron depths of the nextdoor factory, we headed back to the creek. The hundred or so children from St. Joseph the Worker duly appeared according to schedule, a little army in yellow tee-shirts and caps advancing across the oval. Cinnamon spoke to them encouragingly about caring for the creek, and then they marched with us for half an hour or so under a hot sun—in many cases on chubby legs alarmingly unaccustomed to walking—along a section of the valley that was still untended, weed infested. They looked around enthusiastically for native birds, but few were in evidence, and eventually the little troupe departed, flushed but still keen.

We continued on along a sealed stretch of path until we came to another patch of bush. In a clearing here we noticed, in long grass, the dome of a large terra-rosa rock, somehow reminiscent of those old-fashioned tanks of the early days of deep sea diving. Closer inspection revealed that this perfect sphere was cast in concrete, and that several others lay, as if they had rolled there, on the other side of the clearing. There were pressings in the surface of these—a few coins and leaves and such. The effect was quite entrancing. Spheres, after all, have an ambiguous status: occurring in nature, in cosmological contexts as well as in rocky creeks such as the Merri, they also have the geometricality of artefacts. As natural objects which nevertheless bear this mark of intelligent intent, they can bring an aura of the metaphysical, the mythological, to an otherwise ordinary landscape. These spheres, so unannounced, actually deepened the landscape poetically, rather than, as more often seems to me the case with environmental art, intruding upon it.

After an interlude with a flock of firetails—crimson-daubed finches with lipsticked beaks—who took flight and alighted as with one mind, adding another poetic layer to this haven of bushland still within a day's walk of the city towers, we came to the end of the bicycle path. This is where Mahoneys Road almost converges with the major Western Ring Road. After picking our way through the rubble under the Mahoneys flyover, we emerged into a rather heart-stopping no-man's land between the two elevated, walled highways, with earthworks-in-progress and piles of bluestone making the going rough. The creek itself of course was undeterred. It nosed around the various obstacles and eased itself under the speedways, though it did become somewhat gagged with rushes at this juncture. But we followed its patient example, and soon found ourselves in the gloom of the ugly tunnel under the Ring

Road. The creek ran quiet here, with just some sparse, hardy rushes for company, though Cinnamon heard a lone warbler in those rushes as the darkness deepened. We padded through on a conveniently bulldozed embankment, until we reemerged into the light of . . . an industrial horror strip!

This was the moment of truth! We had vowed to follow the creek wherever it led, and now it was leading us into the veritable belly of the beast. Were we up to it? My intrepid companions didn't miss a beat. We pressed on, round the back of warehouses, past dead cars, through truck yards, up into a dirt-track trailbike maze sculpted out of the hillside with thousands of old tires, through spiky holes in cyclone-wire fences, past a hill stripped of everything but a broken-down windmill, which gazed out, from earlier rustic days, over vistas of smoking, grinding decimation. It being Sunday, we spotted few if any actual persons, so no one stopped or challenged us and before too long we were able to return to the creekside, which was now waist high in grass and monster thistles.

And what was this that greeted us? From the very jaws of the city, on the fringes of Campbellfield, the landscape suddenly opened out into a delta of green vastness, a wide valley spreading into a plain that stretched all the way to a green horizon. What joy and relief, like an awakening after nightmare, a vision of what forever lies on the other side of things, the open grassy road that leads back to our beginnings. The thread of the creek wound away across the valley floor, as unfussed as ever, towards an uncluttered skyline.

We beat a path, literally, along the clifftop then down into the wide expanse, leaping a little tributary which Cin christened Pilgrims Creek, until the suburban rooftops of Campbellfield appeared again on the brow of the western wall. It was now apparent that the valley was laced with dipper-style dirt tracks, clearly intended for dreaded trailbikes, but there were few landmarks other than our first river red gum, standing guard over a sandy waterhole, emanating memories of that vanished world in which river reds were the gentle tutelaries of the entire Merri valley. There was also a green pole with spiral moldings and a ventilated cover that turned in the wind, whispering rustily but eerily. What was it? A religious icon, a prayer wheel? Another unannounced sculpture? A sewerage vent? No need for answers.

We rested, devoutly, under the red gum, watching a black-shouldered kite in the heights above us. I had heard that the good people of Campbellfield had recently launched a Black Kite festival. Perhaps one day, I dreamed idly, absorbed in the hovering image, there will be linked bird and animal festivals along the entire length of the creek, singing and dancing the world back into its proper semblance. We stretched out, relaxed. There was peace in the air, but also a certain dissonance. The green pole rustled, the weary old red gum continued its mute witnessing, but the stillness had a sinister edge, as if full of subliminal echoes. Echoes of what? Of the uproar and rage of trailbikes, bulldozers, chainsaws, axes, guns? Who could know. There was just this uncertainty, these unsettled depths. The only certainty was the creek, always making its way at its own pace—the right pace, as Anderson would say—across the land, attending so faithfully to its effluvial business.

It was now that I began to think in earnest about the creek as Taoist teacher, and creek walking as a Taoist exercise. Lao Tzu speaks often of the Tao as the soft Way, the way of water: it resists nothing, but in the end nothing can resist it. "The Softest thing in the world rides right over the Hardest things in the world."[7] Water seeks out the lowest places, never the high, but by doing so it implacably achieves its goal. Tao's presence in the world, Lao explains, is like a great river or ocean, because, like them, it "excels at being low."[8] Elsewhere he puts it as follows: "The highest Excellence is like water. Water, Excellent at being of benefit to the thousands of things, does not contend—it settles in places everyone else avoids."[9] A similar point is made in the *I Ching*. Discussing the appropriate approach to situations of danger, the authors appeal to the example of water: "It flows on and on, and merely fills up all the places through which it flows; it does not shrink from any dangerous spot nor from any plunge, and nothing can make it lose its own essential nature. It remains true to itself under all conditions."[10] So the creek finds its way across the land, singleminded but patient, equable, flowing around obstacles, never forcing the issue. It does not strain or stress itself, but follows existing gradients, wandering or simply waiting until a way forward opens, when it quickens effortlessly again towards its destination. Accepting degraded country as unwaveringly as the pristine, the stream parts for car carcasses just as it does for river red gums and it carries junk as faithfully as it does ducks and ibis. "Doing nothing" then, in this sense, the creek ensures that everything is done—that the work of the world is accomplished. "The thousands of things depend on it for life, it rejects nothing. . . . It clothes and feeds the thousands of things, but does not act the ruler."[11]

Walking the creek, following it along its entire course, really did require, to some small extent, that one enter into this watery spirit. To follow where the creek led, accepting what its course offered, not looking for higher, drier, or safer ground, nor taking short cuts to save time, was indeed to acquiesce, patiently and without judgment, in the given. True, we were walking upstream, "climbing the river" rather than going with its flow, but this did not remove the need for acquiescence, and we could not after all follow the creek, or the Tao, downstream until we had discovered its source, its essence, its true story.

We slept that night in the back streets of Campbellfield, in a local Community Center, to which another kind friend, Noel, ferried our food and gear (and gin and tonics—oh pampered pilgrims that we were!). Noel accompanied us next morning back into the valley and a little way upstream, to the fabled gorge about which we had all read so much in the newsletters of the Committee and the Friends of the Merri. Galada Tambore. Here was wildness of a more typical kind: large boulders, swimming holes, and impressive cliffs, sandstone on the east, basalt on the west. Native shrubs resumed their rightful place, and river gum survivors gathered and huddled in inaccessible clefts. A worthy destination for day trippers, if only a path could be cut from Mahoneys Road through all the intervening rubbish!

Afterwards I discovered that it had in fact always been the (visionary) intention of the Creek Committee to bring the path right out to this wide green horizon, thus opening a leafy through-line from city center to outskirts. This would certainly foster a greater experience of connection with country for the residents of the (traditionally working-class) northern suburbs of our city, deprived as they are of beaches, mountains, and major parks. But wouldn't such pathways be desirable in any part of any city, breaking down divisions between city and country, culture and nature, with all the tendencies towards human self-obsession implied in this separation of humanity from the greater continuum? When, later, I returned home and resumed my usual streamside rambles, I found that my trip to the rural uplands had brought about for me a transformation of perception. Walking the banks of the creek downstream, but feeling its palpable continuity with the waters upstream, which I now knew, I was actually in psychological contact with the uplands. I no longer felt as trapped in the capsule of the city as I had in the past.

After taking leave of Galada Tambore, we walked all day in a between-worlds zone that was in fact the old freeway reserve, generally a kilometer or two wide, with a skyline of factories always visible at its edge, and an incessant background of machine noise. In the creek gully itself, hawthorn blossom reigned supreme, but there was also an abundance of gorse and, in the paddocks on either side, miles of outsize thistles. The Hume highway joined us at one point, and we were within hearing of its traffic for the latter part of our way. But how quickly this dark lining to our silver state of mind was forgotten when we came to the native grasslands—one of the last, miniscule remnants of this most endangered of ecosystems in our state. How absorbed we became in the botanical treasures at our feet. Cinnamon and Maya, far more knowledgeable than I in this connection, put their heads together and identified them. Some I remembered from my childhood, when they were still plentiful on roadside verges, especially the chocolate lilies and varieties of egg-and-bacon. I let the names of others slip by, though I did forge a permanent friendship, I think, with the red-eared kangaroo grass, the original ruler of the Iramoo plain over which the whole of northern Melbourne is laid. (Having encountered the native grasses and wildflowers here in their natural settings, I noticed later, after my return, that I truly recognized them when I saw them in the replantings along the urban banks of the creek—I *knew* them now, in a way I never could have known them through book learning.) I marveled too at how scruffy this precious sanctuary looked—how unassuming an aspect it presented to the casual eye, all its treasure in the detail, as is the case with so many Australian landscapes. And, of course, where the native grasses were, there too were the warblers, firetails, larks, raptors, bluewrens, and other native folk; at one point I surprised a tiny ground hen sitting on three bronze eggs in a woven nest.

It was late afternoon, and raining again, when we arrived at our destination for that day—Walker's Farm (yes, *Walker's* Farm!), next to a sylvan stretch of creek on Craigieburn Road. Margaret Walker, a free spirit who had found release from suburban conventionality on these seventeen acres, lived here with her parents and Arab mares. The family had invited us to pitch our camp by a billabong at the back of their property. The frogs, roused by the rain, were in full cry when we arrived, and that in itself was sufficient homecoming for me. I had not slept the previous two nights, jolted by passing traffic, but on this night, while the sky fell in and flamed with one of the wildest storms for years, I slept cradled and smiling in my tent, my ears tuned to nothing but the crooning of the frogs. Our concerned hosts had offered us the stables (yes, oh pilgrims, the *stables*!), but we were safe beside the river red gums, nestled under a stony ridge. We awoke to find the creek in a high state of chatter, bursting with news, and the billabong brimming.

Much later, almost a year after our pilgrimage, I learned that our campsite that night was located in a corner of a sometime sheep station owned by the founder of Melbourne, John Batman. Batman had signed a treaty with eight elders of the Wurundjeri-willan clan, the original owners of the Iramoo plain, a treaty that was later disallowed by the colonial government in favor of the legal fiction of *terra nullius*. It was reputedly on the banks of the Merri, downstream near the confluence with the Yarra, that the historic signing had taken place. Batman's flocks, the largest in the fledgling colony, had apparently grazed up here on these wide creek flats in the late 1830s.[12] Doubtless the billabong, on the grassy verge of which we had slept so peacefully, was one of the water holes from which the Wurundjeri had been displaced by the early pastoralists.

From Walker's Farm we set out that morning to follow our ripple-robed old guide past the brick quarries that were scalloping, scooping out, the pinky flanks of Summer Hill. After a wet lunch shared with hundreds of millipedes frantic, for some reason, to get off the ground, we found ourselves finally free of highways and industry, and out into farmlands proper. The valley narrowed here, opening out into little ampitheaters now and then, while the watercourse itself was mostly screened by, and often completely buried under, gorse. The red gums however were still in attendance, especially at water holes. Gracious guardians, spreading their arms out to the water, bending low, limbs entwined, their maternal presence blending somehow with the fabric of the black-duck dreamings that seemed to wrap these entranced sites!

As we negotiated fence after fence—scores of them, of every description, generally barbed wire, often electric—we started to work as a team, holding the wires open, heaving our packs from hand to hand, catching each other as we jumped from posts. Our inhibitions began to disappear. There was nowhere we couldn't go, nothing we couldn't tackle! We backed through walls of gorse, hacked our way under railway bridges, forgot about snakes. Dispensing with stepping stones, we simply waded through the knee-high stream when we needed to cross the channel. Anyone looking out from a passing train would now have been unlikely to spot us—we were disappearing into the landscape, squatting under bushes for our tea breaks, acquiring a patina of mud. When we finally arrived at Donnybrook Road, late in the afternoon, we were exhausted but elated. Something was beginning to happen!

We walked the last kilometer to the Mineral Springs Park along a road beside the railway line, while the creek cut through another paddock. We were met, as we approached the Mineral Springs homestead, by a black stallion galloping, riderless, down the dirt road towards us in the twilight. A beautiful white horse was whinnying from a paddock behind us, while a young girl called from the homestead gate. The stallion was visibly torn by the opposing summons but, after thundering along for another moment or two in the direction of the white horse (and us!), he actually stopped in his tracks, turned, and cantered back to the black-haired girl, who slipped a rope around his neck, and ran with him, barely holding his bursting strength, back to the paddock from which he had escaped. The girl was Zantha, and there were other equally impressive children at Donnybrook Park. (The horse was actually a gelding, as it turned out, but bred for harness, which explained his imposing appearance.) The park had recently been refurbished by the children's father, Jerry, who was trying to revive this old pleasure ground, site of the first piped mineral waters in the state. There was a lot of magic here, flawed, slightly out of date, but with its peacocks, parrots, and geese, it was certainly reaching for the indefinable, for the spirit of the lost domain. Its effect on Zantha and her siblings, Chelsea and Gabe, was striking: with their innocent but straight-to-the-heart-of-the-matter questions, they had stepped from the pages of some enchanted tale, but they seemed in consequence more fully present in the world than most of their media-mesmerized contemporaries. We were warmly welcomed, served tea and pavlova from the previous day's wedding reception, and offered refuge from the night's rain on the floor of a lumber room—an offer we gratefully accepted.

Pampered again by another member of our support crew, Cathie, we listened to Jerry's stories of the district while awaiting dinner. Nearby Kalkallo had once, it seemed, been a watering place for bullock teams. Originally named Rocky Water Holes, it had served literally to water the bullocks but figuratively their drivers too, with six or seven pubs in the tiny settlement. The drivers would hole up there on the flood plain of the creek and wait until a sailing ship heaved to in the port of Melbourne town. An old sea captain with a homestead on Mt. Ridley, north of Craigieburn, could see all the way down to Port Phillip Bay with his telescope, and would let the drivers know when sailing ships appeared.

I had sensed a bit of this frontier pub tradition when I had first pulled in to Donnybrook on one of my upland scouts, several weeks before. After the drive from town along the Hume highway—which seemed to hold, in its forty hard-hitting minutes, all the crass aggressiveness of late modernity—I had been astonished to wander into the Donnybrook pub, there to discover, in the persons of Graham and Morrie, the veritably premodern ambience of "outback Melbourne." Chatting with these lifelong local boys, I could have been in a pub in the back blocks of the Pilbara. They told me about old mills and Chinese market gardens, dams and swimming holes, along the creek. I was struck, as I would be more and more forcefully in the course of our journey, by the historical richness of this route. Later, after our return, I discovered that the explorers Hume and Hovell, the first white men to cross the Great Dividing Range, had followed the Merri valley for a day or two on their way down to Port Phillip Bay! How strange to think that our very own creek had been a conduit of colonization in this way. What to make of this equivocal discovery? I was pleased to think that though we were partly retracing this march of colonization, we were doing so *in the opposite direction!*

As we left the park the following morning, we stopped for a ceremonial cup of the spring waters, trickling from a rusty pipe into a stone recess. They tasted metallic but sweet. Delicious! The special distillation of our creek. Holy waters indeed! I vowed to return to collect it in bottles. If Joe's vegetables, grown on the Merri flood plain downstream, were my soulfood, then this would be refreshment for my spirit!

Now we entered a seemingly charmed zone, a parklike reserve and pinery, with lawn down to the water's edge. The creek was at its most alluring here, with stone terraces and amphitheaters, steps and water gardens, shoals of shards and spheres tossed together, like simple petrified souls. How busy, how talkative, the creek was among all these rocks! "The Merri Creek saying the right thing / over and over," as John Anderson had noted.[13] Meadows of purple iris bloomed between the river gums. The pine trees however lent an edge to the otherwise cheerful atmosphere, as if something

were present in the shadows, watching, with an indefinable attitude. A wed-
getailed eagle crossed our path, very close, and the vague sense of menace
was underlined when a falcon dived past with a tiny bird (perhaps a
bluewren?) in its talons.

We were now approaching the foot of the long-visible Bald Hill, from
which, my later reading revealed, Hume and Hovell had first viewed this
entire southern portion of the continent. In his diary Hovell had named it
Perambulator Hill, because the pram device he was laboriously wheeling with
them to measure distances had here broken into pieces. Hovell wrote of the
sight that met their gaze from the hilltop: "This was plains, and open forest,
which served to give them a more beautiful appearance, beyond the reach of
the Eye and as far as we could see With the Spy Glass (say) from S.E. to
West and the land falling with a graduel [sic] descent towards the South,
never did I behold a more charming and gratifying sight, at least not were it
in its Natural State."[14] Others were to share Hovell's enthusiasm. This was
the site of the future city of Melbourne.

At the foot of Bald Hill the railway reappeared, bisecting the landscape
into separate countries. On the west side of the weathered bridge—the side
from which we had come—the land told a gothic tale, full of beauty and sus-
pense, a product of the potent interweaving of European and Australian elements, faerie overlaid on dreaming; on the east side lay a wide plain of native
poa grass, innocent of secrets, open to the sky, the creek no more than a line
of river gums scrawled towards the horizon. The channel of the creek was
full, flush with the grass, long ribbonweed tresses loosed in its stream. Even
the rocks had vanished, though the sheep remained. A little way along, scat-
terings of lace-trimmed rocks reappeared, and a particularly celtic-looking
mound, studded with worn old rock teeth, beckoned to us. Perched on the
crown of Pilgrims Knoll, we were treated to an amazing show of speeded-up
weather: at first storminess impended, and Bald Hill blackened; then it was
as if the sky relented, breaking out into forget-me-not smiles and gilding the
hillsides, only to furrow over, dark and beetle browed again. Enthralled, we
sat and applauded these atmospheric theatrics.

By and by we recrossed the creek, avoiding bull paddocks, and continued
on for some time through an amiable emptiness. Our feet however were by
this stage rather sore. Maya had resorted to placing hers in plastic bags inside
her boots, in an effort to keep them dry. My toes were the shade of ripe
plums, and one of them was turning black. With shopping bags bunching
out the tops of socks, trousers rolled up, collapsed brims of sodden hats, and
a repertoire of funny walks that favored our fitter parts over our failing ones,
we must have looked a sorry little band of water rats. The barbed-wire fences
loomed relentlessly. We swung packs, scaled posts, squeezed through spiky
gaps, did the limbo at a dozen different heights. Finally we arrived at a track

that led to what we hoped was the farm at which we had arranged to spend the night. We broached the flooded ford, and Cinnamon rescued me when, mesmerized by the knee-deep, fast-moving water and topheavy with my gear, I kept gently capsizing, surrendering to the flow.

So it was that, decidedly wayworn, we trudged up to the cluster of roofs and hedges at the center of an immaculate estate, trying, as we went, to stay out of the enclosures of all manner of overly frisky-looking livestock. We did eventually, after various false starts, find the cottage (a tastefully furnished, five-bedroom farmhouse!) in which we had been invited to stay, and we sank gratefully into the floral sofas. We decided, then and there, that we needed a rest day, and when Kate, our generous host, appeared, she agreed without a blink to our request. A whole troupe of our support team soon arrived, with hot food that would have moved less susceptible hearts than ours to sighs of gratitude, and the contemplative pace of the day changed abruptly to one of chatty conviviality. We bedded down contentedly that night under fresh quilts in separate rooms, and I fell asleep wondering at the ancient tradition of hospitality towards the stranger. Even in cultures such as ours, in which this tradition has so thoroughly lapsed, it resurfaces spontaneously, it seemed, as soon as an opportunity arises. In most cases we had only had to ask, and people had offered us their paddocks, stables, spare rooms, their showers, and in this case, their vacant cottage. Our hosts had been people of widely different backgrounds, yet each had responded, in their own way, without hesitation and with utmost graciousness, to the archaic pilgrim call, a call so counter to the demands of "possessive individualism" that frame modern life.

The following day, while nursing my purple toes, I had leisure to ponder further the meaning of our journey. That it was indeed a pilgrimage was clear, and the meaning of pilgrimage itself—in contrast with bushwalking, for instance—was now coming into sharper focus. For bushwalking, in its more dedicated forms, is surely a pursuit of unspoiled nature, an exercise in withdrawal from human relativity and mediation, the better or more directly to experience the ground and unnegotiable context of human existence. Such a withdrawal from society seems necessarily to require an ethos of self-sufficiency and physical austerity. Pilgrimage, by contrast, was shaping up as an exercise in the acceptance of the given. After a single initial choice—that of one's sacred destination—one hits the road. Once on the road, however, one takes whatever comes. There is no preference for the nonhuman over the human here, nor is there any sense that the human is less a part than the nonhuman of the numinous, the sacred, the absolute order. One rejoices in nature and the open skies, but trudges through industrial darkness and urban labyrinths if that is where the way leads. One's dependence upon others is acknowledged, and the alms of rich and poor alike are gratefully accepted.

Tonight might be spent crouched in a wet paddock, but tomorrow night one might be plied with gin and tonics, sitting up, conversing brightly, in front of a blazing loungeroom fire. In this respect, pilgrimage seems, again, to be Taoist in its essence: one follows the Way trustingly, resigning judgmentalism and control, accepting succor from any quarter.

And what does the pilgrim offer in return for this sacred hospitality, I wondered. Well, she *gathers in*. Her journey gathers the people and places she encounters along the way into a sacred story. By journeying to her destination—traditionally a temple, shrine, or other holy site—she draws the entire landscape and its inhabitants, including her benefactors, into the net of its meaning: through her intention, her dedication to that meaning, she binds everything into her wake. In our case, we were gathering all that we encountered into the narrative net of the Source of the Merri, threading people and places, animals and birds and plants, landforms and weather to a single spool, winding them into a poetic unity.

However, though it was true that our journey was undertaken in a pilgrim spirit, it did not coincide exactly with pilgrimage in its traditional sense. For while any devotional journey to a sacred destination may be described as a pilgrimage, the destination of the traditional pilgrim typically lay in foreign lands. (This is reflected in the etymology of the word "pilgrim," derived from the Latin *peregrinus*, foreigner.)[15] The sacralizing force of pilgrimage moreover is not tied in any intrinsic way to landscape itself: a philosopher, for instance, might undertake a pilgrimage to Athens to honor Socrates. His journey would then indeed gather all the elements he encountered along the way into a narrative, but this narrative would knit these elements into a story about the sacredness of philosophy rather than the sacredness of the landscapes he had traversed.[16] Our walk was a pilgrimage, but it was not a journey "to foreign parts." It was on the contrary a journey into our own country; the land itself was our destination and our object was to gather *it* into a poetic unity and thus to make it more our own. Moreover, while a wide variety of modes of travel may serve the purposes of pilgrimage, it seemed that *walking* was integral to the spirit of our endeavor. Our step-by-step contact with the land created an intimacy that bound us to it and it to us.[17]

As I mused on this, sitting in a cane chair looking out over the well-tended pastures of Merri Park, a whole tangle of different kinds of journey started to distingish themselves in my mind, and our own walk seemed to partake, in some way, of each of them. A pilgrimage it certainly was, but it also seemed to tap into the spirit of ancestral journeys—the creative journeys of the mythical ancestors, or "dreamings"—of Aboriginal peoples. These ancestors traveled across empty, primal landscapes, differentiating by their activities dunes and salt pans, rocks, rivers, and waterholes, eventually creating further landforms and totemic species by their own metamorphoses.

Such dreaming stories—stories of long-ago mythical journeys—gather the present landscape into poetic unities for the peoples who inhabit them. Dreaming stories are however in a continual state of evolution, with new stories emerging, so that the poetic unity of the land is perpetually in process of renewal.[18] The unifying function of the stories is reaffirmed by the fact that the journeys they describe are reenacted by the people to whom they belong. Aboriginal people follow the steps of the ancestors, singing and dancing the stories of the primal journeys, reinvesting the land with meaning and coherence, bringing it to life. When the world is thus sung and danced to life, it is possible for human beings to enter into communicative relation with it. Through such journeys then we can truly inhabit our world, belong to it, become its natives, its people.

When journeying is understood in this way as gathering everything in the journeyer's wake into a poetic unity, waterways themselves take on the aspect of prototypal journeys, or journey lines—the journey of water through land to sea. Each creek and river binds the elements of the landscape through which it passes into the story of its own adventure. The landscape is sculpted to this adventure, all its features touched by it and subtly turned to it. Like preexisting songlines then, the waterways knit the land up into narrative unities. It is via such unities that distinct "country" comes into being. But while waterways allow for the discrimination of one such country from another, they also *link* the countries they serve to individuate. These watery storylines thus organize country via a simultaneous action of differentiation and connection: they draw the world into wholeness while at the same time generating difference.[19] In walking a waterway then we are already repossessing all that it has gathered into its narrative terrain. In retracing its primal story, we not only renew that story but expand it, in our turn gathering all that we encounter into the story net of our own journey.[20]

In thinking about ancestral journeys however, I also had to consider how our expedition compared with those other journeys with which our continent is so liberally inscribed—the epic journeys of colonial explorers, such as our precursors, Hume and Hovell. On the face of it, journeys of exploration also served as ancestral journeys, but they did so for the colonizing cultures as opposed to the indigenous ones, marking with dramatic narrative features maps that were as yet, from European perspectives, almost as blank and undifferentiated as were the primal dreaming landscapes of Aboriginal provenance. These journeys of exploration enabled the colonizers to settle the land at the level of imagination as well as at a material level. Moreover, by risking and sometimes losing their lives, the explorers symbolically staked out a *moral* claim to the terrain their journeys "opened up": by their real or perceived heroism, and the epic scale of their hardships, they "won" this new terrain, mythically, for the conquerors.

However, the relation to land that was established by these journeys was of course one of conquest rather than of mutual belonging. The explorers were not pilgrims. Their journeys did indeed gather the people and places, the species and landforms they encountered, into stories, but the reference point of these stories—the center around which they turned—was not a sacred destination but the personality of the explorer, the "hero," himself. If pilgrimage draws everything the pilgrim encounters, including himself, into the net of meaning provided by the destination, the colonizing journey draws everything the explorer encounters to himself—he arrogates the landscape to himself by the force of his heroic will. Instead of walking the world into being then, bringing it all to life in the wrap of meaning that emanates from a sacred destination, the explorer walks himself into being. He enchants and charges up his own personality (and by implication, that of his race and class and culture) by *overcoming* the people and places he encounters, mythically absorbing their life force into himself, rendering them objects of his own triumphalism.

But what distinguishes a journey of reinhabitation from one of colonization? When the children of the colonizers want to belong to the land, rather than have it belong to them in the manner of their fathers, is this merely a further extension of the process of expropriation? If the new, would-be natives ignore the history of the land they wish to reinhabit, then perhaps it is. But if they shut their eyes and ears to the story of the land in this way, then they cannot fully reinhabit it in any case. To belong to the land is to uncover its layers, discover its story, and weave one's own identity into that story. In our case, here in Australia, this story includes chapters of bloody invasion. We cannot enter the land without bringing these chapters to light and acknowledging them. To acknowledge them is also to deal with their aftermath, to seek some kind of justice or redress for those who have survived.[21]

As an exercise in repossession, it also seemed important that our journey was largely through private land. For the subjugation of land by modern societies, and the consequent alienation of culture from "country," is expressed most forcefully through the institution of private property. Private ownership, as it is currently understood, nullifies the mutuality between landholder and land: the land belongs to the holder, but the holder does not belong to the land. Even more importantly, while giving legal control of a portion of land to one or several parties, the institution of private ownership generally excludes the wider public from accessing it. "Trespassers Will Be Prosecuted." Under modern property regimes, the world is no longer in any moral sense *our* world: access to most of the places in our immediate neighborhood is drastically curtailed. How many of the houses in my own street, let alone in the whole of Brunswick, have I seen inside? How much of the

Merri Creek in its upper catchment is even visible, let alone accessible, to the wider public?

This physical exclusion of people from their homelands began in Europe long before it was reenacted on the indigenous peoples of the European colonies. We were of course all indigenous people once, and not so long ago, but we Europeans were dispossessed, by way of the privatization of the commons—the centuries-long process known as the Enclosures—prior to, and concurrently with, the dispossession of indigenous peoples in colonized lands. Many who were dispossessed on their own soil became dispossessors on conquered soil, but the process of dispossession, whether in old lands or new, has always been a corollary of capitalist economics, and continues unabated into the present. This process is perhaps less visible in a contemporary frame, because people generally are today *born* into a condition of dispossession, in the sense that they are from birth denied physical and spiritual access to the greater part of their immediate environment. This deprivation is eased for some by their own exclusive possession of a house or apartment, but many lack secure access to *any* portion of their surrounds, and most, even those who do enjoy some degree of private ownership, are profoundly impoverished in their relation to the larger world. "Home" refers, at best, to a small plot, and for many this word has no tangible referent at all.

Compare this state of metaphysical dispossession with the wealth of indigenous peoples of premodern societies and eras. I remember once standing on the tip of Cape Leveque in remote northwestern Australia, looking out across a string of pink islands of unearthly beauty in a live, primeval sea. This was the "backyard" of the Bardi people, with whom I was at that time staying, a small group of families who had hopped from island to island on ceremonial business, swimming the shallow channels, escorted by tiger sharks through waters plied by dugong and sea turtle, for thousands of years. This wonderland had been *theirs*, their home, their world, the very substance of their soul. And what was *mine*? A tenth of an acre in Brunswick? What did this say about the dimensions of my soul? And I was one of the lucky ones! Even medieval serfs were in this respect better off than most moderns—the world through which they walked was one of wildwoods and commons, spiritually open to them, even if sometimes physically out of bounds on account of bandits and wild animals. Or take the camel nomads of northern India. Until very recently they had the free run of their ancestral migration routes, even though these lands were legally owned by others. Traditional property regimes in this part of the world were regimes of usufruct, allowing for multipurpose, communal access to land, with no one party having exclusive moral title to it. Different groups and peoples were able to participate fully, on spiritual and imaginative levels, in their immediate world.[22]

To be at home in the world, to experience one's immediate environment as one's *own* world—isn't this a basic metaphysical right of all human beings? Isn't denying people moral or spiritual ownership of their world cutting them off at the knees, psychospiritually speaking, condemning them to a most abject metaphysical poverty? Yet this metaphysical poverty seems to be a routine consequence of modernity. Doesn't it show up in a poverty of poetic expression at the level of everyday life—a poverty of expression all too apparent in modern societies? Compare daily life in industrialized modern cities with the daily life of those north Indian nomads, for instance. The almost exclusively utilitarian tenor of the modern city, with its resultant ugliness and discordance, is obvious to anyone standing on a busy Melbourne street, whereas an equally casual glance at a nomad camp reveals a form of life expressive, down to the last detail, of a poetic sense of existence: the most mundane activities are raised, through song and story, costume and dance, to a form of poetic address, an ongoing call to a responsive, mythically activated world. We moderns may be offered abstract or transcendental compensations for our metaphysical disenfranchisement: we are invited to ground our identity and our imaginations in philosophical, religious, nationalistic, or other ideals. But aren't these pale substitutes for the inexhaustible reality of a living, speaking land, a land that greets us as kin as it stretches away and away in every direction, filling our senses and emotions with a richness of experience that no amount of clever abstract thought could ever provide.

To urge the repossession of privately owned land through walking is not to waive the legitimate rights of landowners. The pilgrim will surely seek the owner's permission to cross their land, and will treat their pastures, fences, livestock, and the rest, with all due respect. She is legally a potential landowner herself, and landowners are in any case, in a larger sense, like everyone else in the cultures of modernity, relatively metaphysically dispossessed. There is thus no us/them divide in this equation. By harboring the pilgrim, the landowner is acknowledging an older and truer compact between human peoples and the land, and thereby helping to ameliorate the metaphysical pauperization of our collective life.[23]

Of course, it was not possible to ask for permission to enter *all* the properties that adjoined or were crossed by our creek, and it has to be admitted that the fact that this land was conventionally off limits gave our journey a special frisson: we were venturing into places we would never previously have entered, and passing points at which we would once unthinkingly have stopped. There is danger in giving up the safety of remaining in just those spaces one is by social convention permitted to occupy. If any harm befell us as a result of such trespass, we would receive little public sympathy. And privately owned lands are in a sense a last great frontier, for there is no public record or account of what goes on, or is kept, within such grounds. This lent that edge of unpredictability to our progress that turned our walk across tame farmlands into a trek into a true wild.

It was clear that in the course of this short journey we were beginning to lift the lid on a rich brew of meanings and traditions largely ignored by modern societies. But it was not only the meaning of journeying that we were rediscovering; back at Merri Park the term "day of rest" was taking on fresh meaning as well. It wasn't quite a sabbath, because it was our sixth rather than our seventh day, but we were certainly in need of re-creation. I basked in intervals of warm sun in my cane chair while Maya and Cinnamon went off on botanical business. Magpies mewed in the grass, cockatoos shrieked as they passed, unseen birds chattered to themselves in piping voices all around the house. Our boots and gear were spread over the yard to dry. Later Kate came down from the main house and told us a little about the property. The entrance drive was lined with oaks grown from acorns gathered in the grounds of Buckingham Palace. This formal avenue set the tone for the front of the estate, but over the ridge, out of view of the road, the land reverted to its natural rocks and river reds as it descended to the creek flats. There was a lot of love in the air here, of commitment to land care, to the return of native grasses, to replacement of the dowager red gums. Subdivision was, apparently, inevitable. Farming is uneconomic, and when town water comes to these parts, large landowners will be "rated out." My heart sank at the prospect of this country being subjected to yet another wave of appropriation, but it was some comfort to remember that hobby farmers can in fact prove to be sterling conservationists, establishing more habitat for native species than broadacre farmers possibly can. We considered what it would take to establish a reserve along the entire length of the creek: the consent of all landowners, and $10,000 per kilometer for fencing. Something in the order of $700,000 in all. An impossible dream?[24]

Revitalized, we set out early on the drizzly morning of the seventh day—without glimpsing the legendary white-tailed water rat that lives under the Merri Park bridge. The creek meandered through Scottie's bull paddock (a matter of some concern for me!), then it cuddled up to the road for a way, before striking out across quite empty paddocks, past the back of Barrows's farm. The rocks and river reds had almost disappeared here, and the creek ran bare through grass till it led right up to the back door of a dilapidated farmlet. An assortment of black-faced animals—goats and geese and sheep—greeted us from tumbledown sheds, but no one else appeared. The fences, improvised out of old door frames and bits of tin, proved almost impassable, and it was only after some fancy acrobatics that we emerged onto the Beveridge Road. There we crawled under a wet bush and sat peeping out into the rain like Ratty and Moley in *Wind in the Willows*, sipping our tea in surprising snugness.

The landscape was bleak at this point, but it was also profoundly charged with the proximity of Ned Kelly's house.[25] I had been astounded to discover the existence of this house on one of my reconnoitring trips. Kelly had, it turned out, been raised on the edge of the hamlet of Beveridge, a couple of kilometers west of the creek. I had driven over to the town—presently, inevitably, in the throes of development—and followed signs to the house. Imagine my delight when I found, not a touristified bit of historical kitsch, but a genuine ruin, an early colonial weatherboard with characteristic low ceilings and hand-hewn timbers, its roof collapsed, its boards dangling, patently unsafe to enter. Oh joy! Only the bluestone chimney had been restored. Rotting old hawthorn bushes still blossomed wildly in the yard. A sign on the cyclone wire surrounding the site said that the house had been built by John "Red" Kelly, Ned's Dad, and that the family had occupied it until 1864. I stood at the back of the house, and pictured little Neddy playing there. The country to the south and east—the direction of the creek—was still free of housing development, and I tried to imagine it through Neddy's eyes. He would have known the Merri well, given the affinity between boys and creeks, and he probably fished and yabbied there.

Back at the side of the Beveridge Road, after our teabreak under the wet bush, we found ourselves in a huge paddock, with just a smudge of gorse marking the line of the creek. Soon the ground started to rise, and the rocks reappeared, and with them the hawthorn, still in exuberant bloom. This made presently for a very pretty landscape, in a moody, moorish sort of way: rocky mounds laced with lichen and bowers of creamy-jade hawthorn marked the watercourse as it wound across wide pastures. Sheep completed this celtic tableau, though ebony cattle also appeared, and I finally found myself face to face with a bull—though a youngster, fortunately. He stared big-eyed from his blossomy bower among the boulders, and followed me with his look of fixed astonishment, but did not budge.

Like an emanation of this celtic scene, a homestead now appeared on a ridge up ahead, secluded among pines, but rivettingly picturesque. On the map it was named Camoola, but Wuthering Heights would have been more apt. The creek led us right through its cluster of antique buildings, which included an early bluestone farmhouse, windmill, and huge, two-storey, bluestone barn, small windows set in its high walls. A vehicle stood in the drive, but no Heathcliff appeared, so we trudged on, through gates and yards, past more ebony cows, and out onto another, even more expansive plain. The only landmark on the entire horizon here was a rather odd kind of pointy hut, set like a sentry box in the midst of emptiness. As it was still raining, we made for this apparent shelter, as a likely lunch spot, but on closer inspection we found it to be a rather greasy machine shed, ringed, in good fairytale style, by a moat of mud and a circlet of ferocious thistles.

Maya, ever game, improvised a drawbridge with a couple of planks, but when she stepped on them, they sank. Stranded at the entrance to the grimy tower, with no prince-to-the-rescue in sight, she had no alternative but to splash back glumly through the mud, adding sludge to the cold slosh that already filled her boots.

After more trudging, we spied (yes, we were definitely by now in fairy-tale mode) another cluster of intriguing gables in the distance. This also turned out to be a lost domain, tucked among trees and hedges, with rose-colored lofts and roofs. On this occasion however, the creek did not lead to its front door, so we contented ourselves with gazing at it from a grove of gums in which we spread our lunch. As it turned out, however, this was no ordinary lost domain: I was stunned to discover a few weeks after our return that "Walnarring" was reputed to be the actual birthplace of Ned Kelly, the site of the original Quinn homestead. The Quinns were Ned's mother's family, and the whole Kelly drama had originated here, on the very banks of the Merri.

Ned's father, John (born Sean Ceallaigh near Tipperary in Ireland) had been a convict (transported for the theft of two pigs) in Van Diemen's Land, but in 1848 he was freed, and traveled to Port Phillip. The Irish community that had established itself on the windy plains at the foot of the Great Divide, less than twenty years after Hume and Hovell had stood on Bald Hill and praised the very same country, drew John inland, through Epping and Donnybrook and eventually up to Wallan East. In 1850, Kelly senior "was engaged in splitting and fencing, near the Merri Creek, and chancing to be in a hotel . . . in the vicinity of James Quinn's residence . . . he for the first time encountered the latter individual. . . . The meeting was the commencement of an intimacy which finally gained Kelly admission to the farmer's home."[26] Later that year, John ran away with James's second eldest daughter, Ellen, and the two were married in Melbourne. On the marriage certificate, both gave as their address the Merri Creek. The young couple returned to the maternal household, and built a hut on the banks of the creek, where two baby girls were born. In 1854 the family moved to their own home, a couple of miles to the west in Beveridge. Little Edward was born a year later, either in a house in Beveridge or more probably at the Quinn homestead. Ned grew up in the Beveridge area, on various family farms, with no doubt much to-ing and fro-ing across the Merri Creek to visit and stay in his grandparents' lively household, until trouble between the large Quinn clan and the local police induced both the Kellys and the Quinns to move farther north. That was in 1864. Late the following year, poor John "Red" Kelly, a battler if ever there was one, died at the age of forty-six, and the eleven-year-old Ned, now the male head of the Kelly family, signed the death certificate.

From this point the story of course rises gradually to the level of legend, though I found to my surprise that I actually knew hardly any of its details until I started reading up on it. But in light of its now revealed link with my own country, recovering the full story had become a matter of urgency for me. It was particularly exciting to me that the legendary figure of these parts should turn out to be *Ned Kelly*, for although he is a *white* hero, Kelly has also made his way into the Dreaming stories of some of the Aboriginal peoples of Northern Australia.[27] As one who put up a spectacular resistance to white man's law, and defended those whom that law oppressed, Kelly has been embraced, up in the region of the Victoria River, for instance, as an Ancestor, a mythic exemplar of a larger Law of Life which both black and white can avow. And now, as part of the story of our creek, this wonderful hybrid Ancestor, who holds out the possibility of weaving black and white alike into the fabric of the land, was ours!

Really, what *didn't* this obscure little tributary offer the pilgrim?! Temples, divine colossi, medieval gold-spired churches, festivals dedicated to sacred birds, flora parks and sanctuaries and holy waters, and in addition a string of powerful originary sites! What was going on? It was not as if we had chosen this creek for our pilgrimage because we knew it to be particularly significant. We had chosen it simply because it was *there*. It happened to be part of our local environment. It was not until years after I personally had first bonded with the creek that I started to turn up its unsuspected links with my own family history. My great-grandfather had settled on the flood-plain in Brunswick in the 1860s, and my grandfather and father had been born in the creek's environs, close to where I currently live. The family had moved to the south bank of the Yarra in the 1920s, and not returned to Merri country until the 1960s.[28] I had not known any of this history when I settled down to raise my own son in Brunswick. But the poetic significance of the creek had only continued to grow since I first became entwined with it. What kind of magic was this? Would *anywhere* prove equally rich in significance once one had made it the focus of this kind of attentiveness, once one had become wedded to it, as "country"? And pilgrimage? Is pilgrimage a kind of philosopher's stone that can open up the mythic inexhaustibility of reality to the pilgrim heart, however seemingly banal the route and routine the destination?

After our lunch in the rain at the back of Walnarring, we returned to the banks of the creek. Our little waywender had from here been taken in hand and straightened out, its lazy bends removed and untidy banks smoothed. It parted the paddocks now in a well-behaved, cleancut fashion, though admittedly under cover of thick gorse, until it reached Wallan East. Little remained here of the picturesque place that Hume and Hovell had named Tempe Valley.[29] "In this place the Willow Trees has a very beautiful appearance," Hovell jotted down erratically in his diary, "it resemble at a distance a Lemon or Orange Tree, The Forest below us extend, and I have no doubt but it will open into a very fine Country—the Creak run to the southward— The Native Flax Grow in abundance, it appear where the ground is good, that it is a common weed, and if cultivated it would be equel to the best that is grown at home, we found that the Bronze Wing Pigeon, the King Parrot & the Native Dog are common."[30]

Our own approach to Wallan East was uneventful, our day's travel, minus meanders, being quickly accomplished. To what end? We arrived at the tiny cluster with most of the afternoon still ahead of us. But what in the whole world could compare with moseying through the countryside at a creek's pace? What could substitute for the lure of the unexpected, the bracing discipline of pilgrimage? Certainly not the heartsinking banality of town life, sampled in a pizza parlor in the main town of Wallan, on the far side of the Hume highway. This attempt to find solace in coffee and cake dampened our spirits more thoroughly than a whole month of mornings trudging through drizzling paddocks could have done. Listlessly, we wandered back to Wallan East and flopped in the pub, perking up a little when some of the locals volunteered recollections of the creek in flood. Late in the afternoon, Greg and Kari arrived with our gear and food, and we were finally able to return, gratefully, to our story, making our way up to Bill's paddock.

Bill lived at the far end of the little strip of houses that was Wallan East. Wallan East was marooned on an island between the fierce torrent of the highway and the train line: its reason for existence was the railway station. Bill had grown up here and remembered with immense affection his childhood adventures on the creek—which now lay on the far side of the railway tracks. His grandfather had built the original house and the family had occupied the property—adding dwellings from time to time—for a hundred and twenty years, since first selection. Bill had agreed to let us camp the night in his railside paddock.

We found a spot in dripping grass beside a dam full of very happy frogs. The campsite was a scene of extraordinary activity as we unpacked. Goods vans and passenger trains passed incessantly, blasting their whistles, and a level crossing that led to a broken bridge flashed its lights and rang its bells. To the north, just beyond a screen of scrub, the Hume swept past. With an airfield also operating on the other side of the highway, we were hemmed in by the roar of heavy vehicles. A rather surreal scenario for pilgrims! The clamor of the frogs however made for a nice counterpoint to the trucks, trains, and railway bells. Once night fell, the camp assumed a cinematic aspect, with a blazing gypsy fire in the foreground and the flashing confusion of lighted carriages and black goods vans against the sky behind. Only a bluesy soundtrack was lacking. The rain eased, we dried our wet socks against the flames, and a warm conviviality sprang up in the midst of chaos. When we retired I slept with my ears tuned exclusively to the frog band on the sound spectrum.

The last morning of our pilgrimage dawned gold and remained so, only gaining in thoroughly biblical radiance as the day wore on. I was on the look-out now for an Indian gentleman I had encountered on a previous visit with Cin. Looking for a campsite, we had driven up to the level crossing and discovered the collapsed bridge. (A sign announced that it had not been in use since 7 September 1989.) Taking a liking to the spot, we settled down for a picnic on the creekbank. Just as we were biting into our feta cheese and corn thins, an Indian personage of breathtaking beauty appeared on the opposite bank, flanked by his two young sons. I rubbed my eyes. What was this? What was Krishna doing here out the back of nowhere, by a broken bridge? But he was perturbed, in a very mortal sort of way. What were we doing on his land, he wanted to know, polite but testy. We explained our mission. Could we cross his property? Too much gorse, he said. Later, after I had sent out a letter to landowners there in the upper reaches, he telephoned. Definitely no, he said. Too many snakes! But still, he added, God bless! As fate would have it, the full gypsy horror of our camp was now pitched just meters from his boundary, and I imagined him observing us from the upstairs window of the suburban castle that stood in the midst of his little kingdom of gorse. He did appear, of course; as we set off down the railway tracks, by-passing his property as he had requested, we could see him chasing a goat in front of his house, his face turned towards us.

Two other owners had refused us permission to cross their land immediately north of Wallan, so we followed a vehicle track along the railway easement instead, which fortunately ran in tandem with the creek here for as long as it mattered. We paused to rest in a wildflower garden on the railway verge. Yellow bulbine lilies, milkmaids, chocolate lilies, rice flowers . . . a feast of tiny beauties unfurled out of the raw clay. Now that we were in foothills, the river reds had finally made way for other gums—swamps and messmates, perhaps, though our botanists were not entirely sure. Before the track disappeared under reeds, Cinnamon alighted on a gold ring in the mud. I was ravished by this extraordinary token, but the gift and its message were for her, not me, so I held my peace.

When the vehicle track gave out, we were forced to walk for a little distance on the railway line. We were heading northwards, but the line was also carrying northbound traffic, rather than southbound, as we had for some reason assumed. It was only because there happened to be another level crossing up ahead, which started ringing and flashing, that we realized that a train was bearing down on us silently—and very rapidly—from behind. We just had time to leap from the tracks when the monster was upon us, with an avalanche of noise. Maya squatted only a couple of meters from the wheels, her arms over her head, her hat blown off! Amid all my worries about bulls, rogue cows, territorial dogs, and the rest, being flattened by a train was one fate I had not anticipated!

After the level crossing we returned to our riparian haunt, and found ourselves in a new kind of bush idyll—lightly wooded hills with sunny lawns and meadows browsed by sheep. The creek was here the merest rill in the bed of a wide, grassy channel, shaded by swamp gums and messmates. The road, railway line, and watercourse crisscrossed fairly frequently here, and the creek was lined, for stretches, with big forest, too thick to enter. Small farms proliferated, and although this more settled landscape lacked the moody appeal of the flatlands, I took comfort from the relative density of birdlife that rural subdivision seemed to entrain. We were joined at one point, too, by three tiny yellow dogs, who gamboled and frisked with us through a long dappled paddock, adding that dimension of animal companionship which was the one thing I had really missed on our journey. This, by the way, was our sole canine encounter—three little lap-loving beasties in place of the fierce farm avengers I had dreaded!

Tributaries were now busily joining the creek from different directions, as we were well into the region of the headwaters, but we were resolved to follow what appeared, at each juncture, to be the major channel. This major channel now ceased heading north and struck out to the east, passing several lily-choked billabongs and tunneling under the railway line. (Even Maya was not brave enough to broach the hip-high water in this gloomy pipe.) On the other side of the line the landscape opened into a wide valley. This was presided over by a large suburban house set magisterially just beneath the wooded ridgetop and adjoined by a workshop enclosure. We spread our lunch on the banks of a deep clay gully in the direct line of view of the house, but as in all previous cases, despite signs of occupation, no one stepped out either to greet or to challenge us. Even when, following the gully a little higher, we came to a capacious dam, and Maya and Cinnamon stripped off and, amid ear-splitting squeals, plunged into the chilly water, no one appeared.

By this stage the watercourse had almost disappeared, and a couple of step-wise dams led up to a higher paddock, where it petered out altogether. A sturdy gum and a patch of clover with a snake in it seemed alone to mark the "source." A scattering of dumped cars on an adjacent spur set a final seal of disappointment on the scene. From the very start of our journey I had had a certain ceremonial intention with respect to the source, but to carry it out seemed unimaginable on this exposed slope. Although I accepted that "this was it," and that in this surreal juxtaposition of the sacred and the crass, the ambiguity of the creek's story was contained, I felt a kind of unthinking agitation to get to the treeline, and after a pause we hurried to the top of the ridge. At the sight of what lay on the other side, my heart turned cartwheels! There, in thoroughly sylvan seclusion, was a glittering lake! A quick perusal of the map revealed that another tributary, which we had missed down below the scowling house, led up to this, so the lake was ours! The grand nineteenth-century explorer Sir Richard Burton could not have been more overjoyed when he discovered Tanganyika, the great waters that fed the Nile, than we were to discover little "Pilgrims Lake." We scrambled down to its southernmost shore, and now we *all* stripped, and, in a gilded moment, dived into the Source. For several minutes we swam and circled, our limbs disappearing in the tarnished amber depths, then we returned to the bank and sat, glistening with the Merri waters, like three newborns.

Thus baptised, and flanked by my two dear pilgrim witnesses, I ceremonially asked the creek, its guardian spirits, and the ancestors who still dwell within its rocks and clefts if I could have the honor of bearing its name, to announce our interlocked identities, and to seal my custodial pledge. After I said the words, Cinnamon noticed, out of the corner of her eye, the form of a diver bird, but we could not be sure it was a kingfisher. The sun clouded over, but I sat there, naked and glistening after my christening, my heart pealing with gratitude. One could never have hoped, in one's most optimistic moments, that the Source would turn out to be so generous, so luminous, so magical, hidden as it was (behind a facade of profanity) on the "other side" of reality. How could the story be so true? If the humble Merri could offer this to its pilgrims, what could the wider world offer its people, once they approached it as devotees? The vision-filled lakes of Old Tibet, perhaps? The oracular landscapes of the classical world? Who could know.

And who else knew this secret of the source, the significance of this little sister to Lake Tanganyika, nestled in the foothills of the Great Divide? The people in the house over the ridge? Not likely, judging from appearances. The staff of the Creek Committee? If so, why had they not mentioned it? Those who had drawn up the ordinance map would of course have been aware that the Merri was fed by a sizable body of water, but what would this have mattered to them? From a cartographic point of view, it might just as well have risen among the dumped cars. The cartographers had not grabbed the creek by its lapels, and, staring into its eyes, asked, WHO ARE YOU? They had not trudged for seven days on rotting feet to find an answer to the question. The Merri, the Darebin, White Elephant Gully, Bruces Creek, the Dry, all these would have been the same to them, parts of an undifferentiated Externality, laid out, waiting to be measured, fitted, transcribed, devoid of inner meanings. Suspecting no secrets, failing to address, speaking only to each other over the heads of the landforms they were mapping, the mapmakers would of course have received no revelation. Only those who ask,

WHO ARE YOU?, and faithfully trudge the trail to find out, do so. Only they get to see the "other side" of cartography.

So does it really matter, in the end, if wildernesses and special sites are profaned by the irreverent eyes of the casual, the curious, the touristic? Are not quests for the numinous and unknown always, in essence, quests for revelation, and is not revelation necessarily vouchsafed only to those who come to the world as seekers and supplicants, speakers of a subterranean poetics? A site that remains impenetrably veiled in banality to the hundreds of passersby to which it might be daily exposed may nevertheless choose to unveil itself—in a uniquely revelatory fashion, via dreamlike conjunctions and sequences of circumstances—to the gaze of the initiate. The sacred is surely always in this sense hidden from the eyes of the profane, and who but the initiate can say what is sacred and what isn't? By the same token, even the most exotic sights and sounds encountered by colonial explorers might have failed to count as true discoveries, true inroads into the unknown, if they were perceived simply as part of the same great empirical Externality which had already been so fully charted. Our own expedition, in contrast to these colonial travels, was a journey, not *overland or around the world*, but *into* the world, *into* the land, a walking *through* the appearances into a terrain of speaking that lies beneath those appearances, indeed that utters them. Isn't all in-land journeying then a journey to a primal source? And couldn't we rest assured that while other seekers might make their own way in-land, the secret of the source in this instance, in the shape of this little sister of Lake Tanganyika, as it had been given to us, was forever ours.

The lake itself naturally had its tributaries, and one of these rose in the glade behind our swimming place. At first it consisted of just a pool here and there in a wide, marshy watercourse, but as we climbed into the thickly wooded gully, a rivulet took shape, varying from weedy runnel to springy flat to deep tunnel of erosion in the clay. Here the sunlight was strobed by straight trunks, making zebra patterns on the slopes. The ground was whiskered with moss and maidenhair, and set with tiny venus fly traps. At one point the valley filled with mysterious wooden pallets nailed vertically to trees. After Cinnamon found a couple of green paint balls in the mud, we realized that this area must be used for military training or war games. Suddenly the slanted shadows seemed astir with ghosts and echoes, phantom heads popping out from behind boards, incongruous shouts breaking the intense stillness. We took this in our stride, as the creek did, and passed on. It was no more bizarre than any other episode in the creek's story. At this point however a lone horse loomed up from the depths of the forest. Actually, there were two horses, but one of them was so old and wasted, standing absolutely motionless and matt among the shadows, it could have been a dead horse, propped up. But the other was all too alive and immediately started to shove and harass and push at us. We had already been through this horse business once before, at Walkers Farm, and my heart began to pump, but fortunately a fence appeared out of nowhere, and, contortionists that we had now become, we were through in a flash.

It was time now to fill our flasks. We lay, cheek to the leechy mud, and reached down into a cavity in which water was audibly running. We waited for the trickle to fill our cups, then drew them up. Reaching out to our land in this last tender sacrament, we drank. The water had no taste, but was iced, and clear as Perrier. It was hard to adjust to this fact. The unpotability of the Merri had always been part of our conception of it. This intimate act of drinking had been ruled out—undreamed of—from the very start. How this taboo must permeate our thought! What is it to walk in a world in which the waters are poison and food nonexistent? How can one belong, in any but a sentimental way, to such a world? But now we were breaking through the bindings of this taboo. We reached our flasks down and collected a little of the miraculous draught to carry home.

Soon the orchids began to appear. Cinnamon and Maya found them, of course, and I stooped, speechless, to admire these holy grails of the wild-flower realm. Several different kinds grew up the sides of the gully. There were creamy bridal ones, and others that were port red and green haired, squatting openlegged, like little chthonic goddesses, close to the ground. Further up we were greeted by sky-blue, wide-eyed faces on high stems. What could one say? Could Eden itself, where the primal rivers rose, boast anything more holy than these tiny illuminations from the manuscripts of creation? I had never imagined, never dreamed of receiving, such an access of graces, and I trailed behind my two companions, brainstruck, my head ringing like a Tibetan singing bowl.

The sun was setting. It was time to rendezvous, up at the mountain crossroads, with Greg. We had found the Source. We had swum in it, walked in it, drunk of it. Our hair was still wet with it. We had entered it, and it had stepped forward and received us, kissing us each on both cheeks. For myself, I knew that I belonged to it. There was no turning back. The Tao rises, in infinite beauty, shrouded from view but revealed, in the midst of desecration, to the pilgrim. There are no words for this. There are no maps for this. Everyone invents their own journey to the Source, to find their own revelation and rebirth. The Source, as all the guidebooks agree, is every-where. To find it one has only to ask the right question. But this is a question that has never yet been asked, because it is uniquely one's own. The Tao flows, patiently wending its way around all-that-is-named, down to the great sea of namelessness to which every last thing returns.[31]

Chapter 8

Barramunga: Return to the Doorstep of Night

In a tiny hamlet high on a ridge in the Otway Ranges in southwestern Victoria stands an old house, vacant now, with its memories gently capsizing around it. The name of the hamlet is Barramunga. Although at present it is comprised of only five or six houses, including the empty house on the hill, it was not always so tiny. In its heyday, back in the earlier part of the twentieth century, fifty families were settled in its environs and the little town boasted a post office, a pub, a store and a school, two churches, a butcher, a black-smith, a violin-maker and several furnituremakers! Seventy-five children attended the primary school. Many small timber mills operated in the surrounding hills.[1]

Hardly any trace of all this activity remains today. In the words of Barramunga's last custodian, Norm Gardner, "there's very little sign of civilization now. It is almost forgotten. In most places it is hard to find any sign of that pioneering era. In a few places one can see a few sticks of rotting timber, a rusting boiler and a few crumbling old bricks, overgrown by ferns and blackberry bushes. . . . It's hard to find where the tramlines and tunnels went through the hills. The railway lines have gone and there's no evidence of any railway stations ever being there."[2]

Norm's grandfather had taken out one of the first selections at Barramunga, in 1883. With his son, Norm's father, he had built the house on the hill. Norm was born in that house, when the twentieth century too was still in its infancy; his family witnessed the clearing of the vast virgin rainforests that had rendered the Otways inaccessible, even to the indigenous people, for aeons. The smouldering stumps of mighty myrtle beeches and eucalypts dotted the cow paddocks that surrounded the town while Norm was growing up.

In time Norm had married and, with his wife, May, raised a family of his own in the house that his grandfather had built. The life was hard but they were happy days. After World War II, the forestry commission closed down all the small, privately operated timber mills, and the lively little town started to decline. Norm and May stayed, and when their children were grown, they built another dwelling on the property, and handed over the original house to one of their sons and his family. By the time I arrived on the scene, in the mid-1980s, that son had left and the house had been vacant for a decade or so. Only the front three rooms were habitable, the back of the house being in a state of collapse and ruin. With my friend, Jenny Kemp, I was at that time looking for a rustic retreat in the Otways. Jenny already knew the Gardner family well, and it wasn't long before we were laying fires in the old fireplace and waking up the cold, long-silent house. For many years that hearth was a focal point of our lives, though throughout those years our interludes there were brief. Then, in 1998, I started spending extended periods in the house alone. It is from this latter phase that the following journal entries are selected.

6 Oct 1998

I arrived yesterday evening, just before dark. I have never before spent a night alone in this dire old house. It was a wild night, with drenching rain spells and gusts of wind that lifted the corners of the roof. I retired at 9 o'clock with my dog and cat tucked up in bed with me. Although I was warm enough, I couldn't sleep. Lurid fears stalked my mind, but on the other hand it was patently silly to think that anyone could be prowling around on such a ghastly night. But oh, it was a long night nonetheless. Not that I remained scared; I just kept waking and lying there in the black abyss of this semi-derelict house, with all the roaring and howling and heaving of old timbers going on around me.

Still, today's not too bad. There is a special charm in vistas of grazed green slopes and eucalypt forests glimpsed through ruined doorways and crooked windows. And sitting here in the kitchen I can watch sheep and lambs drifting over the hillsides. I love it when only the sheep—and not the cattle—are here. Oh proverbially gentle creatures. Who ever heard of an angry sheep, a vicious sheep, a sheep on the war path? A lamb, grazing by itself, walked right up to my hand yesterday. But perhaps it was blind—there did seem to be something wrong with its eyes. All the animals here are infirm in some way. Only if one doesn't look too closely is the aspect from the window truly soothing. Still, there is undeniably something pleasing in the overall dilapidation. Everything made by human hands—the remains of sheds, tanks and troughs, car bodies and farm equipment, the house itself—is returning to earth. The ghosts have long since departed and a bright host of birds has taken their place.

7 Oct 1998

How does time pass for a sheep, I wonder? The long, uneventful day of browsing and drowsing stretches imperceptibly into the even longer endurance test of night. For some there is the occasional disruption of mating, and then, for the females, the exertions and emotions of birthing and tending a lamb. Predators cause moments of panic. Unlucky members of the flock are swallowed up in appalling disasters, such as becoming bogged in mudholes or tangled in wire. Such disasters can involve prolonged, uncomprehending, fathomless suffering, when eyes are pecked out by crows, or foxes eviscerate the stricken one before it is dead. For the whole flock there is the stress, not very frequent here, of being handled by humans. But mostly it's just a matter of timeless browsing and drowsing.

I'm starting to feel the rhythm of this life. I'm starting to slip into it. After a cuppa with Norm and May, and the delivery of a load of firewood by a local man named Ian, I walked with my dog, Sashi, down to the lower paddock. The rain had lifted and the woods were sunlit. The air was alive with little "business birds"—robins and wrens and such—and a couple of black wallabies stood at the forest's edge. Although the scars and maulings of recent logging were evident everywhere, the nether valley still opened to view at the foot of the steep wooded slope like a secret country, a lost domain of bright buttercup meadows and fields of watercress leading down, finally, to a creek that can be heard but not seen in the ferny depths of the gully. Even the sheep are drawn to the seclusion here; at birthing time they often brave the treacherous mud track through the trees to reach it.

There is a family of young bunnies under the house. Poor things, they won't last long, what with the caleci virus, the foxes, hawks, and crows. There is one feeding next to the car wreck by the front gate now, as the sun sets.

I look in the mirror over the kitchen sink. Next year I'll be fifty. Sleeping Beauty awakes. This is the age at which the dies that were cast and the scripts that were stamped on one's forehead in one's early years finally run their course and come to an end. The curse that was laid on one in infancy, the finger-pricking oedipal inevitabilities, are finally spent. One has been slumbering since the onset of one's adolescence, sleepwalking through the predetermined dramas foreshadowed by the Family Romance, but now the hundred years are up. One awakes. One looks back on a dream. One looks around at the armies of those still in the dream, still sleepwalking, under the primal spell. But for oneself this is over. The rest of one's life, be it long or short, is one's own. One has lost one's Beauty, but it was Beauty which bound one to the realm of dreams, illusions, oedipal robotics—to the realm of sleep. One's fifty-year-old face and body belong to oneself; they are no longer a public screen for the projection of archetypal desires. One is at last free to be for-oneself. But it is not just the loss of youthful looks that ushers in the slumber's end. There seems to be a biological clock that controls the duration of the curse. As one approaches fifty, the curse expires. It seems to be as simple as that.

Two boys have just walked up the road, stopping to throw stones at the gate. Big boys. No doubt from the schoolcamp up at the corner. Damn! I thought there were no school groups there at the moment. How well the epithets that don't fit sheep fit boys of that age!

8 Oct 1998

Already it's hard to keep track of the days. I'm sinking, comfortably, gratefully, into sheep time. Mists this morning. Lifting off the grass in sheets when the pale sun shone through them. But now the sun has well and truly departed. The sky is white and powder filled with pinpoint rain—forest rain—of a type we never see in town.

The days are so benign, the nights so scary. I so want not to be hostage to my fears....

A whole flock of crimson rosellas is feeding on the sheep-mown lawn outside my window. A few of Norm's chooks who live among the discarded tanks and tumbledown sheds at the back of the house are announcing eggs. Feeding, laying, all the unavoidable business, proceeds despite inclemency....

A whole group from the school camp just walked past, down on the road, all dressed in oilskins. Sashi stood at our little garden gate (as opposed to the big gate down at the roadside) and barked aggressively. Good girl!

I'm not feeling lonely here at all. So long as I can write, I quite enjoy being alone. It is abandonment—the experience of being unacknowledged, unmissed—which, I think, causes the sense of loneliness. But here, where I have put myself out of range of calls, I feel very content, at least so far. There is not even any post. If one can't be contacted, one can't be overlooked.

It seems that this is the tempo for which I've been yearning. At home even the smallest distractions—appointments, messages received and sent, things-to-be-done—disrupt my day. Only now am I experiencing the smooth flow of time that enables me to feel in possession of my life. Even so, there is not excessive time for work, for writing. With all the subsistence chores—the carrying and heating of water and the lighting and keeping of fires, for instance—in addition to the normal domestics, together with tending to animals, daily visits to Norm and May, long walks, treks up to the telephone booth at the main road to make truly vital calls—with all this the daylight hours are far from empty. But still there is this contemplative mood, which pacifies my mind.

A little tribe of wood ducks joined the bower-birds on the cropped "lawn" this morning, where crowds of juvenile crimson rosellas were busily feeding all day yesterday. What do they eat? If there are any grass seeds there they are barely visible. . . .

Logging trucks come up and trundle down the Falls Road all day. I can hear—always—the familiar whine of the chain saw in the distance. Sometimes it is pines that are cut, other times native forest. Blue gums are replanted. Better than pines, but just plantations nonetheless, force fed with fertilizer every three months. Even Norm, who has been cutting timber all his life, does not dispute the short-sightedness of this kind of forestry.

This is surely part of the reason for the sadness that, despite all the changes of mood throughout the day, always seems to linger in the evening smoke here at Barramunga. But if one is to come here at all, indeed if one is simply to live in the present world, one must adjust to this sadness, like people living in a war zone. There is no place in which one can find refuge from it. Everywhere is either ecologically uncertain or in decline. Lands are quietly dying. And the biggest threats are often in the remotest regions. Who could contain this sadness now, or hold it? It is our sky, the air we breathe, the very matrix of our lives. It stares out at us from behind the implacable smiles of our public and private faces, from the eyes that meet ours so intimately in the morning mirror. We are leaking sadness now, like doomed vessels. But here one is swimming in it, the beauty of the landscape floats on its darkness, and the angry ranting of chainsaws in the distance only confirms it.

Oh dear, a blowfly just flew into the cottonwool web in the corner of the window, a grisly torture chamber full of sucked-out corpses. It squealed piteously for a minute or two and is now silent. I notice the legions of other blowfly husks along the window sill. The thick webs around the window frames serve to keep the room quiet, the spiders plump and the blowfies bound for hell.

The rain seemed to have set in after lunch, but I decided to go for a walk anyway, with raincoat, gum boots, and the rest of the works. No sooner had I stepped out, however, than it stopped, just like that, before I could even get my hood up. This kind of accommodation is pretty reliable here. I can imagine it happening on a routine basis and on a larger scale, so that such rapport with the elements became the taken-for-granted basis of our praxis. But this could only be the case if our numbers were vastly fewer. How could the rain accommodate itself to my intentions if there were five thousand other folk, each with their own agenda, in the same rain dome? Here there are only Norm and May and me, and the rain can easily keep pace with us.

It's all to do with attentiveness, with the way everything awakens under the gentle beam of one's sympathetic attention. Being alone here provides the opportunity, effortlessly, for such attentiveness. When one emanates this gentle beam, when everything on which one's look falls is bathed in this kindly light and warmth, then the world walks at one's side, and poetics blossom in one's footsteps.

Raptors with a squeaky-door call oversaw my walk, and crows and wood duck were assembled on the back slopes. We (Sashi and I) found the body of a sheep, only recently dead; its wool looked washed and bright, unlike the wool of living sheep, while its perfect little ears were poignantly pricked.

I felt my first pang of loneliness tonight as I walked up from Norm and May's house in the dark. I had been watching the news on television, and it was this, I think, that touched my vulnerabilities. Everything that appears on that small screen speaks within, and to, a shared frame of reference, a frame of reference to which I am patently here external. Not that I am usually really inside it. I have hardly ever owned a television, and not at all for more than a decade. But just living in the city, or in normal society, serves to bring one to some degree inside that frame. Watching television tonight enabled me to see my situation here from the outside, from the viewpoint of social convention, and to recognize, with fright, just how out on a limb I am. It's not merely that I am alone here. I have stayed alone in several houses, some of them very remote. The transgression is to dare to live alone in *this* house, a house that is only half standing, that is already returning to earth. Yet it is this very overstepping of certain bounds—bounds undefined but to do with dilapidation and somehow related to safety and propriety—that has felt so potentiating over these last few days.

Yes, one has to defer to society. One has to acknowledge its moral claim on one's identity, its ownership of one's self. Yes, it is society that thinks one's thoughts, that dreams one's dreams and desires one's objects of desire. But mustn't one somehow reach through the miasma of conventions and assumptions if one is ever, for the merest moment, to touch the bare face of reality? If there is a door that leads out of this miasma, it is surely the narrow door that stands in the walls of one's fear. One has to step through that door alone. At any rate, that's how it feels here. And I do indeed have a sense that reality, in all its luminescence and poetic eloquence, stands on the other side. . . .

A boobok owl is calling in the high trees behind the house.

11 Oct 1998

Yesterday I arose at 6.30 A.M. into sheer effulgence. The luminosity of the sunrise transformed the landscape into a shimmering veil. I had to broach that glory, so I threw some clothes over my nightshirt and strode out with Sashi into the ethereal fields of gold. With a sense of exultation we both gamboled down the grass road and I thought, ah, I've never been down to the secret valley at this hour or seen it under such a biblical aspect. When we picked our way down the rutted mud track however, my spirits sank a little, as I realized that the valley was still deep in shadow. Nevertheless, we persevered, out of the forest and right down to the creek, but when we turned around and started up that steep incline—a climb of a mile at least—my chest closed tight. I was afflicted by a slight nausea and clamminess, and anxiety replaced my early morning enthusiasm. My thoughts turned to doctors, and, with a new urgency, to my return to the city.

Today I am happy again, though I still feel a little squeezed in the chest, and slightly apprehensive on that account. But the amazing discovery is not diminished: here, away from people and society, I can return to my ground state, which is simply a steady state of cheerful tranquillity. This ground state exists; it has not been depleted, scratched even, by years of overexertion, exhaustion, and neurotic process, and no effort is required to reenter it. All that is required is withdrawal from the jostle of assumptions and expectations that form the matrix of our normal social functioning. Surely return to this inalienable ground state is the goal and aspiration of the contemplative life?

The old apple orchard is a veritable bridal bower of blossom—and consequently a riot of birds. Although the collapsing, lichen-laced trees flower so profusely, they no longer fruit. Perhaps this is due to the parrots stripping off the blooms, but perhaps it is also a case of beauty outliving its function?

I find one of the younger rabbits dead beside the car wreck. Suspicion turns to my cat, Fuji. Twice she has slipped out at night and knocked on the bedroom door hours later. Could she possibly be preying on the little flopsies? These innocents are, of course, at the same time unwitting environmental demons. I am watching one of them now, just outside the kitchen window, so close I can see the passing of expressions across its face and the quivering of its ears. Its little body quakes. In its eyes is the painful incomprehension of one whose sole reason for existence is to provide a meal for others. How can my maternal protectiveness not be aroused?

Some tiny pale yellow-bellies alight on the grass. I've never seen them before. I receive my first visit from a kookaburra!

12 Oct 1998

To my relief and joy the little bunny made another appearance this morning. I didn't let Fuji out last night despite her reproachful growls. It's a very cold day. Quite a few of my bird friends were around earlier, but the rain has now driven everyone away, apart from a few sheep and persistent chooks. Consequently there is none of that humming, happy sociability and busyness of brighter days.

Nonetheless, half a dozen little firetails alight on the front lawn, like dancers from a fairy troupe, with their scarlet masks and the flash of a scarlet petticoat in their tails.

The rain is so heavy this afternoon it didn't stop when I ventured out with Sash for a walk, though it did ease off noticeably, then pelted furiously again just as we returned to the house.

I must say it's very cosy here with the rain whiting out the view from the windows and the world closing in. I feel very happy again, free at last just to exist, to write and think and rub shoulders with the variegated populace around me. These last twenty years I have been pining, fretting, for just the right kind of love, when all the while there was this other door, leading into the tranquillity and companionability of fond solitude, peopled by animals and birds.

Evening mist descends. Magpies carol. Crows caw. The little bunny is still out grazing, close to the car wreck.

13 Oct 1998

A tempestuous night of wind and rain. Yet it was, again, so cosy in the little bedroom—until, this morning, SPLAT . . . right in my face. The roof is leaking over the bed. Oh no! There is a worrying droop in the ceiling already. I imagine water continuing to pool up there and then one night, CREAK CRACK, the ceiling caving in (as it has in other parts of the house) and a hundred and twenty years of accumulated dirt and ratshit and dead things falling on my face. Still, the leakage appears to be small so far, and the rainfall last night was, after all, unusually extreme. . . .

A weird thing is happening with the swallows who are nesting above the kitchen door. Every night at around 9 or 10 o'clock they emerge and flit frantically about inside the enclosed front verandah. Why do they do it? Is it because the light is on? They are obviously agitated. What's it about?

A small tree fern is sprouting under the car wreck. The wreck has been sitting there these last twelve years. It wasn't a wreck when we first moved in. It was just a dead car that had been parked in front of the house to make it appear, from down on the road, as if someone was in residence. But now, when the car is well on its way back into the earth, a fern has found sanctuary from browsers in the niche that the body of the car has made. Inside one of the other wrecks—an ancient Peugot, much more disintegrated—down the hill, a tree fern has completely taken over the front compartment, its fronds entwined with the steering wheel.

Today the weather is utterly forbidding—there is no question of asking it for favors. Complex and serious weather business is clearly under way, leaving no room for lighthearted play.

Despite the sheet rain and ice wind I went down for my daily cuppa with Norm and May and took Sash for our indispensable walk. Norm warned me about walking in the gully on the other side of the road. There used to be a saw mill there, he said. No evidence whatever remains of this now, but under a blanket of bracken and blackberries, apparently, there is a large sawdust heap, providing labyrinthine five star accommodation for armies of rats and snakes. The current owners of the land presumably have no inkling of the true history of their picturesque bush block.

Tonight, absolute stillness. It's really a hermitage here. No phone, radio, television, internet, or other media. No visitors. A hearthfire burning from morning to night. Subsistence activities, like carting and heating water, gathering and stacking firewood, and tending fire. No shower or bath, no flushing toilet. No locks. For company, animals, wild and tame, and legions of birds. For the spirit, hilltop vistas and forest depths, the inexhaustible text of the weather, celestial light.

15 Oct 1998

I notice how important my daily rituals are for achieving a sense of order in the midst of this gentle return to earth. I seem impelled to build a ritual structure in place of the collapsing physical one. I am far more dedicated to routine here than I am at home, where I perform necessary chores in no particular sequence. Here, as soon as I rise, large pans of water are set on the stove, a fire is lit, yesterday's clothes are washed and the soapy water is saved to flush the toilet. Throughout the day dishes are washed as soon as they are used and everything is kept tidied away in its right place. I am positively fastidious about personal hygiene and cleanliness. My bedtime rituals are important too. Preparing the hot water bottle, opening the window to the right height, arranging the curtain, settling Sashi and Fuji comfortably on the bed, lighting the candle, jumping into bed, lying there for a while with the candle alight, then blowing it out. All this feels like a staking out of a holding space, a space of sleeping and dwelling. When there are locks and unbreached walls and fortifications, such ritual securing of space is unnecessary. But I like it anyway, this instinctive negotiation of a place, a safe interior, in undifferentiated, uninhabited, externalized space. I like its unconscious reinvention of the elements of consecration....

Flopsy sits outside the kitchen window again today, sorrowful and withdrawn. She brightens up a little when three juvenile crimson rosellas join her on the lawn to feed. Their company gives Flopsy the confidence to start feeding too. As she chews she looks through the kitchen window at me. She is only about two meters away, on the other side of the mossy glass. As the four youngsters feed together, a black chook investigates, and another chook strolls into view. Through a gap in the hedge, a passing sheep is momentarily framed.

When the little yellow-bellies take off in sunshine, their open wings reveal a yellow spot on their backs that flashes like a gold coin.

A warm and golden morning. As I was bringing in kindling from the orchard, with its pink and white masses of bee-humming blossom, I was again struck to see how beautiful such old, now-barren, lichen-laced ladies could be, more beautiful even than a young, fruitful orchard. What kind of beauty is this?

This is my eleventh day here. I have to go back to the city this afternoon, but I can't wait to return to Barra tomorrow night. To think that all these years have passed without my ever having truly discovered this place. I could have been semi-living here all along, had I not been afraid of it. And now who knows how long remains of our tenure here? Still, if there's one thing that I've learned about the meanderings of the Tao, it is that one should never look back with regret (how do I know that a dreadful crime was not averted in earlier years by my *not* being here on my own then) and one should never contemplate future possibilities with undue attachment (how do I know that our loss of Barramunga will not open up horizons different from any I can yet imagine?).

Listening to the frogs at night it is possible to subside into rapt timelessness and make believe that things are still right, that our world is still turning in time with the other spheres.

16 October 1998

A night and a day in Melbourne. Phone calls, emails, errands, appointments, banking, buying, making arrangements, tracking errors in systems, readjusting arrangements. Administering the infrastructure for life has taken over life itself. How glad I am to step out of it all again, and return to Barra, to Be-ing. My mind expands and my senses feed on the beauty that is worn here, mantilla-like, by every least thing.

17 October 1998

All my assumptions exploded! Outside the kitchen window—*three* baby bunnies! All looking exactly the same as the "one" I've been fretting over. Now my environmental conscience kicks in. After all, I remember reading in Norm's histories of Barramunga that at the height of the rabbit plague a hundred million rabbits were being captured each year in the Geelong-Colac region. A factory at Colac canned rabbits and shipped fifteen tons of meat a week to Melbourne.[3] Even so, these three little flopsies look impossibly sweet all nestled in the grass under the mossy trees.

Today there is loud blowfly music in the kitchen. I can't help wishing the flies a bad fate at the hands of the spiders, but I don't kill them myself. I try to follow Jain principles here, removing insects from the firewood, and such like. I do this even though I know that these principles can only ever have a relative validity. As if one could think otherwise at Barramunga! But it feels impossible intentionally and unnecessarily to snuff out the life of even the tiniest little aspirant. So I will just have to try to like the music. I've heard worse on FM radio!

It's hard to improve on the dog and cat as companion animals. I've tried a number of other species, most notably and recently the pig, but between them the dog and cat provide exactly the services I need to stay here by myself: the dog protects from intruders and the cat keeps rats and mice at bay. How nice it would be though to extend the team, to include a horse for transport, a goat for milk, and ducks and chooks for eggs.

Earlier today I counted, outside my window, fifteen crimson rosellas, in various stages of maturity. And on our walk I encountered a late newborn! A lamb no more than hours old, its little white jumpsuit brand new against the dingier sheep and older lambs. Its joy of life, its prancing delight and expectation of universal jolliness, was as unsullied as its jumpsuit; it has not yet experienced night.

20 October 1998

Norm has just made my day! For some reason I had assumed that although there are always sheep here, there was regular turnover, as old ones were shunted off to market and new ones brought in. But no. Norm has just assured me that this is a *flock*. It was first established on the property twenty-five years ago. So the sheep that I see all around me are those that were here when we first arrived—or at any rate, they are their daughters. They are not just anonymous stock, but individuals, who have been observing us in their placid way these last dozen years. Sisters and aunties and grandmas, all on historic family terms with one another—a maternal clan.

A bitterly cold day today, too stinging even for a walk, though I did keep the daily date with Norm and May, which somehow I can never bring myself to miss. It is part of being here. Norm told me he'd been reading up on philosophy and art last night in his dictionary/encyclopedia and May demanded to be told what mythology was!

I love this misty closing-time of day. I love looking out at the empty road and knowing that now no one will come till morning breaks. How good is the smell of pinewood smoke drifting on the mist at dusk, conjuring folk memories of hearth fires, of gathering in for the night.

21 October 1998

My last full day here. But I'm ready to leave. I've been long enough on my own, for the time being. I'm looking forward to returning for another stint next month.

Fuji catches a mouse in the roof! Hooray! Well, that's a bit heartless, but perhaps it is the one that has been fluffing about in the boarded-up cupboard in the kitchen wall each night, making me nervous.

Oh no! I have just found the remains of the "mouse" and it is some kind of appealing little bush rat, with a face more like a possum than a rodent. Only its head and front legs were left . . . and a string of near-term fetuses!! I feel very, very bad about bringing Fuji here. . . .

It's closing-time again, time for gathering in—not only for folk but for animals too. All the chooks are lined up on their perch in the ramshackle shed, after strutting so jauntily about the paddocks all day. The mother rabbit is out in the back yard taking in the last of the light. Sheep are calling as they look for their nighttime resting places. A few birds are doing last-minute things before retiring. (Others of course are just waking up and blinking their eyes.) Everybody, including me, is busily preparing for the onset of that other world: the night. Each creature understands and obscurely sympathizes with the busyness of others as darkness draws in. I love sharing in that understanding, being part of that general creaturely busyness.

The first thing I do in the morning is build and light the fire, and the last thing I do in the evening is put the firescreen in front of the embers. All day long I tend and feed this living thing at the heart of the house, this companion of my solitude, to whom I return after walks and outings as to the warm and comforting lap of a mother. Isn't the hearth fire the very condition of our humanness? How right it feels to live in its presence, to succumb to its fascination, to gaze, like our ancestors, into the shimmering light of the embers and glimpse there the molten core of creation.

Boo ... book ... boo ... book ... boo ... book ...

Such a chasmic night. No moon, no stars. Just my little lighted ship, becalmed though derelict, in space.

22 October 1998

No one came to the boarded-up cupboard in the kitchen wall last night. I understand those earlier visits now. It was the little bush rat, close to term and therefore busily making her nest. That old disused cupboard must have seemed like the birth-center of her dreams. How sad I feel that I caused those faithful dreams to be destroyed and how I miss now the rustlings that I dreaded only the night before last.

13 November 1998

Back to Barra! Back to reality. In the city one is swept up bodily in a swirling blended soup of eventfulness and social ideality. One finds oneself running, running, talking, talking, but somehow in mid-air, unable to focus one's eyes or compose one's mind. Here I meet reality again, I lean up against the trusty old solidity of things.

Just one little urban incident occurred that brought me back to myself. I was walking from my car to my house when I heard an unfamiliar noise. I looked up. It was a windy day, and there, high overhead in the dingy, turbulent air was a fully inflated white plastic shopping bag, blowing along like a sail with no ship. How strange it looked. A shopping bag, that most trivialized of things, assuming a form and purpose of its own and setting off on a trip.

All my pals are still here. Two flopsies, slightly bigger than before, have appeared outside the kitchen window. The stoical sheep are limping around among mudslides in the rain. On our walk along the back of the ridge Sashi and I surprised a large fox. The tribe of wood ducks is grazing by the nearest dam. Rosellas, bower-birds, maggies, and blue wrens are all at this moment visiting the garden, in spite of the inclemency. And the tree fern colonizing the Peugot carcass down by the sheds is waving its arms out of the windowscreen.

Norm has been showing me more of his photos and videos. He counts off for me all the members of his family who have lived in this house since it was built by his grandfather in 1888. I gaze at a faded image of Norm at age nine, surrounded by sheer desolation—stripped hills dotted with burnt stags, the result of a bonfire that raged for twenty years. I look at the flesh-and-blood Norm across the table and it is hard to compute that I am talking to a pioneer, a man whose family took out the first selection at Barramunga and who himself, as a child, witnessed the fall of that great primeval forest. For half a century the house is surrounded, in the photographs, by completely bald hills, until, as the century progresses, the trees start to reappear. By the time I first started visiting the Otways, in the late 1970s, the forests were back again, tamer, simplified, and more scattered, but back.

Finally, a burst of gold and a crystalline tranquillity, just at sunset. This is the time of call and response for the sheep. Why? Are they trying to find one another before nightfall? I hear this plaintive, bass-voiced bleating, the draughty sound of flames in the fireplace, the derisive cry of a crow, and the odd parrot tinkabell. And nothing else. How good it is, after the systematic inversions of the city, where truth is everywhere and in every way subordinated to the social imperative, to be in among the honesty of sheep and parrots and rasping old crows. I could dwell here happily for eternity. A glad Taoist fool.

14 November 1998

A sublime day. Platinum gold, with a shine in the very air. I am in the little front yard under a struggling tree fern. Two rosellas have alighted on the rusted remnant of a fence, just in front of me; they are eyeing me mildly. I have been sitting here watching the ladybirds in the grass, tiny jeweled flashes down among the roots of things.

The swallows in the verandah are flying in and out, lining their nest with fluff. I put hair from my hairbrush out as an offering.

A history student from my very own university far away in Melbourne was visiting Norm and May this afternoon, seeking first-hand recollections for his thesis on early saw mills. Norm was showing him the albums and the Barramunga videos when I came in. Dear Norm. True custodian. No doctorate or fancy titles for him. Just the realness that all this intellectual culture parasitizes. And when he and May have gone? When only the transient occupants of the weekender opposite and the masseur in the old store and the truck driver in the house beside the store are left? Who will hold the story then? Who will know about long-lost sawdust heaps and tram cuttings in overgrown gullies and iron wheels abandoned at a turn of the creek not visited by anyone for fifty years? Who will remember the children lined up outside the one-room schoolhouse that has now been turned into a youth camp? Who will know that the patch of jonquils on the far hill marks the spot where a house exploded in the Black Friday fires of '39? Who, ever again, will carry in their mind a story map, richly illustrated, like Norm's, showing every detail as fresh as when it was last seen, even if that was decades ago. A few photos and perky reconstructions by observer-outsiders, filed away in theses and libraries, will be all that remain.

To receive these stories from a true custodian however—not as a researcher but as a member of the clan—is immediately to know their significance and to feel the responsibility that is bequeathed with them. One cannot fail to understand that this is how culture and community are transmitted, that the past persists into the present through these detailed memories of place. It is by walking the same hills or streets or desert tracks that our ancestors walked, by reading their traces there, recalling their memories, consciously touching the same rocks or walls that their hands touched, that we experience the presence of the past. By abandoning the places of our ancestors, and hence our contact with the ground of their memories, we abandon our ancestors themselves. When we abandon them, are we not breaking a primal human compact, on which the very possibility of culture rests? For isn't culture transgenerational in essence? Yes, there are the codes and schemas that are transmitted in modern societies by public modes of education. But without that intimate sense of the reality of our ancestors' lives—a sense that is acquired only through living in the richly storied landscapes of ancestral memory—how can we feel any real attachment to the past? The past is for us only an abstraction, an idea, perhaps to be sentimentalized but not to be encountered. Without a sense of its reality, how can we grasp our obligation to hand it on? Consequently the societies of modernity repudiate the past and reinvent themselves to suit their present convenience. Our sense of future generations, of whom it is assumed that they will walk on unknown trails and comport themselves in unimaginable ways, is also abstract: both past and future are remote planets peopled by outlandishly costumed strangers with curious habits.

But can culture be built within that vanishingly small interval between past and future? Within such a compass we can certainly organize ourselves according to principles of utility and efficiency; we can pit ourselves against the past in terms of epistemological and creative performance. But is this culture? Doesn't culture grow from the *cherishing* of world, not merely for the sake of practical requisites, but because world holds some deeper storied significance? Doesn't its preciousness lie partly in the fact that our forebears entrusted themselves to us via this world and its local modality, place? To desert the ancestral places and hence to be deaf to ancestral memory is not only to consign our ancestors to extinction. It is also to undercut the attitude of cherishing which alone renders a set of representations and social practices a culture. Isn't a culture that obliterates its ancestors by abandoning the places in which they walked a contradiction?

But what if, collectively speaking, our ancestors were themselves perpetrators of obliteration, even murderers? Won't the stories then be filled with gaps and silences? In his written history of Barramunga, Norm considers this. Barramunga was, he tells us, named for Barramungah, "an aboriginal who had been shot for stealing a sheep from [Charles] Forrest's 'Warrawie Sheep Station.'" Norm then recalls the last Aboriginal person in the district, a man called Jim Crow. "We knew Jim Crow and respected him," Norm writes. "His people lived around the Colac lakes and they owned all the land until the squatters came and killed them and stole the land. For a day's sport, some Colac squatters rode around shooting them."[4] Norm asks us to remember this.

Does such an ancestral scenario negate the possibility of cherishing? Does it nullify our obligation to reinhabit the places of our dead and thereby to sacralize the ground on which we tread? Surely not. Ancestors are ancestors, for better or worse. The purpose of ancestral stories is to add textures of meaning to reality, not to flatter the vanity of descendents or to bathe them in reflected glory. It is not by being virtuous but simply by passing their memories on to us that ancestors transform the neutral terrain of existence into a place of dwelling. Besides, our own turn for appraisal will come. Won't our descendents look at our photo albums and see not our hopeful smiles but the faces of ecological criminals, folk who followed their own generational lights to the detriment of the planet and the greater part of humanity? Under the appraising force of that future gaze, shall we withhold our tales? No! Whatever the moral tenor of those tales and however we might have cheated our descendents in other respects, our truth belongs to them. Without us they will be deprived of their chance to make a home of this world.

In any case, I know how privileged I feel to have a link, through Norm's living memories, with an earlier era, an era with moral crevasses of its own, yes, but in which, here at Barramunga, people rode home on horseback from weekly dances in the community hall, out into the hills, then signaled their safe arrival to one another by swinging a kerosene lamp in a circle from their doorsteps. Through Norm I feel joined to that world in which, as he puts it, a man might be happy with nothing more than " a horse and a bridle, a dog and a sing song around a log fire."[5] That world is a touchstone for me; to have a living link with it is core to my sense of rightness and proportion - to my very sense of realness.

Something different is always in bloom when I come to Barramunga. At the moment it is a white ti-tree, with flowers clumped in the forks of twigs like little heaps of snow. The peppermint creeper is also in floral mode, trailing purple sprays.

If the smoke rises straight up from the chimney, Norm tells me, it's not going to rain.

18 November 1998

A big walk today, right down to the lower valley, where I scythed this-tles with a stick till I was hot and sweaty. Sashi was chasing sunbeams among the thick buttercups that had grown up in the bulldozer tracks. I felt like chasing sunbeams myself. All was well with the world.

I watched the news this evening down at Norm and May's. There was a meteorite shower, a cyclone in the United States, a wash-up of pilchards somewhere on the coast and the discovery of a gigantic dinosaur fossil-egg. Now that's what I call news!

A burnished evening. I leave again tomorrow.

4 December 1998

Two frenzied weeks in the city. So much going on, yet I felt no impulse to record it. It is only when I am here that I feel the impulse. I am moved to record the things that happen when "nothing is happening," and that, in their relative permanence, least need recording: meteorological moods and lights, sunsets, bird sightings, the adventures of ferns, unremarked deaths.

I arrived last night, just after dark, and when I had unpacked the car I noticed something on the kitchen doormat. I had thought, as I was passing in and out, that it was just a bit of bark or dried leaf, but now I noticed that it was glinting slightly. I stooped down to examine it, thinking it might be a rat's head, but no, it was the body of a tiny nestling, quite naked, no bigger than a cherry plum, but now slightly squashed, as either Sashi or I must have trodden on it. Then to my dismay I saw other little bodies on the mat—three altogether. Tiny homunculi, their eyes sealed but visible as huge black circles under the skin of their skulls. They were very newly dead, and had obviously fallen from the swallows' nest directly overhead. The parents were present and highly agitated, dashing in and out of the verandah. As I was still kneel-ing down examining the surreal little bodies, one of them started to move! Was this a dream? I gazed in fascinated horror as it weakly paddled its miniature arms and legs. Okay. I picked it up, wrapped it in my hankerchief and placed it very carefully in my shirt pocket. I fed Sashi and Fuji, had a quick bite to eat myself, then popped the little fetus, warmed by my body, into a nest of cottonwool in a jar. I took the jar to bed with me, and slept with it under my arm all night. In the morning, yes! The baby was alive. But how to feed it? Swallows are insectivores. The insects are presumably mushed into a paste of some kind before being fed to the young. So, I rea-soned, I would try Sus—for that was the hatchling's name—on dried dog food, soaked and then administered by dropper in a solution. It took a long time to entice this minute being, barely any bigger than the top joint of my thumb, to open its (very wide) beak, but eventually it did, and then hung onto the dropper hungrily. It is now mid-afternoon, and Sus seems fine. She's excreting, and cheeping when she's hungry. I gaze down at this scarcely born creature, struggling so hard just to breathe, to lift her head on a neck that has no more strength than a piece of string, and I feel like a marsupial tending the fetus in its pouch.

All the small birds love the dead prunus tree that has capsized into the adjacent lemon tree. I look straight into it from my living room window, where I sit to write. It's a dense tangle of perch twigs; and blue wrens, yellow rumps, and the occasional flame robin are its main patrons, though honey eaters stop by too. It's like a scene from a medieval tapestry. I have just been watching a pair of blue wrens sitting pressed together, preening and grooming in cosy conjugal fashion.

A full moon had already risen when I arrived last night. It was hidden when I stepped out of the car to open the gate, but as I turned to look it sashayed up, with arms outstretched, from a hedge of dark clouds. And the rabbits! Oh, they scattered in my headlights as I drove to the house—a whole troupe of them, large and small.

The swallows have disappeared today. They have abandoned the beautiful nest they worked so hard to prepare. I can only infer that they themselves tipped the hatchlings out of the nest *because* I arrived. Why? They did not seem to object to my presence throughout the nest building. In any case, how could anything that I might do be worse than this? Perhaps it was my reappearance *after* an absence that upset them.

I can't stop gazing at Sus. I hold her in my cupped hand, which she likes, because it's warm skin contact, such as she would enjoy with other nestlings. I can see the tiny feathers appearing under her skin, like five o'clock shadow on a man's face. Her wings—exactly like arms, just two little dark, bent stick-limbs—are strengthening, and she is using them to move herself around. She struggles to stand up against my tilted palm. Caring for her still feels like a dream. I have never before cared for such a miniature creature. Her arms and the ridge of her spine are dark and thinly plated, like the back of a slater. Withal, she is human-like. Caring for her is like caring for a human baby who could fit inside a walnut. This is why it feels like a dream.

5 December 1998

Sus is alive but doesn't seem as vital as she did yesterday. She's eating and excreting and her five o'clock shadow is even darker. But her little body seems shrunken somehow. Perhaps the Meaty Bites are not going to do the job. If she can only hold on till next week, I can get some food from a specialized supplier.

6 December 1998

Sus died today. My delicate little bud of life. Perhaps it was my fault. I left her in a bag above the fireplace when I went out, but the fire burned down too quickly and the bag was cold when I returned. Sus was still alive, but though I quickly put her under my jumper against my skin, she soon died. I gazed and gazed at the tiny form that had resumed its egg posture in death. Though the form was tiny, I was wholly inside it, as I remember being inside my baby's face when he was born. I could not believe I would not see her move again. How to retrieve myself. . . . ?

7 December 1998

Early today I found a dead sheep under the cypress trees to the north of the house. Rigor mortis had not yet set in. When Sashi and I returned from our walk, the big fox was already there, gnawing away at the head. He fled when he saw us, but then I felt worried about the chooks, who were clucking about cheerily not a stone's throw from the corpse. So I reported all this to May, who said she'd ask Norm to put some bait in the sheep. That would do for the fox. But what about Sashi, I wondered, and the crows, and perhaps other birds who might feed on the sheep? The round of death is neverending, whether one intervenes or not.

This merry-go-round, or rather sorry-go-round, continues. Norm has now set a pair of traps for the fox. Since it was I who informed on the fox I can hardly protest. Besides, mercy for the fox means likely death for the chooks. Why, why, does life rest on such a cruel premise? Death, okay. The decks have to be cleared, and so on. But suffering, why? A little might be useful, yes. But it occurs in such vast, unnecessary quantities. This is the question of questions. The question of suffering, the point of departure for all attempts to make sense of life, philosophical or spiritual. It is the chapter on which I am currently working, "Suffering and the Tree of Life." And every which way I turn, it confronts me.

8 December 1998

This morning when I walked down to the decomposing sheep carcass I saw two crows hopping about, their legs in the irons. So now it was their turn to suffer and die. Of course, there was a certain poetic justice in this, given crows' habit of pecking out the eyes of newborn lambs. But still, I turned away. By intervening on the chooks' behalf I was about to cause the death of how many crows? Would the fox even show? I felt defeated by it all.

Soon after the crows had been dispatched, there was a great cawing. Crows gathered in trees around the spot where the two black bodies lay. They were in a great uproar. The cawing had the same flat note as ever, so it was impossible to decipher any particular emotion, but their agitation was evident. The outcry did not last long, however. The gathering soon dispersed, and now there is neither sight nor sound of crows anywhere.

I had no sooner sat down to steady myself with a cup of tea than a blowfly flew into a web right under my nose. A black spider hurried down and started urgently wrapping, while the fly gave out its high distress signal.

Then the spider tucked the bandaged body under its arm, and hastened back to its den, there to devour the poor creature at its leisure, no doubt.

It is as if the brutality that Lucius portrays in *The Golden Ass*, about which I am currently writing, is manifesting all around me. "Look," the world is insisting, "don't underestimate this brutality. It is inescapable, and you are implicated in it whichever way you turn. Who are you going to side with, the fox or the chooks, the farmer or the fox, the crow or the sheep, the baby rabbit or the land it destroys, the spider or the blowfly? It is impossible, impossible, to side with one or the other. Compassion does not solve the dilemma. So what are you going to do....?"

Although it is a bright-winged day, I feel tired and confused. It's the difficulty of saying yes and no to things, of being tangled in barbed double binds.

9 December 1998

A superb day, but my mood is depressed. A dead rabbit in the front garden this morning, one of the youngsters. A wound in its head—possibly a severe peck. This evening another crow in the traps.

As I was walking down to the valley this evening, the warm amber light was slanting across rippling lines of grass. Tiny songbirds were trilling amid the blossomy white of the ti-tree. One could scarcely imagine a more enchanting scene. But it struck me that all this dear beauty of nature, which affords such inexhaustible consolation and uplift, is after all nothing but a function of the evolutionary history of the eye and brain, selected as they are to find terrestrial homescapes pleasing. The lifescapes of other planets, with their reds and purples and transparent membranes instead of greens and blues and opaque skins and surfaces, might leave me aesthetically unsettled, repelled even, but would no doubt afford inexhaustible delight to the natives.

14 December 1998

A few days in Melbourne. I returned yesterday to a luminous pink evening. I have brought Rosie, my galah, as well as Fuji and Sashi, as there is currently no one at home to look after her. On the road we looked like a one-car circus, with the cat in the front seat and the dog and galah in the back.

It is remarkably cold and wet today, given that it was 41 degrees only two days ago, when we were all gasping for breath. Now it's back to hot water bottles and hearth fires, with rain and mist enveloping the hills.

A distilled moment on our walk today. A silver sun shone through the mist to illuminate, in a black and white sort of way, a nostalgic tableau: a little posse of sheep, dark against the ethereal ebb and flow of the grass, wending its way up a long, long slope at the top of which the roof of the old milking shed gleamed as worn, smooth, and lustrous as the doorstep of heaven.

The winds last night were so strenuous that the path to Norm and May's front door was littered with enormous fallen roses.

15 December 1998

The weather grows icier. The rain rolls across the hills. But I am snug in here.

16 December 1998

The lights come on, and wonderland opens up shop again. I walk over to the new (bulldozed) track in the forest on the far ridge. The big trees have been taken out, but oh! the sylvan glades to which one has thereby been given entry. I sit in bright little fern-lined clearings strewn with white-star and orange flowerets and edged with bush violets. Diminutive forget-me-not butterflies flit and kookaburras emit strange electrical sound effects somewhere over my head. It's hard to remember that I'm alone here, because I feel such plenitude, as though I'm in love. I keep looking over my shoulder, as if to speak to an intimate companion who is always with me. But, ever to my surprise, there is no one there.

17 December 1998

A goldleaf morning. Another page in this illuminated Book of Days. I cannot believe how lucky I am! I cannot believe how happy I am! The magpies are yodeling, the crows rasping. Fuji, Sashi, and Rosie are here beside me. Why did I never notice this simplicity so close at hand!

18 December 1998

But now Fuji has killed a flame robin. I see that I must, *must*, overcome my phobia about rats and mice, for I must not, *must not*, continue to bring cats down here. She has made the kill despite being hung like a Christmas sleigh with bells. I scolded her furiously and she dropped the little bird. I held him in my hand. Still warm, without obvious wounds. Dead from shock. Till minutes ago he was hopping about on this spectacularly beautiful day, no doubt bursting with a glad sense of purpose. Now there is a stunned little mate out there. Perhaps a doomed clutch of nestlings. And all this is totally my fault.

19 December 1998

A warm evening. Restless, I walk the hills in the late dusk. I hear, for the first time ever, sounds of voices, of partying, from the cabins on the adjoining property. This may be my last evening here for some time. I too will soon be heading home for Christmas....

24 November 1999

Back to Barramunga! How I have missed it this past year! My thoughts have been caught in a negative groove over the last few weeks. Perhaps I can reconnect with my joy here. After an overcast day the sun came out auspiciously, just as I was arriving, and the hills were suddenly drenched with pink. The approaches to Barramunga were powdered with white ti-tree blossom. I am sleeping tonight in Norm and May's house. A brutal crime has been committed in the area and I prefer to stay with my dear adoptive kin.

25 November 1999

I awoke early to the glory of a Barramunga morning, after a safe, daughterly sleep tucked up at Norm and May's. Sashi, banished to the cold car for the night, jumped for joy to see me. It was 7.15 A.M. and the hills were already wide awake. Magpies were caroling. I could immediately feel the old simplicity, the rightness of things. I lose it when I return to the city. There I can only remember how Barramunga *looks*. I forget how it *feels* to be here. There is no image for that feel. So it is an effort to extract myself from the city, to return. But as soon as I do, I sense the presence of the Tao again. Why? Because things are still, by and large, following their natural course. In town all processes are thoroughly deflected towards premeditated human ends. The Tao is rerouted, the energic field choppy with cross currents, cross purposes, no longer following its proper streams and swirls.

26 November 1999

I saw him today! The lone crane of Barramunga! I've seen him before, often, over many, many seasons, but I didn't realize it was always the same bird, that he lived here permanently. It was Norm, of course, who told me, yesterday. He said the crane had lived here for years. Always on his own. I remembered when I realized that it was always the same sheep I saw, that the same flock had inhabited this land, grazing, lambing, babysitting for one another, dozing, dying, for twenty-five years. They were not just generic sheep, as I had assumed, bought and sold annually, but particular individuals, repeatedly encountered. Now I discover that the cranes I have seen here over the years are also not just generic passers-by but a single individual, a Barramunga crane, old and solitary.

4 December 1999

Last week Jenny was here for a few days. After taking our longish walk down to the local reservoir, we were trudging back up the steep bush track, deep in conversation, Sashi leashed for fear of snakes. I was walking hunched, my eyes on the ground, sightless, my mind absorbed in talk. Suddenly, my sight switched on. There at my feet, filling my entire field of view, was the head of a tigersnake. I have its super-real image impressed on my memory: yellow eyes fixed on me, head raised, tongue blazing. Snake and I were both momentarily suspended, shocked, magnified in each other's gaze. After a protracted instant—an instant seemingly of transference—I managed to break the spell and leap back. Jenny stood there for another long instant with Sashi on the leash, registering the situation, then she too backed off. Sashi managed not to see the snake at all. Presumably the snake itself was too confused by the numerous legs within easy range to know whose to strike.

Old Man Crane was high in a dead tree when I drove up through the paddocks from Norm and May's this morning. He flapped off into the haunting mists as the car approached.

A new bird! A black and bronze honeyeater with a long, curved beak and a brown spot on its white throat.

An amazing and delightful discovery. I had started imitating the chatter of the birds around the house, unthinkingly making little word-calls to match their vocalizations. Suddenly I realized that these words, and the birdlike way of calling them, had the ring of Aboriginal speech. Then I wondered whether here was a key to Aboriginal pronunciation. I tried it out on a string of Aboriginal words and names I happen to know, and there they were, not in their dragged-out, flattened English pronunciation, but with an authentic singing, consonant-condensed Aboriginal intonation. Language so adapted from birdsong patterns seems to depend on strong differential emphases and the availability of different notes. I once studied Pitjanjatjara briefly, but this new discovery offers a kind of attunement to the language that I lacked completely then. What aspects of the Anglo-Saxon homelands do the long flatnesses of English match, I wonder? Or have these flatnesses resulted from a loss of fit, a gradual dissociation, from the emanations of landscape?

5 December 1999

Sprawled in the warm, scented grass on the hillside, I was thinking, what could heaven offer that is as dear to me as this? What kind of immortal beauty could compare with the beauty here? And I fell to thinking again about the functional adaptation between what we find beautiful and our own physiological processes. Isn't it ultimately the fit between my own lifeflow and larger, environing lifeflows that moves me? Isn't it because the world is a vast and inexhaustible elaboration of my own flow that I am carried out into it, psychically traveling with its curves and swoops, branching into its filigrees, expanding across its plains, outpouring with its showerings? In earthscapes everything is shaped by the forces that inform me; therefore every land- and plant- and animal-form resonates with the deepest sources of my own life. This might not be the case in alien environments—on other planets life might have evolved through an entirely different set of dynamics, into forms that would seem coldly unreceptive, dissonant, to us. More relevantly, it is not the case in modern built environments either, in which structures and artefacts are purely self-referencing, their forms drawn not from the sources of life but from the ad hoc, decontextualized, abstract ideas of their human designers. Perhaps this is why the landscapes of modernity so often present a staccato, grid-locked, block-to-block aspect, in which psyche cannot find the contours of its own deep dynamics. Where this is the case, there is no flow in one's looking, no soaring, swooping, cruising, cascading. No beauty. No delight.

Yes, the beauty of these sheep-mown slopes and wooded hills is, for me, purely and simply heaven. To be here, without the weight of griefs or worries from any other quarter, affords a delight greater and sweeter and dearer than which none can be imagined. But looking, as I am, beneath the appearances, intuiting, as I am, that the appearances produce these plenitudinous feelings because they align me psychically with the flow patterns both of my own being and of the energic configurations into which I fit, I begin to glimpse how "heaven" is possible without any sensory aspect at all. If, when I die or shut down sensorily into meditation, I feel myself ebbing into a larger pattern, my awareness dissolving into a larger field of flow, will I be filled with this sense of beauty even though the "doors of the senses," as Buddhists say, are closed?

And isn't this too why the experience of beauty is erotic, because what is eros but a psychic harmonizing, streaming, with the energies of others? Beauty at the level of appearance cannot help inviting the erotic response, but erotic engagement—the finding of the energic fit—can take place in the absence of sensory stimulus, and will produce the same plenitudinous feelings as beholding beauty does. Isn't this what Psyche is taught, in the Eros and Psyche story that I am currently unraveling in my writing here—that she cannot rely on the beauty of her own appearance to win the fickle god Eros, but must transcend the developmental closure of reflexiveness to open herself to larger flows?

I find a gilded beetle on my shirt. Its hard wings seem crusted with greeny-gold tinsel, so sparkly are they in the sunlight. When I take it outside to let it go, it flies off my hand high up into the air, as high as the treetops, till it disappears.

I am also seeing a great deal of Crane. He has his regular beat around the house. It's not surprising that he's settled here, really, what with the dams and full tanks and the wonderful crane-trees, great white-and-grey skeletons into which cranes can blend tracelessly. What is it like to preside over such a domain yet never to be mirrored back to oneself—to exist in so solitary a state, one of a kind? He is perched on the lower gatepost as I walk out the front door. He watches me, but warily. Good! Let him not come to trust me. Boys with guns are not unknown at Barramunga. What but betrayal ever comes to wild creatures who respond to human overtures?

6 December 1999

Keeping company with Norm and May has sensitized me to the relative invisibility of the very old in the mise en scene of modernity. Where are they, the octogenarians and nonagenarians of contemporary society? How rarely do they appear on streets, in restaurants, aeroplanes, cinemas—public places. How often are they to be encountered even at the family dinner table? Ageism is surely hard-wired into the modern attitude, the modern preference for the ideal over the merely given, and hence for that which is not yet shop-soiled by contact with reality. Aversion to age is merely the flip side of this infatuation with the ever-new which is the definitive orientation of modernity. So it is for us profoundly threatening to catch glimpses of a gaunt and wrinkled face looking back at us from mirrors. To appear old like this is, we fear, to forfeit respect and love. But all this could be turned around. The value of things could be seen to increase with age. Things—and people—assume increasingly precious significance as they are woven into the tapestries of our lives. Those who have been around the longest could be regarded, other things being equal, as more precious than those who have newly arrived, since the old folk have become inextricable from world, wearing its truth in their faces, its destiny in their stoop. To love the world is to love the old.

I remember how, as a child, I loved my own grandmother's oldness; how moving I found the gnarledness of her hands, for instance. Though my mother's relative youth was also precious, my Nana's oldness elicited in me a special brand of affection. She wore age as a mantle of dearness. But dearness, unlike the beauty of youth, is a function of close acquaintance: we can appreciate the beauty of total strangers but need to know a person relatively intimately to consider them dear. Were we to become attuned to this dearness of age however, we could recognize its possibility in unfamiliar older faces. And in the face in the mirror. How comforting it would be to look into the mirror and observe one's face becoming dearer, more cherishable, year by year!

This love of old people is growing in me now, a love of their stoop and weatheredness, of the fact that their pretensions have long since been discarded, along with youthful looks and supple minds. But the loveliness of age seems intimately tied to context, to living in place—the very conditions forsaken by modernity. There is such an aura of affection around Norm as he trudges, gum booted and bent double, across the paddocks he has walked and worked throughout his life, surrounded by the gently decomposing debris of the years. Similarly with May, sitting by her fireside, wearing the insignia of age with grace, because, in its context, such agedness has correctness and prestige. What is Barramunga without these old folk? The place loves them, holds them close, glows around them; in them it is distilled, given human expression. How empty, how deserted, is country without its oldtimers, its faithful keepers and companions. Norm *is* Barramunga. These hills that have bent his back and etched themselves into his every expression and gesture, this sky that is reflected in his clear-sighted eyes, these constitute his grace, his measure, his true face. But all this is lost if we accept the decontextualizing terms of modernity, with its standardized "aged-care" provisions, its custom-made "units" and nursing home solutions producing shrunken cores of might-have-beens, the diminished elderly folk who might have been as place-wrapped and grace-endued as Norm and May.

Afraid of our fate, of this diminution, this abjection, that awaits us in the obtuse institutions of modernity, we fret about our personal attractiveness. We lavish restorative effort, inordinate resources, on our faces, our bodies, our houses, while the world around us is stripped to the point of uninhabitability. We follow the Hollywood example, the face lifts, the orthodontic smiles, the interior decor—and the cities that are bleak, toxic wastelands, to be negotiated only via the time-and-space capsule of the car. I think, by contrast, of the Bardi people in remotest northern Australia, with whom I once lived briefly. Gap-toothed, their bodies following the innate proclivities of bodies, their houses gutted, perfunctory, devoid of ornamentation, they lived in spectacularly beautiful country, chains of pink, mystical islands in a primal sea; the eloquence of this country lived, was at home, in the people's time-sculpted faces. Who is the wealthier of these two parties, who the more beautiful? Who would one rather be?

Besides, when people are not allowed to grow old, or if, when they finally do, they are hidden from view, then places themselves never come fully to life. Places need to show their age, their history, if they are to feel like real places. When the people remain artificially youthful—straight-backed and cosmetically enhanced—then the place itself feels artificial, without life. In communities in which residents do visibly age, and where the deformations of time are unashamedly and cheerfully paraded on the streets, there is a sense of vitality and context, for the warping of the human frame into singular shapes and attitudes contributes to the character of place, while the character of place provides the necessary context, the meaning, for such deformations.

A bit of excitement this morning. Just after I had finished eating my toast, I caught sight of Mr. Fox down by the gate, boldly approaching Norm and May's house, flitting like a sniper from shed to shed over sparkling fields of dew. I pulled on my gumboots, and Sashi and I ran down the hill to give him a fright. He actually climbed the mesh wire of the sheep fence in his panic, then streaked across the road and into a thickly wooded gully.

I have long been harassing Norm about the need for a fire plan. The CFA has made it plain that we'll all be on our own if the red devil passes by, so we need to work out strategies in advance. Barramunga is a high point in the Otways, so fires, being disposed to climb, would head for here from every direction. It seems my nagging has paid off. Yesterday Norm and his son, Errol, created a little dugout down by the quarry. Or rather, Norm, in his inimitable style, located a natural, moss-lined hollow in the side of the hill. It was the interior of a huge, long-vanished stump—one of the giants from the primal forest, no doubt. No sign of this cavern was visible from the outside, but, with the help of his son's shovel, Norm uncovered it and dug a track down to the entrance. Who but Norm would know that it was there?

7 December 1999

After checking on the dugout yesterday evening, I went into the mouth of the quarry to let Sashi swim, scattering the wood duck. It's a still, hushed world of blackwater in there, with its high rock walls fringed with different kinds of fern and the entire pool in canopy shadow, a canopy of eucalypt, wattle, and pine. Blue metal was extracted from this pit, early in the century, to construct the road down to the falls. Now water laps right up to the walls, as in a remote gorge, so there is no way to enter, except by getting wet—and who but a dog would brave those unlit deeps! Sometimes I see Crane leaving this netherish domain, slowly climbing the air to reattain the lookouts and crane-trees up on the ridge. As I walked from the mouth up around the outside rim, an animal in the scrub took fright. I heard it scuttling through undergrowth, then PLOP! It had leapt from the top of the rockface into the pool. Gingerly I crawled to the thickly wooded edge and peered down. Ripples were spreading in the gloom, but the animal must have taken the precaution of swimming under water, for no other sign of it was to be seen, though I later heard it scamble out at the quarry mouth.

How I love it here! I wish I could live like this forever, poised on this brink of an ending, with Norm and May, old but never-failing, safely ensconced in their kitchen just down the hill. How comforting it is to be able to think, whenever I have a question, *I'll ask Norm.*

10 August 2000

Back to Barramunga! It's been many months since I was here. In fact I've only been back for a couple of weekends, with either Jenny or my son, since I was in residence last year. Of course, as soon as I arrived I was back in Barramunga time, the Barramunga eternity, and it was as if I had never left, never lived anywhere but here. May and Norm were sitting quietly by the fire in their kitchen when I arrived, just the same as ever, not visibly changed in any way. However, when I drove up and checked out our house, it seemed to have *slipped* a bit. In the unused middle room, which has been in ruins since long before we moved in, there has always been an antique mantlepiece set above the fireplace, inlaid with many large and small mirrors—the last adornment in this otherwise stripped-back house. I found that this mantlepiece had crashed to the floor since my last visit. It must have happened during a storm. Shards of mirror were scattered everywhere. The house felt on the brink of no longer being livable. However, after some concerted scrubbing and sweeping, I've laid these misgivings to rest and settled in as usual.

Still, I can't ignore the fact that the house is in the process of returning to earth. Each time we come here, and wipe away the mold and dust and dry the damp air, we intervene in this process, arrest it for a while. But return is still only a step away. Dwelling here then one is making one's camp in the empire of decay instead of insisting on the new, the fresh, the undefiled; one is lying low, finding one's fit with the dirt, the ground, out of which things emerge and to which they revert. The gods of decay are indeed the presiding deities here, and I am a devotee in training.

20 August 2000

A visit from Jenny and a return trip to Melbourne. On the morning of my departure, when I was moving an old mattress that had been propped up against the bedroom wall for years, I discovered a bat. I was immediately reminded of a night at Barramunga about eighteen months ago. I was spending the weekend here with my son, painting the outside walls of the house. In the middle of the night I awoke suddenly; I had been sleeping on my side and without aforethought I had put my hand to my upper ear. Something large and squishy was sitting on it. I leapt up and violently shook my head. Whatever-it-was however became stuck in my long hair and . . . squeaked! I screamed. I had not screamed for many a year, but I had no trouble finding my screaming voice. I screamed three times. Since this failed to summon anyone, and since I had tried to light a candle but not succeeded, I got to my feet and, in a state of terror, made my way through total blackness to the other room to wake my son. But whatever-it-was had gone by then. Months later, after various other visitors to the house had been dive-bombed in bed, I concluded that my assailant that night must have been a bat rather than a mouse.

On that occasion I had been sleeping on the sofa in the kitchen. Bats could enter the kitchen at night by way of the chimney. I considered, after that weekend, not returning to Barramunga at all. Fruit bats, I knew, carry the fatal lyssa virus. I phoned the department of fisheries and wildlife to find out whether other bats do so too. The lady on the phone assured me that though they did, wild bats would never trouble one if one did not interfere with them. I felt the grumpiness that country people feel in the face of city-dwelling textbook "experts," who flatly and complacently contradict actual experience. What had my bat been plotting, I pondered, while it sat on my ear? Was it just about to sink its fangs into my throat and implant the virus? In the end I managed to persuade myself that, whatever its strange intentions, I would be safe if I confined my sleeping to the bedroom.

But now here was a bat in the bedroom. Perhaps it was the same one that had made itself at home on my ear. It was presently in a very torpid state however—perhaps in hibernation. I placed it in a plastic box to relocate it, but this resulted in its waking up and flapping about. I had a chance then to observe it closely, and I must say I can see why bats are associated with hell: it was opening and closing its mouth in monstrous but inaudible screams and the expression on its face was one of alarming ferocity. I was chilled to think of this very creature creeping about on my defenseless head. But what to do with it? If I put it out in one of the ruined sheds it would no doubt fly straight back to my bedroom. But what else could be done? Besides, I was pressed for time. So I walked out, in a squall of hail, and released the protesting bat into the shed by the entrance gate.

It was dark when I arrived back here on Friday night, after several days in Melbourne. I had just unpacked the car when the bat struck. It swooped down on me, brushing my cheek as it flew past. It careered back and forth on the verandah then zipped into the kitchen, repeatedly diving toward my chest then veering off again. One enraged little torpedo! I hid out of range behind the front door till it had calmed down and the coast was clear. Then I locked myself into the kitchen. By the time I reemerged, late, the bat had gone.

The next morning—yesterday—I had to drive into Colac. I took the opportunity to purchase a mosquito net, and last night, when darkness fell, I was ready, in full bat-combat gear: gloves, scarf, and netted hat totally shielding my face! Ready for anything, no skin exposed. But the bat didn't show. Perhaps it has vented its anger, made its point, and is now ready to make other arrangements.

Bat horror notwithstanding, I still wake up each day jubilant just to be here, down among the sheep, rather than up there in town, among the shops.

Ah, sheep! My passion for these gentlest of animals continues to wax. I idolize them, am potty about the lambs. I long, ache, to gather them up and hug them to me. How inexpressibly sweet is their joie de vivre—admittedly so quickly dowsed in their struggle with the elements here. In these sodden hills the mothers become plastered with mud, and the lambs have to thrust their little muzzles into the dark tangles to get at the milk. Some of their faces are black in consequence. But I try to enjoy the exquisite moments of frolic, of nose-to-nose closeness, the low talking between aunties and sisters and little ones.

I remember how Jenny and I once found a newborn lamb on another farm down by the falls. The mother had died giving birth and the lamb was abandoned. I put it under my jacket and carried it back to our house, where we rigged up a bottle with a rubber glove for a teat. It was Norm's birthday and we had promised to drive him and May out for afternoon tea. I carried the lamb in a fluffy blanket into the tea-house. No one demurred, but the other tea drinkers were visibly startled when eventually a loud baa-ing emanated from the swaddled bundle in my arms. Alice-in-wonderland-like, I feigned innocence, which was not hard to do, because the soft little pink-and-white face at my breast seemed at least as natural, and irresistible, as that of a human child. My body was in hormonal flurry, remembering the triggers, the long-ago laid-down pathways, of lactation. I would happily have adopted that lamb, as mother animals occasionally adopt babies of other species, but the common sense of friends prevailed, and I was induced to leave it in good hands.

I am noticing now that when I go to town, people are all starting to look alike to me, while here the sheep are acquiring individual faces. Why did I never notice the incredible variation among them before, particularly between the round, pouchy-cheeked kind and the rangy, angular ones? Also I'm feeling increasingly affronted by the universal contempt for sheep's intelligence. Just as everyone insists, without a shred of firsthand evidence, on the intelligence of pigs, so everyone is convinced, despite an equal lack of personal experience, of the stupidity of sheep. Isn't this "stupidity" in fact relationality? Isn't the proverbial conformity of sheep in fact the manifestation of a profoundly intersubjective mentality, a capacity to move and flow within a field of communicative "interbeing"? Isn't this just the mentality that we eco-preachers are prescribing, endlessly, for humanity? But confronted with actual relational beings, which exhibit all the virtues of peaceability and mutuality that we would expect from relationality, what do we do but curl our lips and sneer?

After the various bat episodes, I have been wondering about Barramunga as an instance of the gothic. It's not just the bats and the moss, the storm-shattered mirror, the roiling mists and solitudes, but also the tenacious soul of this old house. Oh, and the wuthering! Never have I known such a place for wuthering! When the wind is up and the night is deep, the wuthering in the treetops along the highest ridge can drown out every other sound. Gothic it does seem. But what is the meaning of gothic, I wonder?

Well, let's see. "Gothic" originally characterized a style of medieval architecture—steep pointy roofs, flying buttresses, and so on. In this sense it referred to a premodern aesthetic. But the gothic imagination of the eighteenth and early nineteenth centuries was part of a Romantic vision of a world built in gothic style but also peopled with all kinds of horrors: vampires, werewolves, ghosts, the waking dead, troubled souls, murderers most foul, and other necrotic phantasms. Such horror, although associated with decay, has in addition a supernatural aspect. The gothic universe is an enchanted universe, animistic, indeed panpsychist, in tenor. Clearly the gothic is a repository for the repressed elements of modernity. But why is there this alignment between horror and enchantment? How and why do these modalities come together in the modern unconscious?

Enchantment, in its traditional European variants, entails shape shifting—the metamorphoses of humans, animals, plants, and objects into one another. Things that are capable of undergoing such metamorphoses lack an immutable identity and integrity of their own; their shape is not fixed, definite, in any permanent sense. There is no yardstick of intactness, no essentiality, in the enchanted scenario: everything is fluid, forms are evanescent, one's identity is permeable to external identities. Intactness then is threatened by enchantment just as it is by decay. If decay disintegrates our initial intactness, our essentiality, enchantment deprives us of such essentiality from the start. But the modern is deeply invested in immutable essence. She is infatuated with the new, the as-yet unshopsoiled, particularly in the case of artefacts, because the new still matches its platonic prototype; it is still what it was meant to be. The modern desires to make the world over in accordance with abstract design not only in order to improve on the original, to "progress" beyond the given, but, at a deeper level, to *possess* the original, to encompass it fully, in the way that we can encompass the ideal. We possess the ideal because it is transparent to thought; it is not endowed with conativity, with a telos of its own. As moderns we are attached to the new then because it is still close to ideality and hence can be appropriated by us. It has not yet been claimed by the world. It still presents the appearance of something that can be grasped, epistemically subsumed, by thought. It is bad enough that, even in a materialist universe, things lose their apparent essentiality and grow old, despite our best efforts to arrest them in their pristine state. An enchanted universe is worse, from the viewpoint of the modern imagination, for in it everything already belongs to a larger world, is already permeated by other forms. There is no essentiality, and hence no prospect of epistemic possession. In such a universe the individual subject is cut adrift, in flux, its own identity and its capacity to subsume the world under siege. This is indeed, from a modern point of view, nightmare psychic terrain, but why is it characterized as gothic?

Remnants of the original—medieval—gothic period are of course ancient, and hence associated with decay. For that reason they already affront a modern sense of decorum, propriety, order. But gothic architecture also expresses a figurative, enchanted cosmology rather than a geometrical, rationalist one. The gothic thus combines two of the elements most threatening to modernity: enchantment and decay. Yet the sensibility of the gothic, in this Romantic sense, was charted against a background of scientific enlightenment so unassailable that this sensibility was never really more than a titillation, an alluring "transgression," rather than a serious challenge to the modern mindset. In this sense the modern imagination is never more modern than when it is indulging in the gothic.

From the viewpoint of the panpsychist imagination however, it is conceded from the start that everything is already unfolding within a wider dynamic field and informed with the unfoldings that are other things. There is thus no essentiality through which things can be grasped. We are here to encounter the world, not to possess it. There is conativity, but conatus is energic, dynamic, signatory, rather than substantival. In encounter, we engage conatively with the subjectivity of others, and are ourselves continuously re-formed via the synergies we create. In this sense we are inveterate shape shifters, permeated by our transmorphic conversations. There is thus no horror for us in either decay or transformation. Despite its accommodation of death and decomposition, bats and rats and shattered mirrors then, the imagination of panpsychism does not embrace the gothic.

So we may contemplate decay, senescence, without the horror of the gothic. But what emotion does it then inspire? Decay, we know, is the flip side, the reverse face, of fertility. Through decay the ground for the new, and for the permeation of the new by the spirit of the old, is prepared, so that the old is transmuted rather than obliterated. Old age is preparation for literal return to earth. As we advance in age we become more and more deeply rooted in our place. We take on its hues and moods, its attitudes, meanings, nuances. Our world reclaims us, and our hearts move with increasing willingness away from the embrace of self into world's embrace. Our conatus is transmuted, gradually, into a force for the renewal of world. In this sense our souls become cosmic fertilizer, nourishing the psychic terrain of reality. Deprived of the opportunity to make this final transition, we are robbed of our metaphysical significance, and reality itself is impoverished.

So, in the latter stages of life, we can shed vanity and ambition, doubts and disappointments, and reach out towards the greatness of the world, not only through custodial fit with our own place, but through journeys into the psychic terrain of the real. Now, when our work is done, our families grown, our personas discarded, we have the opportunity, at last, to take to the road. If not now, when? we ask ourselves. And so, off we go, out into the uncharted, finding paths not marked on the maps of the socially approved, maps which, for all the bravura of youth, cannot be entirely disregarded when one is still in search of employment and matrimonial partners. In setting off on this adventure, in a spirit of cheerful and intrepid trespass, our elders in fact render their last and greatest service to the society they desert. For by their example they loosen the grip of convention, of social representation, thereby bringing their society into closer contact with the real. In the regimes of modernity, with their wholesale preference for ideality over the epistemic inexhaustibility of the actual, such elders are surely more desperately needed than ever. They embody, in their agedness, their scathedness, everything that modernity has repressed, everything that it is trashing the world to keep at bay. As those with the least investment in this modern mindset, they are best placed to point the way to the unencompassable terrain that lies beyond it.

It is our elders then who, by cocking a snoot at social imperatives and entering the portals of the real, can keep us on the metaphysical rails. If we are to become elders at all, and not mere shadows of our younger selves, we need to be set free into the world, both to lose ourselves in its inexhaustibility and to grow down into the landscape, to learn the language of the poetic order and pass this sense of the poetic, this existential wellspring, on to posterity.

23 August 2000

Yesterday a boy named Flynn came to batproof my bedroom, though the bat hasn't been back, in offensive mode at any rate, since that first night.

Flynn told me that, according to the chronicles of William Buckley, a tribe of pale-skinned Aborigines had frequented these parts in the earlier decades of the nineteenth century. Normally no one actually lived in the forest. It was far too wet and dense for comfort. Forays into it were occasionally made by the tribes who hailed from around the Colac lakes. But for a number of years this anomalous pale tribe was ensconced in these very gullies. They were outcasts, in some sense, from Aboriginal society. And they defied the Law: they were cannibals. Eventually, around 1840, the surrounding tribes, on whom they preyed, ambushed them and burned them out.

After Flynn had gone I looked up some of my local history books and found a somewhat different story. There mention was made of a "brutal and savage" tribe, the Mirrynong, that alone inhabited the Otways on a permanent basis. The Mirrynong had been formed by a couple of outlawed members of local tribes; they had stolen women and formed a small clan in the inaccessible depths of the forest. According to this account, the group was massacred by a party of white surveyors in 1841.[6]

In the space between the stories, I speculate. Had the outlaw tribe in fact been formed by whitefellas shipwrecked on the treacherous Otway coast? But why would these whitefellas hide away? Perhaps they were convicts, like Buckley himself, but, unlike Buckley, preyed on the local tribes rather than cooperating with them? The fact that they were pale skinned and disregarded Aboriginal Law so flagrantly was certainly suggestive. I look around me with slightly altered eyes. Oh, the endless ambivalence of the face of Barramunga....

24 August 2000

I continue to take delight in the little spaces of order I have created in the wreckage of the house. My bedroom is cosy now, since Flynn fixed the ceiling. I retire to this haven with complete satisfaction. And what pleasure I take in my sturdy kettle and teapot, the old pink Persian rug in the kitchen, the little rituals of fire lighting and water boiling that keep things comfortable and clean despite the general ruination. To create this sweetness of home, of safety and order, in a place that is now so intimate with earth, is strangely enchanting. It is to dwell between worlds somehow, in a zone of the indefinable.

A while ago old Crane came to visit me. I was sitting here in the corner of the room, between two windows, gazing out through a veil of rain. The hills were hidden in mist, but everything in the foreground was still visible. I glanced up from my work to see Crane perched on the roof of the old dairy sheds close to the house. The sheds are wet and grey and streaked with rust, all hatched with vertical and horizontal lines, with a wall of faded brown weatherboards between two walls of upended corrugated iron. Crane, wet and grey, with his vertical conformation and long beak at right angles to the rest of him, seemed as much an emanation of the old sheds as of the bush. He stood there, solid against the mist, looking down at me through the window. Guardian spirit of Barramunga, standing quiet and composed in the fine rain among the ruins. And he notices me! He really does. When I saw him last week down by the quarry, he called out, a loud, excited cry that lasted while he flew in a wide semicircle around me. Yesterday he perched on the tin-topped telegraph pole in the orchard to watch me walk up the hill. Each time I see him, I call out and talk to him. In return he watches me, acknowledges my presence.

27 August 2000

A beautiful evening. There should be church bells here. Actually there were once, before the 1939 fires. I wander back from Norm and May's in the dusk. All the valleys and gullies are white with mist, and a thin mist is settling around the house, behind which the big pines stand somber guard. Even bigger gums drape their foliage on the surrounding slopes in elegant dishevelment. Apple trees in white lace cluster like a great white wedding among the huddle of old sheds around the house. Clumps of daffodils and snowdrops dot the lawns the sheep have made. There are arum lilies too among the rusting bits of farm machinery and scraps of tin. All over the hilltop and the long hill-shoulders mothers are calling babies in, babies are pleading for mothers to come. They turn their sweet faces to me as I pass. It is so heavenly to dwell in these fields of maternalism, little parties of mothers and aunties everywhere, lambs, all related, playing together, scampering, as only lambs can scamper. Could anything be more haunting than this old house decomposing among the debris of its own past turned by the wand of a misty dusk into something of such surpassing beauty?

28 August 2000

Why do I want to come away alone like this, I wonder? And when I do, why this preference for old shepherds' huts or abandoned camps or shell-shocked farm houses? Is it that staying close to the ground is the price of entry into the real presence of the land? Does one have to face austerities and dangers to win the favor of the land just as one does to win the hand of the princess? Is it somehow by passing dark nights and wandering under vast skies, alone, that one comes into the presence—the inner presence, the nurturing, beautiful, poetic presence—of reality? Is this what all those fairy tale tasks and initiation ordeals are really about? Can it be that they are not primarily, as commentators have assumed, psychoanalytic in their significance? Do they direct the seeker not to self-realization but to the gates of the real? There is, after all, from the present perspective, no such thing as self-realization. If our desire is for nothing less than reality itself, then perhaps the journeys and ordeals must be undertaken in a literal sense. Embarking on vision quests in our living rooms, chaperoned by therapists, is no substitute for broaching the actual world. This bride will not lift her veil till we pass through the perilous jaws of the land and step up to her alone and disarmed, holding out our life in our hand. When she receives us into her presence, isn't this the moment of realization-by-reality? And isn't this experience less a matter of pleasure or happiness than of a kind of wand-struck astonished plenitude?

30 August 2000

Today was Norm's birthday—his eighty-eighth—and this evening I went down to make a roast dinner as a little celebration. I cooked it in the woodfire oven . . . mmmm! I was amply rewarded by Norm's appreciative face farewelling me out into the night. "We'll be thinking of you."

As I came out into the black paddock at the back of Norm and May's, I found myself in a strange scene. Gone were the snowdrops and daffodils and sheep antics of gentle dusk. The world no longer looked or felt real at all. It was as if I had been transported into a noumenal realm, a chasmic Bardo zone perhaps, of black space filled with pale mist. Directly overhead there was a clearer strip of sky in which a few stars glimmered. The mist was thickest around our house that loomed up, a blacker-than-black shape, on the hill. From the porch a light shone, beaconlike. The mist separated the light out into long spooky rays. I walked up through the blackness, mesmerized by this play of mist and void and lighthouse beams and the sense of ethereality it created. My perennial questions queued up in my mind again: what is it to exist? What is this night world which looks and feels, after all, like nothing so much as the inside of someone's consciousness? Whose consciousness is it? How can we remember that this is the sea, the field of dark interiority, on which the bright appearances of daytime float? When I finally reached the lighted house, I felt pierced yet again by the difficulty of trying to live this ambivalence, this split-level existence—trying to fit within the discursive imperative, on the one hand, the inescapable frame of social prescription, yet being drawn all the while to reality's door, called to direct encounter with this veiled presence. Can't one already hear the dry rustling of all one's ambitions as they fall, in the wake of this encounter, as they shrivel and scatter, hastening towards oblivion? Can't one hear their pitter patter and feel the draughts of that autumn dawn into which these dead prescriptions disappear?

Afterword

Singing the Ground

Let us return now to the question with which we began: how do we treat the ground beneath our feet? What is the attitude of modernity to the ground on which we walk and live? Ground is always, of course, part of land, and the approach of modern civilization to land, as we have noted, has been to treat it as a tabula rasa on which individuals and societies are free to impose their own designs. This is true in every society that has been subjected to regimes of modernization: land, in all its ecological, topographical, and geological particularity, has been reduced to a neutral substrate to be divided up in accordance with abstract geometrical principles.

This approach has often been described as a Euclidean one: it imposes a conceptual grid of straight lines on land, and land is then parceled up into the discrete, usually rectangular "blocks" of the surveyor's plan. The blocks are treated as separate entities, generally leveled or otherwise physically modified to constitute the blank sheet that can then accommodate the designs of its subsequent "owners." In this process little if any account is taken of the contents even of adjoining blocks, let alone of the character of the region at large. The bumps and curves of actual things, the particularity of the actual ground on which we stand, is regarded as incidental, contingent; the world as it is given to us is mere scenery, a manifold of appearances that can be replaced and rearranged, like theatrical backdrops, to suit our convenience. All the world is indeed, from this point of view, a stage.

If we are to respect the world as it is given to us however, if we are to adapt our thinking and our practice to the "lie of the land,"[1] following the original contours of the environment rather than imposing our Euclidean grid, then we need a metaphysics which, unlike the materialism of modernity, affirms that the world as it is given to us possesses self-presence and a certain integrity of its own. From the viewpoint of such a—broadly panpsychist— metaphysic, the ground beneath our feet will harbor its own ends and meanings, ends and meanings that it can share with us. Such a view of reality, as invested with a subjectival dimension and potentially communicatively open and responsive to us, of course suggests the possibility of new forms of praxis and a new poetics to match.

Does environmentalism hold the key to such a praxis and such a poetics? In its traditional forms, hardly. As Aboriginal philosopher Mary Graham says, environmentalism is just another Western "ism."[2] It is just another grid that we impose on the world, failing to notice the contours of the given. In this sense it is as decontextualized as the rest of modern praxis. Consider, for instance, the attitude of environmental organizations to their own "premises"—the offices or centers that are indeed the ground of their activities. Typically these spaces are as standardized, as abstracted from the lie of the land, as all the other work-spaces in the marketplace, and accordingly treated by staff in as instrumental a manner. For such organizations then, "the environment" lies elsewhere; it is not the great rolling, rippling back of the world-serpent, on which one stands, right here and now. "The environment" is all ideality; it is a scenario in the minds of environmentalists, a hoped-for end point or a lost beginning, but not reality. Reality is, for the environmentalist as much as for the capitalist, just the raw stuff out of which human dreams are fashioned.

In order to begin truly to respect the world as it is given to us, to regard it as a "spirit thing" with ends and meanings of its own which it can in principle communicate to us and in which we can participate, we can simply honor and cherish the place in which we find ourselves, whether that place happens to fall in the degraded heartlands of the inner city or the pristine expanses of the outback. To affirm the life and integrity of the world is to *reinhabit* it just as it is, via the local modality of place. To reinhabit the places in which we live is not to raze the smokestacks and freeways that we might find there but to fit them back into larger unfoldings of land and planet and cosmos. It is to embrace our own role in those unfoldings, both at the level of sustainable practices and at the level of communicative exchange: by engaging with place communicatively, by singing it up, as indigenous people say, we encourage it in its unfolding and become implicated in its ends. In this way a dialogical poetics begins to evolve out of a praxis that turns around engagement with the given. Indeed, praxis and poetics become inseparable, because all the praxes of everyday life constitute interactions with world, and hence in a reawakened world all these interactions will have a dialogical, and hence a poetic, potential.[3]

One example of such an integrated praxis-and-poetics of reinhabitation in an urban context is CERES (Center for Education and Research in

Environmental Strategies), the environment park in my neighborhood in the inner city of Melbourne. CERES differs from most environmental organizations in that it is first and foremost a *site*. That is to say, it is not merely *housed* on a site; its identity is inextricable from the site itself.

CERES started out twenty years ago on a degraded ten-acre lot on the banks of the Merri Creek. In its early days it was used by a number of community groups—the chook group, the bicycle group, the gardeners group, for instance—for small environmental projects. As these groups had few resources, they had no alternative but to work with the site as it was, adapting their plans to the contours of the land and to the materials at hand. No master plan prevailed. In consequence, the site developed *organically*, taking shape by a kind of natural selection of appropriate initiatives rather than by any premeditated design. Since the site was in charge of its own regeneration in this way, it soon assumed a life of its own, emanating a palpable presence. Attuning to this presence, people developed a sense of loyalty to the site, a loyalty that also generally translated into loyalty to CERES' organizational aims. By inducing this custodial sentiment in people, the site enabled CERES, as an organization, largely to transcend ideologies of the political left and right and to attract a true community to itself on its own account.

CERES then represents an instance of environmentalism in a custodial and dialogical mode. The role that *naming* has played in the "singing up" or "en-chanting" of place in this instance is notable. "Ceres" is, of course, the Roman name for the Greek grain goddess, or goddess of fertility, Demeter. The original choice of this name—on the one hand an allusion to an ancient fertility goddess of the settler peoples and on the other an acronym for a thoroughly technical exercise in scientific management—accurately portended the unique blend of techno-environmentalism and reenchantment that would in time give rise to this now blossoming locus of reinhabitation. The name functioned not only descriptively and predictively in this way, but also as an *invocation*, a *call* to the sacred forces of renewal in the land. In this sense CERES' intent was dialogical from the start. Though the call was drawn from the mythic memory of a colonizing culture, it was nevertheless addressed to *this* land, as it now is; it was thus less a homage to a foreign past than an attempt, in an only dimly remembered idiom, at dedication to an indigenous presence. The resacralization of this degraded site via its dedication to Demeter has in any case been uncannily successful: Demeter's myth is being played out with extraordinary appositeness in its present antipodean setting.

What is this myth? It is, of course, a fertility myth and hence a myth of descent and return. Demeter loses her beloved daughter, Persephone, to Hades, god of the underworld. In her desolation she withdraws the life force from the land; plants wither; animals cease to thrive or give birth. The goddess retreats, in her grief, to Eleusis. Eventually Persephone, who has married Hades and thus become Queen of the Underworld, is restored to Demeter, but only for part of each year. Reunited with her daughter, Demeter rejoices and her rejoicing renders the land fruitful again; thereafter Persephone's descent marks the onset of winter, her return the arrival of spring.

The CERES site itself started out, in colonial times, as a quarry, a hole in the ground, a gateway to the underworld. Subsequently, it was a tip—the very image of waste, desolation, blight. Then, twenty years ago, the goddess Demeter was invoked and fertility was thereby reinstated as the guiding principle of the culture that the fledgling venture CERES was dreaming. The process of renewal began. The soil, originally compacted and barren, gradually became fruitful again. The ground sprouted with gardens and groves; animals (particularly pigs, creatures sacred to Demeter) made their home there; and people, especially schoolchildren, came from far and wide to visit the site and learn about the ways of renewal, exemplified in windmills and solar generators, methane digesters and grey water systems, worm farms and native permaculture. There was music and dancing and art, as the devotees of Demeter understood that cultivation—cherishing the ground—involves sacred address as much as it does the regime of hoe and plow. There were many festivals, notably the annual Kingfisher Festival.

In classical times, the cult of Demeter and Persephone gave rise to the most revered and hallowed event in the religious calender of the ancient world: the initiation rites at Eleusis. There, where Demeter was believed to have grieved for her daughter, a large-scale enactment of the descent of the goddess was conducted each spring, for the purpose of revealing to initiates the promise of regeneration hidden within the mystery of death.

In an almost eerie resurrection of the Eleusinian Mysteries, adapted to the present place and time, the Return of the Sacred Kingfisher Festival is held at CERES each spring. The recent return of this little azure bird, the sacred kingfisher, to its homelands along the Merri Creek, after the long winter of colonization/development/modernization, affords an appropriate indigenous Australian expression of the sacred daughter's return.

The festival brings hundreds of local performers of different ethnicity and cultural provenance—schoolchildren, dancers, and artists—together with thousands of local residents, environmentalists, and activists, in a cathartic, high energy reenactment of the retreat of the kingfisher in the face of ecological holocaust and its return in response to the efforts of local people to regenerate their "country" through revegetative healing. The return of the kingfisher symbolizes the beginning of a new season of peaceful coexistence between people and land in this locality. Mythic elements from Aboriginal culture are woven into the proceedings, and the Aboriginal custodians who lead the entire performance "initiate" nonindigenous Australians into ancient local rituals of place, thereby inducing a more custodial consciousness in the new peoples, and inviting all, indigenous and nonindigenous alike, to become reconciled as one people through their common commitment to homeplace. With a blend of forms faithful to the land and its first and later peoples then, but also to the archetypal meaning of its eponymous goddess, CERES both celebrates and powerfully invokes, via this festival, the return of life, of fertility, to our blighted planet.

The Kingfisher festival is an instance of a participatory poetics, an event conceived and presented wholly *in place*. It is an event that could not be held anywhere but at CERES. Each year, moreover, the festival comes closer to being a *ceremonial* event, with audience being invited to process along the creek, light tapers, and perform other ritual actions in the context of the kingfisher story. Audience is evolving into participant congregation. Each year too the site joins in, adding cicada choirs and rainbows, for instance, with dazzling appositeness, at strategic junctures.

In so greatly expanding its original environmental brief, so that it encompasses the mythopoetic in addition to the technological, and takes as its starting point the actual ground beneath our feet—the living carapace of this spirit thing that is our world—CERES is perhaps pointing the way, not only for environmentalism, but for something much larger than environmentalism, in the twenty-first century. As churches are being closed and sold off throughout much of the Western world, perhaps it is time to see centers like CERES, that answer to the increasingly ecological and grounded tenor of contemporary spiritual sensibilities, springing up in their place. In such centers people could come together to experiment collectively, both practically and poetically, with new, locally specific ways of being at-home in the world. Out of the fabric of their devotion to place and their conversations with it, couldn't we expect new local myths—like the still-evolving myth of the sacred kingfisher—to grow? In the energy fields of these myths, wouldn't a new consciousness constellate? Unlike the inchoate consciousness of modernity, fed only on the illusory fare of everchanging discourse, a consciousness that forms within the container of place takes on a definite shape. It follows the contours of its container. Within that shape its own unique, multihued mythos will crystallize. In each such mythos—the blended distillation of a people and their place—the energy of reality itself will inevitably be present. This then will be a mythos which sustains. It will not be empty form. People who live inside such a mythos will be filled with this force of animation, this energy. Not for them the enervated condition of the modern, whose consciousness, despite discursive over-feed, is strangely unsupported, shapeless, "uncultivated." No. Communities who cultivate the ground are in turn cultivated—energized, defined, mythed and refined—by it.

In this small, previously degraded site on the banks of the Merri Creek then, the various thematic threads of the present book tie together. If culture, in its deepest sense, involves a cherishing, specifically a cherishing of ground, then culture revolves around the tilling or otherwise tending of soil, of land. To tend the land in a spirit of devotion is to maintain or increase its life, its integrity, its fertility. There is thus a root connection between culture and the promotion of fertility. But decay and death are a precondition for fertility, so the reverent embrace of decay and death, in their rightful roles, will be integral to culture. To cherish the ground however is not merely to tend it at the material level but also to sing it, to be in poetic rapport with its inner dimensions, to awaken it and evince its poetic response. It is also to think in concert and collaboration with it, to consult it on foundational existential questions. In its root sense then, culture, according to the present usage, is simply this tending and singing and thinking and returning to ground. The strength of our relation to the universe at large is a function of the strength of this foundation.

As centers such as CERES spread, perhaps people in modern societies might begin to negotiate a new covenant with reality that will not only sustain the environment but will recover, in a contemporary idiom, the votary relationship with ground that is perhaps indeed nothing less than the deepest source of culture and hence of our own humanity.

Notes

NOTES FOR CHAPTER 1

1. This dualistic premise of course had a long history before it crystalized fully in the mechanistic worldview of the early modern period. The separation of mind from matter began, in the West, in Greek philosophy and progressively evolved under the transcendentalist influence of Judeo-Christian spirituality.

2. For an elaboration of this argument, see the prequel to this book, *For Love of Matter: a Contemporary Panpsychism,* State University of New York Press, Albany NY, 2003, chapter 4.

3. For an account of a custodial form of economics, see for instance Vandana Shiva and Maria Mies, *Ecofeminism*, Spinifex, Melbourne, 1993, where Shiva details the sacredness of soil in certain subsistence economies; also Carolyn Merchant, *The Death of Nature*, Harper and Row, San Francisco, 1980, in which Merchant traces the history of mining from premodern through to modern times to illustrate the way in which praxes informed with reverence for the earth gave way, in Europe, to praxes that were purely instrumentalist in tenor. Also Maria Mies and Veronika Bennholdt-Thomsen, *The Subsistence Perspective*, Zed Books, London, 1999.

4. A profit-driven economics might also take a socialist form, inasmuch as profit might accrue to the social collective or to the state rather than to the individual. When socialism takes the form of state capitalism, as it has in most contemporary societies that have described themselves as socialist, socialism is unquestionably a mode of modernity, resting on a materialist view of matter. However, the way materialism undergirds state capitalism is rather different from the way it undergirds individualistic capitalism—the economics of possessive individualism—where it is the latter story that is traced in the main text.

5. Relinquishing metaphysics, rulers may attempt to rest their conceptualiza-
tion of the good, and consequently their framings of polity, on a concept of human
nature considered by them the most adequate and objective. But within the terms of a
materialist frame of reference, such a concept must be determined by science. As scientific understandings are by their nature continuously subject to contestation, no
enduring set of institutions and laws can be founded on a particular tenet of science.

6. This expansion is exponential because the greater the technological base for
innovation, the greater the capacity for technological innovation that results: each
new innovation itself paves the way for further innovations.

7. See, for instance, Jean-François Lyotard's account of the self-legitimizing
nature of science as the basis for enlightenment, in *The Postmodern Condition*, tr.
Geoff Bennington and Brian Massumi, Manchester University Press, Manchester,
1984.

8. It is particularly in the *philosophical* thought of the modern period that the
dualist tendency that materialism represents is pushed beyond the realism implicit in
the praxes of modernity to a more extreme logical conclusion. For dualism, as many
contemporary thinkers—particularly feminists—have demonstrated, effects not
merely a severing of mentality from physicality, but a progressive elevation of the
former at the expense of the latter. Or rather, the severing of mind from matter *entails*
such a value differential. For mentality is, by its nature, that aspect of things which
confers meaning on them, so that severance of the mentalistic aspects of reality from
the physical aspects robs the physical aspects of meaning. Modern philosophers have
taken this backgrounding of physicality a step further. Not content with voiding the
physical world of intrinsic significance, as materialism does, they have voided it of
independent reality altogether. Matter is demoted from the merely inert, a backdrop
to the drama of human affairs, to the entirely nonexistent. Its very reality, or at any
rate its knowability, is denied. This movement towards "derealization" in modern
philosophy is not only consistent with the normative force of dualism; it is in fact an
epistemological consequence of a dualistic metaphysics. For when mind is categorically divided from matter, an epistemological chasm opens up between subject and
object: how can a subject infer from its own (mentalistic) experience to the nature or
even existence of (physical) objects? So although derealization seems prima facie the
antithesis of materialism, substituting the insubstantial for the solidly substantial, it is
in fact only the logical conclusion of the dualism on which materialism rests. This
argument is elaborated in *For Love of Matter*, op. cit., ch. 2 and Appendix 1.

9. See *For Love of Matter, op. cit.* In a helpful survey of panpsychist threads in
the history of Western philosophy, published at the time this book was going to
press, David Skrbina defines panpsychism rather differently from the way I define it
in *For Love of Matter*. According to Skrbina's usage, "panpsychism" denotes any view
which ascribes mentality, in some sense, to all objects. Such a view need not insist
that mentality is intrinsic to materiality: a contingent but universal coincidence of
mentality and materiality would be sufficient to actualize panpsychism in this sense.
In other words, panpsychism, according to Skrbina's usage, is compatible with dual-

ism. The way I am using the term, here and in *For Love of Matter,* makes that term necessarily nondualist. See David Skrbina, "Panpsychism as an Underlying theme in Western Philosophy," *Journal of Consciousness Studies* 10, 3, 2003, pp 4-46.

10. It is to Irigaray and other French feminists that we owe the brilliant and now well-known analyses of the "logic of the one"—the logic of phallocentric thought.

11. I first came across an elaboration of this point, and its implications for the scientific testing of animal cognition, in Xenophon Barber, *The Human Nature of Birds,* Bookman Press, Melbourne, 1995. Barber pointed out a basic tension between scientific method, which aims to uncover lawlike patterns of behavior in things, and the evidential nature of intelligence: intelligence is often best manifested in *deviations* from lawlike patterns. It is when an animal is presented with situations sufficiently novel or unfamiliar that neither instinct nor conditioning supplies an appropriate response that the animal is likely to stop and *think.* Experiments that require animals repeatedly to find their way out of mazes or push buttons to acquire food are clearly not of this kind; communicative encounters, by contrast, *are* of this kind. They can be recognized only by close attention to the particularities of the encounter situation.

12. Thanks to Debra White for sharing this story with me. It might be wondered whether the way I am using the categories "Aboriginal" and "modern" here in fact elides the differences within these categories in just the way that I am charging moderns with doing. In other words, am I not lumping together diverse groupings of people under these categories in a way that fails to respect the differences among them? In reply to this it can be pointed out that it is epistemologies rather than peoples that are at issue here, and these epistemologies are being characterized as ideal types more than as the practices of specific peoples. At this level of generality certain key contrasts can indeed be fruitfully drawn. To what degree a particular people or social group instantiates a given ideal type is a further, empirical question.

13. It might be objected that prime importance does, after all, attach to feet in Aboriginal systems of representation, since the activity of tracking is central to Aboriginal praxis. It is thus not surprising that, in societies that live by hunting and in whose art animals and people are often represented by their tracks, individuals should recognize one another by the soles of their feet. See Gary Presland, "A Reflection on Aboriginal Tracking," *PAN (Philosophy Activism Nature),* 2, 2002. While this has to be conceded, the case of the man in the morgue was only one—particularly striking— example of the capacity of traditional Aboriginal people to register a degree of particularity in their perception of objects and beings that seems, to nonindigenous people, extraordinary. For an account of this general sensitivity to particularity, see Deborah Bird Rose, "Taking Notice" in *Worldviews* 2, 3, 1999.

14. As an aside here I would like to note the ideological investment of our current government here in Australia in its Goods and Services Tax that was introduced at the beginning of the 2000/2001 financial year. To implement this tax had been the abiding ambition of Prime Minister John Howard and sections of his party for many years: John Howard had defied electoral unpopularity, wrath even, in his tenacious

pursuit of this tax. Why was he so keen on it? Not, presumably, simply because it was an alternative source of government revenue. As such it would not have been worth the electoral cost. Howard's persistence can, I believe, be more plausibly explained in ideological terms: the GST transforms every activity that involves financial return—no matter how incidentally—into a *business* activity, where business by definition exists *for the sake of* financial return, i.e., for the purpose of making money. Through this tax then, the government has redescribed many kinds of activity or occupation that are normally undertaken as ends in themselves as *businesses*: the poet whose work is published by a hand press or included in an anthology is ideologically converted into a *businessperson* and has to register himself or herself as a business.

15. Later many of these activities were harnessed to military ends, and a number of contemporary sports, such as fencing and discus throwing, are adaptations of old military practices. The basic activities however—walking, running, jumping, throwing, etc.—were undoubtedly originally dialogical modalities.

16. Fitness itself may be understood in either a materialist or a dialogical sense. Fitness in a materialist sense is achieved mechanistically in the gym or on the running track. Fitness in a dialogical sense is achieved via an encompassing of country: by walking, running, or climbing in country we strengthen our muscles and bones, yes, but we also undergo another kind of self-increase—an encompassing of space and landscape within our psychophysical being. Our "fitness" then is an expression of this gathering in of country, this enlargement and amplification of our being. What a minor thing is the mere mechanical stimulation of muscles by comparison!

17. This is not of course to say that sport cannot have positive aspects and effects. It can be indispensable as an arena of physical exercise, for instance, in a sedentary, urbanized society. Given the high cultural status it already enjoys, it can be an important avenue for individuals and social groups and even entire peoples to gain self-confidence and recognition. Team sports—which I have excepted from the above critique—are particularly valuable, wherever they are still practiced at a local level, for their powerful community-bonding effects.

NOTES FOR CHAPTER 2

1. The philosophies in question include those of deep ecology, ecofeminism, social ecology, bioregionalism, and the land ethic.

2. For a sampling of different conceptions of nature, see Holmes Rolston III, "Following Nature," *Environmental Ethics*, Temple University Press, Philadelphia, 1988, and Andrew Brennan, *Thinking about Nature*, Routledge, London, 1988.

3. Arne Naess describes this condition as that of "free nature." See Arne Naess, *Ecology, Community, Lifestyle*, Cambridge University Press, Cambridge, 1989. Translated by David Rothenberg.

4. See my paper "The Soul of Things," *Terra Nova*, 1 (4), 1996, pp. 55–64.

5. This contrast between the artefactual and the natural, though significant, is not absolute. It could be said that it is part of the disposition of things to be susceptible of manipulation by abstractive agents, and to respond to such manipulation in determinate ways. In other words, it is already part of the nature of things to respond to our interventions in the particular way they do. These responses are thus not against "nature." While this is no doubt a fair semantical point, it overlooks the significance of the patterning that occurs when things are not subjected to manipulation compared with the failure of such patterning when they are subject to arbitrary human interventions. There is a major distinction to be marked here, whether or not it is absolute.

6. To defend this genetic claim against the constructionist tenor of much contemporary philosophy would take me too far afield here. Suffice it to say that at a minimal level, this claim is self-evidently true: hunger, thirst, sociability, disposition to learn and use language, to build cultures, to live collectively, are all transcultural aspects of human life even though they are differently expressed in different cultural contexts.

7. See *For Love of Matter*, State University of New York Press, Albany, New York, 2003, chapters 2 and 3. See also *The Ecological Self*, Routledge, London, 1991.

8. See again *The Ecological Self*, ibid., ch. 3, and *For Love of Matter*, ibid., ch. 3.

9. This is not to say that when things are left to their own devices, the interests of individual organisms and smaller-scale ecosystems might not be subordinated to those of greater ecosystems or the biosphere as a whole: competition, predation, and disease may further the ends of the greater systems at the expense of the smaller ones. But by and large, when individuals are following their own innate individual patterns or principles of self-realization, the self-realization of the greater system is assured. Of course, contingencies can also occur. The kind of contingency that immediately suggests itself in this connection is that of the life-shattering asteroid. Although qua system the biosphere is sufficiently largescale to instantiate the kind of greater whole whose own conative unfolding is constituted by the conative unfolding of its elements, it does not necessarily have an answer for everything. On the other hand, the likelihood of this kind of catastrophic contingency occurring is extremely small.

10. It has been put to me (by Robert Young) that most people would happily employ abstractive thought to avert a natural disaster that was going to kill a lot of people, even though this led them to move against nature in the present sense—to manipulate events, by large-scale engineering measures, for instance. I agree that most of us would undoubtedly react in this way if we were faced with the choice in these terms. But to ascertain our true values in this connection it would be more telling to confront us with a choice between two types of society: one which possessed such measures, and consequently had the capacity eventually to despoil the planet's biosystem, and one which did not, and was consequently set to live within the ecolog-

ical terms of that system indefinitely, even though it was unable either to avert catastrophes, or to save as many individual lives in the short term, as the other society. Couched in these terms, I do not think it is nearly so obvious which choice most people would make.

11. I have observed a similar attitude to junk and rubbish in Aboriginal communities in Australia. Lots of litter and old machinery and cars and fridges and so on are left lying around in some of the remoter communities, apparently on the assumption that these things, like all others, have their place in the world, so there is no point in pretending that they do not exist by putting them out of sight. They will in time, again like everything else, be received back into the land, back into the cycles of life.

12. In his book *The New Nature*, Viking, Melbourne, 2002, biologist Tim Low offers innumerable examples of "nature" colonizing the cracks and crannies of cities without regard for ecological purity (indigeneity) and with an exuberance sometimes unmatched in the wild. Environmentalists in Britain have also realized that brownfields, vacant urban sites—often heavily polluted through earlier industrial uses—are among the most biodiverse sites in the contemporary landscape. See for instance "A Bleak Corner of Essex," John Vidal, *The Guardian*, Sat. 3 May, 2003.

13. We might wonder what the implications of letting-be would be for objects that have served as perennial instruments of torment in our lives—for example, the father's strap hanging on the nail behind the door; the barbwire fence surrounding the compound; the bed of the unhappy, abusive marriage. Consideration of our attitude to such objects might suggest that things become precious to us on account of their association with positive experiences rather than on their own account. But while certain objects and places might indeed become highly emotionally charged for a particular individual on account of either positive or negative experiences with which they are associated, it seems that all the remaining things and places that belong to one's immediate environment acquire a positive glow simply on account of constituting the scene of one's life. As long as one values one's life one will be inherently positively disposed towards the things and places that furnish its context, although painful experiences may alienate one from particular aspects of that context. It is this net positive association however that perhaps provides the psychological basis for custodianship.

14. As noted in chapter 1, a socialist economics is also consistent with the underlying values of modernity. In its attitude to matter, socialism does not differ significantly from capitalism: matter is there for us to use for our own purposes. A socialist regime will in principle however be less inclined to foster consumerism and an ethos of disposability, since it is not as committed as is capitalism to the maximization of profit. Nevertheless, socialist states have in practice been as exploitative of the environment as capitalist ones, though less for reasons of principle than on account of inadvertent inefficiencies.

15. Vandana Shiva offers a beautiful account of the incompatibility of the profit motive with ecology in *Staying Alive: Women, Ecology, Development*, Zed Books, London, 1988.

16. In his influential book *Beyond Left and Right: The Future of Radical Politics*, Polity, Cambridge, 1994, Anthony Giddens has explored the breakdown of the left-right distinction in the context of globalization, and has identified the conservative element of ecological politics. He regards ecological politics however as an essentially confused response to the new global situation of detraditionalization and the humanization of nature; no extension of it, such as is proposed here on the basis of a new metaphysical premise, holds any kind of key. The way forward in the new global context, according to Giddens, is via a multivalent approach that draws on both conservative and socialist thinking.

17. See *For Love of Matter*, op. cit.

18. Again, Tim Low offers many examples of waste products that are, often inadvertently, recycled to the benefit of other-than-human species. In a study of the ecology of sewerage, for example, he details many ways in which wildlife thrives even on untreated waste. Albatrosses used to travel from as far afield as islands east of South America to fatten up on the abattoir wastes that were once pumped into the ocean through Sydney sewers. As many as seven hundred birds would congregate to feed on the "plume of lard" that was discharged raw into the harbor. In the 1970s Sydney upgraded its sewerage treatment plants and the albatross population plummeted. The wandering albatross is now on the endangered list. See *The New Nature*, op. cit., chapter 5.

19. While such commercial use of wildlife certainly illustrates the principle of synergy, I think any in-practice proposal to harvest wildlife must be subjected to rigorous scrutiny. Commercial harvesting holds many, many dangers for wildlife as it will rarely be undertaken on a genuinely synergistic basis or respect the social and age profile of a species; for this reason well-meaning ecological proposals can result in destruction and harm for wildlife.

20. Neil Byron, a commissioner at the Productivity Commission of Australia, has said that in many parts of Australia, " farmers are trying to produce bales of wool and bags of wheat, and not making a great deal of money out of it, and it may turn out to be much better for land and much better for the farm family to produce a few less bales of wool and bags of wheat and a bit more environmental services, whether that's in water quality or yield, or wildlife conservation services, or any of this set of ecosystem services." Interviewed on ABC Radio National, "Sacrificial Lands," *Background Briefing*, 8 September 2002.

21. This represents an alternative solution to the question of what moral value to assign to "restored nature," where this is a question that has long exercised ecophilosophers. See, for instance, Robert Elliot, "Faking Nature," *Inquiry* 25, 1982, pp 81–93; Eugene Hargrove, *The Foundations of Environmental Ethics,* Prentice Hall, Englewood Cliffs, 1989; Eric Katz, "The Call of the Wild," *Environmental Ethics 14,* 1992, pp 265–273.

22. See *The New Nature*, op. cit., p. 93.

23. See "Letting the World Grow Old: An Ethos of Countermodernity," *Worldviews* 3, 2, 1999, and "Becoming Native: An Ethos of Countermodernity II," *Worldviews* 3, 3, 1999.

24. Mary Graham, Interview on Aboriginal Perspectives, Caroline Jones and Stephen Godley, *The Search for Meaning*, ABC Radio, 1992.

NOTES FOR CHAPTER 3

1. Such a proposal may be vastly enriched via public dissemination, where possible and appropriate, of the indigenous totemic overlays of landscapes. For a specific proposal for public education of this kind, designed to inculcate totemic and custodial consciousness in local populations, see Deborah Bird Rose with Diana James and Christine Watson, *Indigenous Kinship with the Natural World in New South Wales*, Report prepared for the National Parks and Wildlife Service, New South Wales. In the report the authors propose that the NPWS provide literature and signage that would enable people traveling the Barrier Highway, which traverses the study region, to experience it not merely as "a road to be travelled as quickly as possible but rather as a field of motion along which travellers . . . can learn to appreciate the holistic and historicised ecology which the highway bisects." This literature and signage would serve the following purposes:

> "Indicate the creation stories that also travel in the areas
>
> Point out features that define country and people within the Aboriginal scheme of ecological belonging. Thus, stands of Belah and Nilya trees could be pointed out, as could changes in soil type.
>
> Indicate approximately where the country of one mob finishes off and another mob takes over.
>
> Offer information on the wildlife likely to be seen in the area (this would include brief histories of introduced domesticated animals, ferals such as foxes, and would discuss native animals, many of which also have cultural significance).
>
> Tell some of the stories of the Darling and other rivers where the road crosses or runs adjacent to them.
>
> Provide information on current changes in land and water, and current efforts to ameliorate environmental damage.

2. For a place-renaming proposal, see Val Plumwood, "Decolonizing Relationships with Nature," in *PAN (Philosophy Activism Nature)*, 2, 2002.

3. Jeff Malpas has offered a detailed and sensitive phenomenological exploration of the mutually constitutive relation between self and place in *Place and Experience: A Philosophical Topography*, Cambridge University Press, Cambridge, 1999.

4. For a comparable account of the way the land claims its native sons and daughters in the framework of an Aboriginal world, see Deborah Bird Rose, *Dingo Makes Us Human*, Cambridge University Press, Cambridge, 1992, and *Nourishing Terrains*, Australian Heritage Commission, Canberra, 1996.

5. From "The Old Man of Verona" by Claudian, circa 370–405, tr. Helen Waddell in Ivo Mosley (ed.) *Earth Poems*, Harper, San Francisco, 1996.

6. See Val Plumwood, *Feminism and the Mastery of Nature*, Routledge, London, 1993.

7. To say that one is "internally" related to one's homeplace is to say that one's identity is logically rather than merely causally a function of the identity of one's homeplace.

8. See Susan Bordo, "The Cartesian Masculinization of Thought" in Sandra Harding and Jean O'Barr (eds.), *Sex and Scientific Inquiry*, University of Chicago Press, Chicago, 1987.

9. See, for instance, Jessica Benjamin's adaptation of the object relations approach to psychoanalysis in Jessica Benjamin, *Bonds of Love*, Virago, London, 1990.

10. The modern may attempt to impose coherence on her experience by sub-scribing to a single ideology or creed and trying to make her life entirely consistent with this. Although such an impulse to "make sense of things" may be healthy, the outcome is not: it is likely to entrap the self in fundamentalism or fanaticism.

11. Simone de Beauvoir is one philosopher to have developed a theory of the self as a narrative construct. See Edward Fullbrook and Kate Fullbrook, *Simone de Beauvoir: A Critical Introduction*, Polity, Malden Mass, 1998, for a very full account of her theory as dispersed throughout her writings. Alasdair MacIntyre offers a different version of the narrative self. See Alasdair MacIntyre, *After Virtue*, Duckworth, London, 1981.

12. For deep ecology accounts of the ecological self, see See Arne Naess, "Self Realization: An Ecological Approach to Being in the World," and Bill Devall, "The Ecological Self" in Alan Drengson and Yuichi Inoue (eds.), *The Deep Ecology Movement*, North Atlantic Books, Berkeley, CA, 1995; Warwick Fox, *Towards a Transpersonal Ecology*, Shambhala, Boston, 1990.

13. See "Community and the Ecological Self" in Freya Mathews (ed.), *Ecology and Democracy*, Frank Cass, London, 1996.

14. See *For Love of Matter*, op. cit.

15. Nevertheless bioregionalism has unquestionably laid the groundwork for the philosophy of nativism that is being developed here. The notion of the native, or of becoming native, is central to the work of Kirkpatrick Sale, Wendell Berry, Gary Snyder, and many others. Edward Goldsmith adapts indigeneity as a template for environmentalism in *The Way: An Ecological Worldview*, University of Georgia Press, Athens, 1998. In Michael Vincent McGinnis (ed.), *Bioregionalism*, Routledge, London, 1999, a range of objections to bioregionalism and elaborations of it is also

canvased. In the present chapter my aim is simply critically to explore some of the deeper dimensions of the native condition.

16. For a book-length exploration of this dilemma—which does not however opt for any "position" on the issue—see Peter Read, *Belonging: Australians, Place and Aboriginal Ownership*, Cambridge University Press, Melbourne, 2000.

17. Contemporary instances of such reinhabitation are provided by the inspiring British grassroots organization, The Land Is Ours, whose members squat on abandoned and derelict sites and bring them to blossoming life. See the TLIO website for information: www.tliio.org.uk

18. Although material equality is not a guiding principle of nativism, it should be remembered that certain egalitarian tendencies are nevertheless incidentally implicit in the principle of sufficiency. For when people become committed to the given, they are no longer bound by the acquisitive and consumerist imperatives that drive economic competition, and hence underlie the material inequalities that result from such competition. Even existing inequalities are likely to be ameliorated under the influence of the principle of sufficiency, as those who were initially materially favored cease to covet and accumulate more, contenting themselves with conserving what they already possess, while those who were initially materially deprived seek whatever they require to satisfy their vital material needs, and to render that which they do possess increasingly bountiful and beautiful. In this way, the lot of the initially materially favored begins to converge with that of the initially disfavored, though the initial disparity may be so great as to foreclose the possibility of actual convergence.

19. Susan Murphy makes a similar point in "Feel Free to Look Around," *Blind Donkey: Journal of the Diamond Sangha*, 18, 1, 1998 and reprinted in PAN (Philosophy Activism Nature), 2002.

20. This kind of objection to bioregionalism is made by Andrew Brennan, "Bioregionalism—a Misplaced Project?" and Nina Witoszek and Peder Ankar, "The Dream of the Biocentric Community and the Structure of Utopias" in *Worldviews*, 2, 3, 1998.

21. See, for instance, the studies in David Seamon and Robert Mugerauer (eds.), *Dwelling, Place and Environment: Towards a Phenomenology of Person and World*, Nijhoff, Dordrecht, 1985.

22. For a wry and amusing exploration of a fierce form of domestic territoriality that nevertheless seems entirely lacking in environmental implications, see the film, *The Castle*.

23. Robin Eckersley raises this objection in *Environmentalism and Political Thought*, State University of New York Press, Albany, 1992.

24. Thanks to Gabriel Ball for this clarifying distinction between the global, in the sense of the hegemony of a singular dominant influence, and the multilocal, in the sense of the interpermeation of local influences.

25. A beautiful example of the feasibility and enduring advantages of local urban food production on a massive scale is given by Peter Kropotkin. In *Fields Factories and Workshops*, Putnam, New York, 1909, he describes the growers of nineteenth-century Paris who supplied the city with fresh vegetables cultivated on vacant lots in the suburbs. The growers created their own soil through organic methods and carted it with them as they moved from site to site in response to development pressures.

26. Thanks to John Mathews for helping me to appreciate the force of this argument.

27. In this respect, contemporary nativism parallels to some degree the nativism of many precolonial non-European indigenous peoples. For unlike the village dwellers of premodern Europe, who often had little contact with the world beyond their borders, the peoples of Polynesia, for instance, or Aboriginal Australia, engaged in great rounds of gift giving (in the case of Polynesia) and ceremonial exchange (in the case of Aboriginal Australia) with neighboring peoples throughout the year. In his classic work *The Gift: Forms and Functions of Exchange in Archaic Societies*, Cohen and West, 1970, Marcel Mauss describes the great round of visiting and alliance forming undertaken throughout the year by indigenous peoples such as those of Polynesia.

NOTES TO CHAPTER 4

1. In formulating a socialist version of ecofeminism, Carolyn Merchant has reinstated reproduction as a central category of socioeconomic analysis alongside the category of production, which has traditionally been the axis of Marxist analysis. See Carolyn Merchant, *Radical Ecology*, Routledge, London, 1992. Vandana Shiva has also pointed illuminatingly towards the need to reinstate categories of fertility or regeneration at the heart of our social analysis and critique. See Vandana Shiva, *Staying Alive*, Zed Books, London, 1988, and Vandana Shiva and Maria Mies, *Ecofeminism*, Spinifex, Melbourne, 1993.

2. Chance may reign at the quantum level, randomness in quantum processes resulting in statistical regularities that appear as order at the macro level. But the elements of quantum processes—the various subatomic particles—already embody a degree of order that ensures the smooth unfolding of cosmos. Order is in this sense indisputably built into the foundations of physical reality. From the viewpoint of physics itself, this order is entirely contingent. Physics cannot explain it.

NOTES TO CHAPTER 5

1. There are a few exceptions to this generalization in traditional philosophy—for example, Spinoza and some of the Romantics, Schopenhauer, Fechner, and process thinkers such as Whitehead and Hartshorne. In his survey of panpsychist cur-

rents in Western philosophy, David Skrbina identifies panpsychist tendencies in many canonical philosophers, but he also admits that few of these philosophers are interpreted as panpsychists by modern commentators. See David Skrbina, "Panpsychism as an Underlying Theme in Western Philosophy," *Journal of Consciousness Studies* 10(3), 2003, 4–46.

2. Similar points have been made by David Abram, *Spell of the Sensuous*, Vintage, New York, 1996, and more recently by Val Plumwood, *Environmental Culture*, Routledge, London, 2002.

3. Cameron and San Roque have written their own account of the event. See Craig San Roque and John Cameron, "Coming into Country: The Catalyzing Process of Social Ecology", *PAN (Philosophy Activism Nature)* 2, 2002.

4. If there is a spiritual transaction taking place here it is not of the comforting "Jesus loves me" genre. Country is tough. One doesn't go into it looking for solace or salvation. Country reflects us back to ourselves. If we have demons it calls them forth. If we have depths it takes us into them. If we have wounds it opens them. Country says, *who are you*? It doesn't judge us but it deals in truth. It is not interested in our theories, our speculations, but in our own concrete reality, our unique fit in the complex scheme of things. The reality of our own particularity, rather than the transparent film of thought with which we seek to wrap the world, repackage it, is the starting point for its metaphysical exchanges with us.

5. From a Western point of view, a world that speaks to us of the particularities of our own lives is scarcely metaphysically credible. Wouldn't a psychically activated universe have more on its mind than my childhood traumas or your secret desires? Aren't we back again in the realms of anthropomorphic projection, wish fulfilment, or worse, sentimental romanticism? Why would the universe bother to orchestrate the world order just for the sake of keeping us company? To this one might reply that the world order is *already* being orchestrated for our benefit simply by being arranged in the almost infinitely complex configurations required for our existence. The input necessary to sustain a dialogical engagement with us seems minor in comparison with the investment needed to create and maintain the circuitry, the neural labyrinths, that undergird the conversation. In this sense the world already "cares" for its creatures; it is already involved with the finest minutiae of their existence. It *is* each particular thing as absolutely as it is the sum of everything. So why would it not be interested in the existential questions at the heart of each and every thing?

6. In his essay, "The Journey Home" in Anthony Weston (ed.), *An Invitation to Environmental Philosophy*, Oxford University Press, Oxford, 1999, Jim Cheney speaks about the need for a "ceremonial" context for philosophy, by which I take him to mean something like the invocational context I describe here.

7. The idea that philosophy has been from its inception an essentially indoor modality in need of release into the outdoors recurs in the work of David Abram. In " Merleau Ponty and the Voice of Earth," (*Environmental Ethics* 10, Summer, 1988, pp 101–120), Abram speaks of Merleau Ponty's thought as having never quite left

the city; in *The Spell of the Sensuous* (Vintage, New York, 1997), he reflects on the urban and academic provenance of Plato's thought. In this book he also takes up the motif of the *ground*, attributing to Merleau Ponty the realization that the ground of all our thought—the ground for which philosophers have perennially but unsuccessfully sought—is none other than the actual ground beneath our feet. While latter-day deconstructionists aim to effect a deconstruction of *all* philosophical foundations, Abram notes, "Merleau Ponty's work suggests that, underneath all those admittedly shaky foundations, there remains the actual ground that we stand on, the earthly ground of rock and soil that we share with the other animals and the plants.....We would do well, then, to keep our thoughts and our theories close to this nonarbitrary ground that already supports all our cogitations." (p. 281, note 17)

NOTES TO CHAPTER 6

1. Willa Cather, Preface to Sarah Orne Jewett, *The Country of the Pointed Firs*, Jonathan Cape, London, 1927.

2. From *orektos*, stretched out (for) < *oregein*, to desire, stretch after. See F. E. Peters, *Greek Philosophical Terms: a Historical Lexicon*, New York University Press, New York, 1967.

3. I have explained and analyzed this notion of eros at length in *For Love of Matter*, chapter 6, op cit.

4. I am here following the object relations account of identity formation offered by theorists such as D. W. Winnicott, Jane Flax, and Jessica Benjamin.

5. See *For Love of Matter*, op. cit.

6. Which party "kills" and which is "killed" in sexual exchanges seems, in contemporary Western as in many other societies, to be strongly linked to gender: men are more likely to assume the sadistic, women the masochistic, role. There are many possible explanations for this complementarity. From an object relations perspective, male infants who cathect to a mother are "killed" by an other with whom they disidentify, whereas female infants who cathect to a mother are "killed" by an other with whom they identify. In later reenactments of love as it has been imprinted on them in this primal encounter then, boys kill the other whereas girls kill the same—that is, the self. However this gendering of the sadomasochistic pattern is explained, sadism and masochism are obviously two sides of the same "killing" coin.

7. Australian Aboriginal practices of childrearing provide a model in this connection. Although Law is imposed rigidly on adults and harsh punishments are meted out for transgressions, young children are generally treated very indulgently. Anthropologists Ronald and Catherine Berndt confirm this generalization. "Aboriginal parents are, on the whole, very indulgent. They pet and spoil their children, and stand a great deal from them in the way of bad behaviour, or even disobedience. When they do punish them, it is likely to be severe—a sudden slap or a blow,

when a mother or father loses patience: but punishment is rarely carried out in cold blood. In western Arnhem Land, drawing on a conventional theme from local mythology, a mother may threaten her child with a thrashing 'in spirit.' This means, simply, hitting his footprints or a tree, making a fine display of rage without touching him at all. It is a warning of what she *could* do, if provoked, but would prefer to avoid. The myths of this area contain many references to the danger of neglecting or ill-treating children: and in fact adults do go to some lengths to avoid denying them what they want. In north-eastern Arnhem Land a child who does not get his own way throws himself down on the ground in tantrums, writhing and kicking, crying or whimpering for hours at a time, ignored by everyone nearby, except that every now and then someone may turn and scream exasperation at him. A few girls continue to do this even after puberty. Boys have fewer opportunities after their first initiation rite, because from that point onward responsibility for disciplining them begins to pass from the boy's immediate family to the adult men of his particular *mada* or *mala*. But when a child is young, it is his own mother's or father's business to punish him— or not." R. M. and C. H. Berndt, *The World of the First Australians*, Ure Smith, Sydney, 1964, p. 165.

8. Note that the connection between sexualization and sadistification here is contingent. If it were possible for the nonhuman to act as agent of socialization, cathexis to the nonhuman might result in sadistification of eros even though it would not result in the sexualization thereof. In practice however, cathexis to the nonhuman is likely to result in neither a sadistified nor a sexualized erotic orientation.

9. Feminists have to date focused on the difference that gender standpoint makes to metaphysical outlook. So, for instance, there has been a great deal of feminist analysis of the methodology and metaphysics of science, pointing to the ways in which scientific worldviews reflect and serve masculinist psychological profiles and needs. Little attention has been paid to the ways in which contemporary gender categories are themselves premised on certain metaphysical assumptions. In other words, while gender is often used to deconstruct metaphysics, metaphysics can also be used to deconstruct gender! This is a fact not noticed by most deconstructionists.

10. There have been attempts in the last decade to argue that sex itself is culturally negotiable. See, for instance, Judith Butler, *Gender Trouble*, Routledge, London and New York, 1992. The development of sexual organs and function has been shown to be sensitive to social and cultural influences, and sexual organs themselves can be mixed and matched as a result of medical intervention. However, this degree of variability does not alter the fact that the organs themselves are dimorphic, and fixed by the requirements of reproduction.

11. This point has been elaborately made by feminist object relations theorist, Nancy Chodorow, who also emphasizes the consequences for gender identity of the infant's identification or disidentification with the primary parent. I would certainly include these dynamics in a general theory of gender identity formation.

12. To say that the experience of self is basically energic is not of course to say that it is basically biological; the energic encompasses psychic energy patterns as well as bodily ones.

13. In societies of a generally ontic orientation, individuals may still be organized along traditional gender lines, but masculinity and femininity will be less prescriptive as discursive overlays on the struture of psyche, because they will not be held in place by existential imperatives. Sexual relations within such societies are likely to be either entirely formalized, serving reproductive and kinship purposes only, or fully erotic, which is to say, intersubjective and unsadomasochistic. Either way they will be less psychically intense than sexual relations in societies in which eros is exclusively invested in sexuality.

14. The sadististic impulse can of course be directed either towards others or towards the self. When directed towards the self it is described as masochism. But masochism is still sadistic—the one killed identifies with the killer and vicariously enjoys the power the killer exercises. The masochist may also derive a sense of power from her effect on the sadist: it is his desire for her that leads him into the psychic extremis that his sadistic behavior represents; in this sense the masochist feels herself to be more powerful even than her subjugator.

NOTES TO CHAPTER 7

1. I am of course not alone in harboring such deep childhood memories of a creek. The childhood significance of creeks and rivers, even for citydwellers, has been documented by many writers See for instance Thomas Campanella, "The Lost Creek" in *Terra Nova* 1,4, 1996, 113–19, and Robert Pyle, *The Thunder Tree: Lessons from an Urban Wildland*, Houghton Mifflin, Boston, 1993. According to Peter Steinhart, most people have a creek in their deepest memories. "Nothing historic ever happens in these recollected creeks. But their persistence in memory suggests that creeks are bigger than they seem, more a part of our hearts and minds than lofty mountains or mighty rivers. Creektime is measured in strange lives, in sand-flecked caddisworms under the rocks, sudden gossamer clouds of mayflies in the afternoon. ... Mysteries float in creeks' riffles, crawl over their pebbled bottoms and slink under the roots of trees." Peter Steinhart, "The Meaning of Creeks," *Audubon*, May, 1989, 22–23.

2. Another such adventure into the heart of the given is described by Roger Deakin in his book, *Waterlog*, Vintage, London, 2000. Having undertaken to swim his way across Britain, Deakin searched out rivers, swimming pools, and water holes of every kind, embarking on a watery quest wilder at heart than any eco-tour into South American cloudforests or the Siberian taiga.

3. Johann Wolfgang Von Goethe, *Faust* Part II, translated by Phillip Wayne, Penguin, London, 1959. p. 258.

4. John Anderson, *The Forest Set Out Like the Night*, Black Pepper, Melbourne, 1997, p. 13.

5. "Merri" is the Wurundjeri word for "rocky."

6. His full name was the Venerable Thich Tinh Dao.

7. Michael Lafargue, *The Tao of the Tao Te Ching: A Translation and Commentary*, State University of New York Press, Albany, 1992, p. 102.

8. Ibid. 136 and 120.

9. Ibid. 16.

10. Richard Wilhelm (trans.), *I Ching*, Arkana, London, 1967, p. 115.

11. Lafargue op. cit., p. 138.

12. See Helen Penrose (ed.), *Brunswick: One History, Many Voices*, Victoria Press, Melbourne 1994, ch. 1.

13. Anderson op. cit. p. 14.

14. Alan E. J. Andrews (ed.), *Hume and Hovell 1824*, Blubber Head Press, Hobart, 1981, p. 203.

15. See Kate Rigby, "The Politics of Pilgrimage," *PAN (Philosophy Activism Nature)*, no. 1, 2000.

16. Rigby makes this point. "There is no necessary link between pilgrimage to … culturally co-constituted sacred places and an enhancement of ecological consciousness, let alone eco-political activism. However, where pilgrimage is reconfigured as a journey in which we honour, not only particular cultural mediations of the sacred, but also and especially the underlying order of ecocosmic creativity within which such mediations are enfolded and by which they are sustained, then it might indeed contribute to the rehallowing of the whole Earth, and to a renewed commitment to its continued flourishing." Ibid p. 30.

17. We were "walking the world into being," to use the wonderful title expression of an episode of the ABC Radio National program, *The Listening Room*, broadcast in 1991. (No other details available.) Satish Kumar also emphasizes the importance of such step-by-step contact in his spiritual autobiography, *No Destination*, Green Books, Devon, 1992. "Pilgrimage is best," he says, "when you put your body on the pilgrim's path. The Tibetans go on pilgrimage by prostrating themselves every inch of the way. They start by standing, their hands held in prayer, then they kneel and, bowing down, lie facing the earth and touching her with their forehead in humility. Then they make a mark on the ground with their nose, stand up and walk up to the spot marked by the nose (to ensure that they do not miss a fraction of the path). Then they stand and repeat the process, and this they do all the way to the temple, which might be one hundred miles away" (p. 176),
I was moved by Kumar's account of a pilgrimage he had taken around the sacred sites of Great Britain. Kumar was born in India and spent his early life as a wandering Jain monk. It is apparently an Indian tradition that in one's fiftieth year one makes a pilgrimage to the holiest Hindu and Buddhist places of India. (I was gratified when, later, I remembered this Indian tradition, for the Merri walk had fallen, not at all by design, just after my fiftieth birthday.) By the time Kumar himself reached fifty however, he had long been resident in Britain, and was settled in Devon with a British

family. Undeterred, he made his pilgrimage to the holy—Christian and pre-Christian—places of Britain instead. He describes the intention behind his four-and-a-half month walk as follows: "In India, before you enter a temple you go around it. There is a precinct for that purpose, and by going once, twice, three times round you prepare and centre yourself. You leave your negative thoughts behind. When your body, mind and heart are ready, then you may enter the temple. Similarly, I am making a journey around the temple of Britain, so that I may enter into its mysteries. This pilgrimage is a pilgrimage to Britain, to its rivers, hills, moors, dales, fields, to all its natural beauty" (p. 180).

In the early 1960's Kumar had embarked on an even more impressive journey, a peace march from India to the four nuclear capitals of the world, Moscow, Paris, London and Washington. He and his companion travelled only by foot, at least where the route lay overland, and, most astonishingly, they carried no money. Reflecting on the eighteen month walk, Kumar wrote, "[i]n wandering I felt a sense of union with the whole sky, the infinite earth and sea. I felt myself a part of the cosmic existence. It was as if by walking I was making love to the earth itself. Wandering was my path, my true self, my true being. It released my soul-force, it brought me in relation to everything else." (p. 110) As a result of his walking around the world, it seems that the planet itself became "country" for Kumar.

18. Discovering new stories or revisioning old ones is essential if the power of stories to unify the land is to be maintained. Roger Deakin's swimming journey through Britain is a beautiful contemporary example of revisioning country, perceiving it through a new poetic frame and in that sense *re*discovering it, *re*possessing it.

19. For an account of the way in which Aboriginal songlines or "strings" function as lines of both discrimination and connection simultaneously, see Deborah Bird Rose, *Dingo Makes Us Human*, Cambridge University Press, 1992.

20. When the role of waterways as creators of country is appreciated, the ancient Greek perception of rivers as gods becomes more comprehensible: as an agent of creation—poetic as well as physical—the river has an undeniably mythical status. See Harry Brewster, *The River Gods of Greece : Myths and Mountain Waters in the Hellenic World*, I. B. Tauris, New York, 1997. Why not honor it then in a mythic idiom—by deifying or otherwise personifying it? How might the Merri respond if we addressed her as a goddess?

21. Kate Rigby brings out the complexity of pilgrimage in colonized lands in "The Politics of Pilgrimage," op. cit.

22. See Robyn Davidson, *Desert Places*, Viking, New York, 1996, for an account of the history and culture of one group of such peoples.

23. A significant step in the politics of repossession and reinhabitation would be to campaign for public access to all the waterways in our state and ultimately across our continent. Waterways are, as I have remarked, the natural pathways through the land, and if people are to "walk their world into being," then a primary desideratum is that they should have access to the waterways. Such access has apparently been legislatively

assured in New Zealand: a colonial law affording a twenty-two-yard strip of public access along the banks of every river in the country has recently been reenacted. (The law is known as "the Queen's chain" because it was originally requested by Queen Victoria.) See Deakin, op. cit., p. 34.

24. In August 2000 the Victorian National Parks Association and the Friends of the Merri put forward a proposal to encompass the entire length of the Merri creek, up to Wallan, in a linear park. The park would be 2500 hectares in area and would link all the significant biological and geological sites along the creek.

25. Ned Kelly is Australia's most famous bushranger and people's hero.

26. G. Wilson Hall, *The Kelly Gang: The Outlaws of the Wombat Ranges*, G. Wilson Hall, Mansfield, 1879. Quoted in Keith MacMenomy, *Ned Kelly: The Authentic Illustrated Story*, Currey O'Neill Ross, Melbourne, 1984, p. 11.

27. Deborah Bird Rose, *Dingo Makes Us Human*, Cambridge University Press, Cambridge, 1992.

28. After I published a little account of our journey in a local newspaper, I received a phone call from a man who wanted to know what had first attracted me to the Merri Creek. It turned out that he was a genealogy buff, and amid his researches into his family tree he had come across a forefather of his, one George Mathews, who had been swept off the bridge that crosses the creek at Heidlberg Road during a flood in 1854. George's body had never been recovered, so his bones, or at least his ghost, presumably still lay in the bed of the creek. Was I related to George? I don't know. The Mathews branch of my family were arriving in the area at around that time, so George may well have been an uncle or brother of my great-grandfather.

29. This was no doubt named after the sacred Tempe Valley in ancient Greece. See Brewster, op. cit.

30. Andrews, op. cit., p. 201.

31. I would like to offer my heartfelt thanks to all who helped us reach the source of the Merri. Our support team: Len O'Neill, Noel Blencowe, Vyv Rodknight, Cathie Nixon, Thais Sansom and family, Gerard Farmer, Saer Lachey, Greg Milne and Kari. Our hosts: the Coburg Scouts Club, the Campbellfield Community Center, Margaret Walker, Jerry and family of Donnybrook, Kate and Stephan Adey, Bill of Wallan East. The Launch at CERES: Tony Faithful of MCMC, Ray Radford of the Friends of the Merri, and Alan Reid of the Gould League. We also acknowledge our incalculable debt to those who belonged to the creek before us, and belong to it still, and who are our teachers and elders in creek matters as in so may other respects, the Wurundjeri people, both ancestral and of the present day.

NOTES TO CHAPTER 8

1. Norm Gardner, *A History of the Gardner Family and Life at Barramunga*, Colin Greenwood, 1978.

2. Ibid. p. 40.

3. Norm Gardner, *A History of the Gardner Family and Life at Barramunga*, Colin Greenwood, 1978; *Back to Barramunga*, photocopy, 1990.

4. Norm Gardner, *A History of the Gardner Family and Life at Barramunga*, Colin Greenwood, 1978, p. 25.

5. Norm Gardner, *Back to Barramunga*, photocopy, 1990, p. 7.

6. Jack Loney, *Otway Memories*, A Marine History Publication, Geelong Vic., 1979.

NOTES TO AFTERWORD

1. See Paul Carter, *The Lie of the Land*, Faber and Faber, London, 1996. In this book Carter offers a beautiful analysis of the place insensitivity—the *ungroundedness*—of modern civilization. "We do not walk with the surface; we do not align our lives with its inclines, folds and pockets," he says. "We glide over it; and to do this, to render what is rough smooth, passive, passable, we linearize it, conceptualizing the ground, indeed the civilized world, as an ideally flat space, whose billiard-table surface can be skated over in any direction, without hindrance." (p. 2)

2. Mary Graham, Interview on Aboriginal Perspectives, Caroline Jones and Stephen Godley, ABC Radio National, 1992.

3. Paul Carter also argues that we need a place-sensitive poetics that renounces the colonial "nostalgia for horizons, focusing instead on the ground at our feet, beginning to pay attention to its folds and inclines." op. cit. p. 14.

Index

Abram, David, 216, 217
abstractiveness, 27–30, 32, 38, 42, 108, 209
aging, 31–32, 34, 36, 51–56, 93–94, 97, 167–68, 177–78, 187–91, 193–95
Anaximander, 105,
ancestors, 178–79
Anderson, John, 138–39, 143, 147, 219, 220
Andrews, Alan, 220
Anker, Peder, 214
artefactual: contrasted with natural, 27–28, 209
artifice: contrasted with nature, 27–30, 32

Barber, Xenophon, 207
Bardi people, 153, 189
Barramunga, 165 ff
Batman, John, 145
Beauvoir, Simone de, 213
Bell, Julia, 87–91, 98–100
Benjamin, Jessica, 213, 217
Bennhodt-Thomsen, Veronika, 205
Berndt, Ronald and Catherine, 217–18
Berry, Wendell, 213
bioregionalism, 72, 79, 213, 214
"blockmindedness", 15–19; sport as instance of, 19–20

Bordo, Susan, 213
Braeside, 5, 7–8, 15
Brennan, Andrew, 208, 214
Brewster, Harry, 221, 222
Butler, Judith, 218
Byron, Neil, 211

Cameron, John, 109, 216
Campanella, Thomas, 219
Camus, Albert, 133
Carter, Paul, 223
Cather, Willa, 115, 217
cathexis: definition of, 118; to world, 117–29
CERES, 135–36, 138, 200–4
Cheney, Jim, 216
Chodorow, Nancy, 218
Christianity: and principle of fertility, 92–93
civilization: definition of, 29–30
Claudian, 56–57, 63, 80, 213
countermodernity, 46
culture: the ground of, 20–23, 25, 46–47, 83, 126–29, 178–79, 201, 203–4

Dao, Venerable Thich Tinh, 219
Davidson, Robyn, 221
Deakin, Roger, 219, 221, 222

deep ecology, 69, 72–73, 213
Demeter, 92, 201–2
Democritus, 105
derealization, 12, 206
Devall, Bill, 213
Drengson, Alan, 213

Eckersley, Robyn, 214
ecopolitics: and nativism, 72–74
Eleusinian Mysteries, 93, 201–2
Elliot, Robert, 211
environmentalism, 26–27, 30–34,
    37–38, 41–43, 57, 68, 73, 79–80
eros: definition of, 118, 187, 217; in
    relation to other-than-human, 119ff;
    sexualization and sadistification of,
    120ff, 217–19. See also self, erotic
Eros and Psyche, story of, 187
Evans, Cinnamon, 136 ff

Faust, 138
Fechner, Gustav, 215
fertility, 91–100, 195, 201–4; as condi-
    tion for worldhood, 95–96
Flax, Jane, 217
forgiveness, 73, 89, 91–93
Fox, Warwick, 213
Freud, Sigmund, 119, 121
Fullbrook, Edward and Kate, 213

Gardner, May, 166 ff
Gardner, Norm, 165 ff, 222, 223
gender categories: metaphysical presup-
    positions of, 218
gender identity, 122–26, 218
Giddens, Anthony, 211
given: affirming the, 21–23, 25, 29–32,
    34–48, 50–58, 67–68, 73, 75–76, 81,
    91–92, 94, 97–98, 121, 137, 143,
    149–50, 158, 199–200, 214, 219; con-
    trasting attitudes to, 63; rejecting the,
    11, 22–23, 29–30, 60–61, 96–97, 187,
    193–94, 100; sufficiency of the, 53,
    58, 75–77, 81, 214. See also letting-be
globalism: in relation to nativism,
    80–83

Goethe, J. W. V., 138, 219
Goldsmith, Edward, 213
gothic: meaning of, 193–95
grace: as modality, 21–23, 128–29
Graham, Mary, 48, 212, 223

Hall, G. Wilson, 222
Hamilton Downs, 108 ff
Hargrove, Eugene, 211
Hartshorne, Charles, 215
healing, 41, 98
Heraclitus, 105,
Hovell, William, 147–48, 151, 158–59
Hume, Hamilton, 147–48, 151, 158–59

I Ching, 143
identity politics: nativism as, 68–72
inaction, 22, 35, 45
Inoue, Yuichi, 213
Irigaray, Luce, 207

James, Diana, 212
Jewett, Sarah Orne, 115, 126, 217
journeying, 77–78, 133–64, 195, 197

Katz, Eric, 211
Kelly, Ned, 156–58, 222
Kemp, Jenny, 166, 185, 190–92
Kingfisher Festival, 136, 202–3
Kropotkin, Peter, 215
Kumar, Satish, 220–21

Lafargue, Michael, 220
Lao Tzu, 143
Latz, Peter, 109
letting-be: as comparable with Aborig-
    inal modality, 47–48; as conducive to
    votivity, 45–47; as consistent with
    mode of agency, 39–45; as emplace-
    ment, 53–54; as meaning of "nature,"
    27–30; as "returning to nature,"
    30–39; and undermining capitalism,
    34–36
liberalism: as resting on materialist
    premise, 9, 10, 13, 45; and nativism,
    78–79

Loney, Jack, 223
Lowe, Tim, 42, 210, 211
Lucius, 183
Lyotard, Jean-François, 206

MacIntyre, Alasdair, 213
MacMenomy, Keith, 222
Malpas, Jeff, 212
materialism: definition of, 9–10, 106; as premise of deconstruction, 13, 46; as premise of modernity, 9–15, 17, 20–21, 36–37, 45–46, 49, 60, 63, 79, 121–22, 127–28, 199–200; as premise of socialism, 210
Mathews, Freya, 205, 206, 209, 211, 212, 213, 217
Mathews, John, 215
Mauss, Marcel, 215
Mayfield, 2, 5, 6, 48
McGinnis, M. V., 213
Merchant, Carolyn, 205, 215
Merleau Ponty, Maurice, 216–17
Merri Creek, 133 ff, 201–2, 219, 222
Mies, Maria, 205, 215
Mirrynong, 196
modernity: definition of, 11, 37; as modality, 7–9, 11–15, 20–23, 25, 30, 34, 37–39, 42–43, 45–47, 59–61, 63, 73–76, 78, 80–81, 83, 92–97, 112, 115, 122, 126, 154, 178, 186–89, 193–95, 199–200, 205–6, 210; and philosophy, 101–4. *See also* self, modern
Mosley, Ivo, 213
Mugerauer, Robert, 214
Murphy, Susan, 214

Naess, Arne, 69, 208, 213
nativism: contrast with modernity, 125–129; as identity, 57–59, 63; deconstructive objection to, 61–62; as identity politics, 68–72; other objections to, 74–83. *See also* self, native
nature, definition of, 26–30; return to, 31–34
nomadism, 77

orexis: definition of, 118–119, 217

panpsychism: definition of, 14, 27–28, 49; as metaphysical premise, 20–28, 30, 36–37, 45–47, 53, 56, 58–59, 62, 67, 77, 79, 95, 104–8, 119, 121–22, 126–28, 194, 199–200
Penrose, Helen, 220
Persephone, 92, 201–2
Peters, F. E., 217
philosophy: definitions of, 113; in context of modernity, 101–4; in place, 108–14; origins of, 104–7
pilgrimage: meaning of, 149–52, 158
place: account of, 53–55, 173; engaging with, 25, 50–56, 89–91, 108–11, 200–4; and identity, 55–63, 115–29; and journeying, 150–54, 158, 162–64; love of, 7–8; and old age, 187–89, 195; and "living", 63–68; philosophy in, 108–14; as primary other, 117–22; relation to ground of culture, 177–79; sense of, 52, 79–80, 108–09, 135
Plato, 217
Plumwood, Val, 212, 213, 216
Presland, Gary, 207
production: as principle of social organization, 96–97
progress, 9, 11–12; as undermined by letting-be, 35
Pyle, Robert, 219

Read, Peter, 214
reconciliation, 74
reinhabitation: example of, 200–4; journey of, 152–54; psychology of, 126–27
Rigby, Kate, 220, 221
rivers: as gods, 221
Rolston III, Holmes, 208
Rose, Deborah Bird, 207, 212, 213, 221, 222

Sale, Kirkpatrick, 213
San Roque, Craig, 109, 216
Schopenhauer, Arthur, 215

Seamon, David, 214
self: discursive, 117, 120–21, 123–129; ecological, 69, 213; erotic, 126–29; medial, 124–26; modern, 16–17, 22, 56–57, 59–64, 67–68, 71, 78, 128–29, 203, 213; native, 56–59, 125–29, 151–52; native, as contrasted with modern, 59–68; native, and identity politics, 68–72; native, and ecopolitics, 72–74. *See also* nativism
sexuality, 118–26, 128, 217–19
Shiva, Vandana, 205, 210, 215
Skrbina, David, 206–7, 216
Snyder, Gary, 213
Spinoza, Benedict, 215
Steinhart, Peter, 219
sustainability, 40, 97–98, 200
synergy: economics in synergistic mode, 40–41; environmentalism in synergistic mode, 41–43; as panpsychist modality, 39–45, 118–20, 127, 194, 211; politics in synergistic mode, 43–45

Tao, 35, 45, 47, 56, 111, 129, 137, 140–41, 143, 150, 164, 174, 185
Thales, 105
The Castle, 214
The Land Is Ours, 214

Vidal, John, 210
votivity: as panpsychist modality, 23, 25, 45–47, 73, 115, 204

Walker, Margaret, 145
Ward, Maya, 135 ff
Watson, Christine, 212
Weston, Anthony, 216
Whitehead, A. N., 215
Wilhelm, Richard, 220
Winnicott, Donald, 217
Witoszek, Nina, 214
wu wei, 45
Wurundjeri people, 145, 219, 222

Young, Robert, 20